BRAND REAL

BRAND REAL

How Smart Companies Live
Their Brand Promise and Inspire
Fierce Customer Loyalty

LAURENCE VINCENT

American Management Association
New York • Atlanta • Brussels • Chicago • Mexico City • San Francisco
Shanghai • Tokyo • Toronto • Washington, D.C.

Bulk discounts available. For details visit:
www.amacombooks.org/go/specialsales
Or contact special sales:
Phone: 800-250-5308
E-mail: specialsls@amanet.org
View all the AMACOM titles at: www.amacombooks.org

This publication is designed to provide accurate and authoritative information in regard to the subject matter covered. It is sold with the understanding that the publisher is not engaged in rendering legal, accounting, or other professional service. If legal advice or other expert assistance is required, the services of a competent professional person should be sought.

Library of Congress Cataloging-in-Publication Data

Vincent, Laurence.
    Brand real : how smart companies live their brand promise and inspire fierce customer loyalty / Laurence Vincent.
        p. cm.
    Includes bibliographical references and index.
    ISBN 978-0-8144-1676-1 (hardcover)—ISBN 0-8144-1676-4 (hardcover)
    1. Branding (Marketing) 2. Customer loyalty. I. Title.
    HF5415.1255.V55 2012
    658.8'27—dc23   2011049757

About AMA
American Management Association (www.amanet.org) is a world leader in talent development, advancing the skills of individuals to drive business success. Our mission is to support the goals of individuals and organizations through a complete range of products and services, including classroom and virtual seminars, webcasts, webinars, podcasts, conferences, corporate and government solutions, business books, and research. AMA's approach to improving performance combines experiential learning—learning through doing—with opportunities for ongoing professional growth at every step of one's career journey.

Printing number

10 9 8 7 6 5 4 3 2 1

For my mother, Kathleen Callihan Morris,
who taught me the Midwest value of doing what you say you will,
and inspired me with the promise of unconditional love.

CONTENTS

ACKNOWLEDGMENTS

....

This book shouldn't be in your hands. If not for the steadfast belief and encouragement of Ellen Kadin, my editor at AMACOM Books, I assure you that it would never have found its way to bookshelves. Several months after I began my work on this project, my wife and I learned that a new tumor was growing in my daughter's spine. Jordan had been fighting a rare cancer that affects the brain and central nervous system for seven years, but until we received this new news she had enjoyed a brief period of remission. I lost my concentration and stopped writing as I shifted into Daddy mode. When my deadline approached, I knew I was going to miss it. It would be the first time I didn't meet a deadline in my writing career and I was ashamed. I did what any writer would do. I called my agent and asked her to deliver the bad news. Cynthia (my agent) called me back within the hour and told me not to worry. She said that Ellen completely understood and that AMACOM wanted to stick with the project whenever I was ready to continue. I felt a sense of relief, but it paled in comparison to the way I felt when I received my next call . . . from Ellen. "Editors are people, too," she said. "I can't imagine what you're going through, and I don't want you to give a second thought to writing deadlines." I made some apologies and fumbled for the right thing to say, before Ellen interrupted me. "Be good to yourself, Larry. This book shouldn't be your priority right now. I know that you'll come back to it when you're ready."

Sadly, when Jordan's health recovered, I found it hard to come back to the book. I would miss my deadline two more times before it was all said and done. And each time, Ellen refused to give up on me. One night, in a bout of complete exasperation, I made up my mind to throw in the towel and walk away. I even wrote an e-mail to Ellen explaining my reasons. But I didn't hit Send on that e-mail because I thought about the loyal mentor on the receiving end. Despite all the setbacks and unfortunate circumstances, she motivated me with kindness, faith, and unbelievable patience. So, instead of sending that e-mail, I hunkered down and got serious about writing this book. I was inspired by my editor and my friend, and I'm very grateful to her for believing that I would eventually keep my promise.

I am also thankful to the rest of the great folks at AMACOM, especially freelance editor Louis Greenstein, who helped me assemble so many scattered pieces of the final manuscript and find the story while we both sped forward on a challenging race to finish. If you can imagine the writing of this book as a Hollywood-style "buddy cop" movie, think of Louis as the lovable partner assigned to work with the cop who has a reputation for "working alone." In the end, they work so well together that you hope for a sequel. I'm also grateful to Barry Richardson, who played the role of our sergeant, providing Louis and I with lots of great coaching, support, and encouragement during the final stages of development. I'd be remiss if I didn't also thank my agent, Cynthia Zigmund. Truthfully, it feels strange to refer to Cindy as my "agent." She's a friend and a confidante. It was Cindy who convinced me that I had another book in me. And when I was uncertain whether the book was shaping up to be what we'd originally intended, Cindy was the one who kept saying, "Write the book you want to write, and the rest will fall into place."

Three men—true characters, indeed—played large parts in the story of this book's development. The first is Alan Siegel, the Chairman of Siegel+Gale. It was a privilege to work for Alan. When I told him I was thinking about writing a new book, he was the first one to encourage me. In fact, his encouragement never wavered. Whenever I'd fall behind in my writing, Alan was usually right there to ask, "When are you going to finish that book?" When my phone rang and the name on the display was "Alan Siegel," my palms would sweat because I knew he was going to ask me again. Truthfully, the fact that he even cared provided plenty of motivation to keep going. Alan is one of the great pioneers of the branding trade, and I consider it an honor to know him and to have learned from him. He's a role model and one of my most cherished mentors.

The second influential man in this story is Jason Cieslak, the managing director of the Los Angeles office of Siegel+Gale, and my former boss. When I told Jason I wanted to write another book, I wasn't sure he thought it was a good idea. But once I got started, he proved to be one of my biggest cheerleaders and sounding boards. One night early on in the project I sent him a chapter, and he sent me back an e-mail that said, "Man, I love it when you write!" Without friends like him, I don't think I'd have the courage to keep doing it.

The third man in this ode to mentors is Jeremy Zimmer. Jeremy was once my client, but he convinced me to leave my gig at Siegel+Gale to join him on a new adventure at the United Talent Agency. I thought the idea was crazy at first, but I accepted his offer because I respected him so much and I was kind of dumbstruck by his confidence in me. In the final stages of writing this book, he had an uncanny ability to say just what I needed to hear to keep at it. On one particular occasion, when I was feeling frustrated and defeated, he looked at me and said, "Listen, what are you worrying about? Go write the rest of that book. If you're writing it, it's going to be great." It's hard to explain what it feels like when a guy who brokers power deals for some of the biggest names in Hollywood tells you you're going to do great. Suffice it to say, you feel a little cocky.

Thanks to Matthias Mencke and Eisuke Taki for helping me create the illustrations in this book and providing me with their perspective on the challenges involved in designing great brand identities. And many, many thanks to my friend Nikolas Contis for his great insights on naming . . . and for naming this book!

Finally, I am so grateful to my family. I couldn't do anything without them. Thank you, Lucas, Jordan, and Jeanette. You inspire me daily. We have been through so much together, and I am humbled by your boundless love and support. You have no idea what it meant to me when I'd come home after a long day and one of you would ask, "How'd the writing go?" I love you.

BRAND REAL

INTRODUCTION

....

The world does not need another brand. We've got plenty of them, and to be honest, many are underwhelming. After twenty years in the branding trade, I wrote this book because I'm as frustrated as the average consumer by the way so many brands consistently disappoint. Not *real* brands, mind you. Real brands are excellent at fulfilling, and often exceeding, our expectations. They are so focused on keeping promises that they define the very concept of "brand"—they make tough strategic decisions about what to offer customers (and what not to offer them), they attract and retain employees who care, and they grow without straying from the sense of purpose they symbolize. It's the real brands that inspire fierce loyalty.

It takes great discipline to create and manage a *real* brand. But you'd never know that by the way a lot of managers talk about branding.

A while back, I was interviewing a prospective client. During our discussion I asked him questions that I refer to as the *reality check*:

- How indispensable is your brand to your customers?
- What's your rate of employee turnover?
- What does your brand do better than any competitor, and why does it matter?

- How easy is it for competitors to replicate your brand experience?
- How easy is it for customers to do business with your brand?
- If your brand disappeared tomorrow, why would anyone care?

On this particular occasion, his answer stunned me. He said, "I'm not looking for a management consultant. I'm talking to you because I need a nice new brand to make up for the problems you just asked me about." And there it was: the trouble with modern branding, right there out in the open, staring back at me without any sense of irony. My prospective client ran a company that was being commoditized. He couldn't keep good employees because "they all end up wanting too much money." His company was engaged in a constant race to keep up with competitors, so he relied on "cost management" (i.e., cutting corners) and aggressive pricing tactics as his means of differentiation. And doing business with his company was a nightmare. He'd outsourced and subcontracted so many pieces of it that a customer was apt to believe the company was schizophrenic. Yet somehow he believed he could solve all of these real problems by hiring someone from the outside to design a better logo, tidy up the website, and clean up the advertising. That's not branding. That's stagecraft.

Needless to say, we didn't end up working together. He thought I was arrogant and expensive, and I thought he was delusional. The experience agitated me because that kind of thinking is widespread, and it poisons the well for all brands. So I began writing a manifesto about what it takes to be a *real* brand. Real brands make and keep a *promise,* and they deliver simple-but-powerful experiences. My manifesto began as a guideline for the strategists who worked for me, but before I knew it, my notes became the outline for this book. My goal: to show you what it takes to make and keep a brand promise.

I'm fond of a quote by F. Scott Fitzgerald: "Don't write because you want to say something. Write because you have something to say." I have a lot to say about branding. I invest a little bit of myself every time I work with a client to create or strengthen a brand, and I find it rewarding when the effort results in a stronger relationship between the client's brand and the audience it serves. I suppose that's why I take it personally when I hear branding described as a graphic design exercise—a cosmetic attempt to manipulate the truth. Brands should stand for something or they shouldn't stand at all. If you want to create a real brand, you have to make a promise and be willing to bet the farm on it. It doesn't matter whether you're a small business in Peoria or a large corporation with offices in every corner of the globe.

Real brands make promises they intend to keep. This is as true for a brand that stands for a product as it is for a brand that stands for a person. Everything you may already understand about a brand—names, logos, advertising, package design, retail experiences, customer support, and so on—is really just an extension of that promise in action.

We'll start in Chapter 1 by debunking one of the most common assumptions about branding: that names and logos can solve business challenges on their own. In Chapter 2 we'll explore the mind of your audience to understand how they remember brands and recall them when it really counts.

In Chapter 3 you'll discover the common ways that a brand can make or refine a promise. After more than one hundred years of brand evolution, you'll see that there are some useful patterns at your disposal.

Chapter 4 looks at one of the most bothersome branding challenges: how to create a brand architecture that provides room for growth without sacrificing the essence of the brand's bond with customers. For rapidly growing brands, architecture—the purposeful organization of brands and subbrands within a portfolio—is often a nagging issue. You'll find some specific ways to make brand architecture a tool for growth instead of an obstacle to progress.

In Chapter 5 we'll examine how to position brands within a competitive category. We'll discuss *establishment brands* and *challenger brands,* and how they engage in an ongoing battle for category leadership.

Chapter 6 will help you better understand the minds of consumers.

Specifically, you'll see how consumers attach their identities to brands and why it's more important to be relevant than to be liked.

In Chapter 7 we'll explore the power of brand narrative and how brands rely on storytelling to communicate a promise and connect with consumers' identities.

Names and logos attract a lot of attention. In fact, they're often mistaken for the brand itself. But in Chapter 8 you'll learn the truth about the role that names and logos actually play in branding. And we'll see that a brand's identity serves an important purpose that's often overlooked.

In Chapter 9 we'll see just how much the brand experience affects consumers' future decision making. We'll look into the thoughts, feelings, and behaviors of branded experience to provide you with a better perspective on how to prioritize your brand's operating plans.

Finally, we'll discuss the critical importance of aligning a brand internally and the most effective ways to engage people on the inside so they can deliver the brand promise to the people on the outside.

A brand, at its heart, is a promise to deliver. When the brand experience doesn't live up to that promise, customers take their business elsewhere. This book—intended for anyone on the inside of a brand—is a practical guide for making a brand's promise stand up when and where it matters most: at every customer touch point.

···

CHAPTER ONE

REALITY CHECK

It's Time to Move from Brandlore to Promising Brands

f branding began as a way to mark cattle and claim ownership, today it is a way to mark minds and claim "mindshare." When it works, it is quite powerful. The trouble is that many marketers aren't clear on what a brand actually is, which is why we are in a dangerous state of overbranding. In a recent advertisement for a leading smartphone, I counted no less than twelve features of the phone that were branded with clever names or graphic symbols. Including the brand name and identity for the phone itself, that means this one product embodied thirteen brands. During a stay at a popular hotel chain I was surprised to see that my bed, my shower, the room service option, and even the air in the room were all marketed with unique brand names. This penchant for elevating ordinary things—and often their subparts as well—with shamelessly clever brand identities threatens to dilute the value of all brands.

One reason I decided to write this book was to clarify the relationship between brand behavior (what brands do and why it matters) and brand identity (how the brand looks and feels). Though there are many brands that own beautiful logos and distinctive names—think of the mythological symbolism of the Starbucks logo or the clever repurposing of the word *blackberry* to name the famous Research In Motion (RIM) device, the Black-Berry—there are just as many successful brands that use logos that are little more than a word mark (Facebook) or that are identified by names that are blandly descriptive (General Electric). Believing that the aesthetics are the substance of a brand is as much a mistake as assuming that a penguin can fly simply because it has wings.

When he was twelve years old, my son Lucas was struck by an entrepreneurial impulse. He decided to launch his own photography studio and asked me if I would buy him a copy of Adobe Photoshop so he could create his brand. (This anecdote proves that the apple does not, in fact, fall far from the tree.) My first instinct was to grab my chest and rail about the price of Photoshop, then a $700 piece of software. But I decided instead to seize the opportunity to learn what he thought a brand was.

"Dad, you know what a brand is. That's what you do."

"Oblige me."

"You know. It's a cool logo and stuff."

Intrigued by my son's interest in my profession, and nauseated from having it reduced to "stuff," I asked him to tell me more about the business concept behind his brand. How was he going to service his clients? What kind of value would he provide? This conjured some eye rolling because in his mind it was painfully obvious. People would want to hire him because he'd post really great flyers around the neighborhood. He'd use his brand to make them look so good that customers would be inspired to call him, and when they learned that he charged only $25 for a photo, the price would win them over. All he needed was a great logo, he said. That's why he needed Photoshop.

"Why do you think people would be willing to pay *you* $25 for a photo?"

"Because it's cheaper than going to one of the professional studios," he said.

"But if I'm a potential customer, how do I know that the photo you take for me will be worth $25 or more? How can I trust that you know what you're doing?"

More eye rolling. "Because I'll have a good brand."

While I found Luc's circular logic amusing, I was set on using it as an opportunity to educate him about how business actually works and how brands stand for value. (I did not provide him with the requested seed money, by the way. I decided this was also a good opportunity to teach him a lesson on venture capital.) But in that conversation, my smart kid raised illuminating questions. For instance, he asked why I spent so much money to buy the first model of the iPhone when I knew it had inferior battery life, poor reception in our home, and no compatibility with my office e-mail system? Wasn't that proof that I was just buying a brand instead of value? Why did I sometimes select a bottle of wine that I had never tasted before simply because I liked the name or the design of the bottle's label? Wasn't that proof that names and logos mattered? Luc reasoned that I made an awful lot of decisions based solely on how much I liked a brand's aesthetics, or not. He surmised that a lot of consumer behavior is irrational and unpredictable, driven mostly by reaction to creative presentation, not substance.

BRAND CONTAMINATION

If Luc had observed Congress's lengthy debate over what to rename the legislation formerly known as No Child Left Behind (NCLB) or the social media frenzy that ensued after retailer Gap changed its logo, he would have valid proof points for his observations.

When Representative George Miller (D-California) suggested in a 2007 interview that NCLB might be "the most negative brand in America," he caught my attention.[1] Though it's not unusual for lawmakers to point fingers at brands, there wasn't a household name sitting in the congressional hot seat. It was No Child Left Behind (NCLB), legislation that had enacted standards-based education reform in 2001.

As chairman of the House Education Committee and one of his party's leaders, Miller had a dilemma on his hands. Every Democratic colleague making a run for the White House had pilloried NCLB in stump speeches, decrying it as a clear indictment of President George W. Bush. In truth, NCLB had been championed for years by advocates on the left, most notably Democratic stalwart Senator Edward Kennedy of Massachusetts. As the rhetoric increased, Miller found himself in the awkward position of defending the act on the one hand, while maintaining solidarity with his party on the other. What was a Democratic leader to do? Rebrand, of course.

Representative Miller suggested that NCLB suffered from a classic case of brand contamination. He argued that the act had become an extension of the George W. Bush brand, and as the president's approval ratings slid, NCLB became less popular by association. He believed the situation might improve if it was given a new name—one freed from association with an unpopular administration. The idea stuck. By 2009, when President Barack Obama's new education secretary, Arne Duncan, tackled the issue on his own, he dusted off Miller's strategy. "Let's rebrand it," he said in an interview for the *New York Times*. "Give it a new name."[2]

Within days the Beltway was buzzing with suggested names, including more than a fair share of sophomoric puns on the acronym. Three of my favorites included REDO (Resourcing Educational and Development Outcomes), AACAAA (All American Children Are Above Average), and NEW TEST (Not Even We Think Educational Standards Teach).[3]

If national opinion polls were any indication, however, Americans didn't seem to think rebranding was the answer. A 2009 Gallup Poll found that nearly half of Americans believed the legislation had made no difference in public education. More than half of those familiar with the act said it made education worse, and one-quarter of Republicans agreed with them.[4] Even Marian Wright Edelman, the founder of the Children's Defense Fund—an organization whose tagline, "leave no child behind," had inspired NCLB—publicly stated that the act "dismantle[d] all of the gains we have made for children."[5] Though the experts and the public seemed to believe there was more to the challenge than rebranding, in 2010 No Child Left Behind was renamed the Elementary and Secondary Education Act.

MIND THE GAP

On October 4, 2010, a lot of Gap customers questioned the logic behind the change the iconic retailer made to its logo. Though it was somewhat unceremoniously introduced that day, it didn't take long for customers to light up social media with vitriol. "Your new logo makes your brand look cheap," one customer wrote on the company's Facebook page.[6] Another customer contributing to the growing Twitter frenzy tagged it an "atrocity." By day's end, the rancor had attracted the attention of major news media, and an army of branding experts and identity designers tripped over themselves to explain why the new Gap identity was a "crap logo."[7]

Gap certainly didn't see it that way. Spokesperson Louise Callagy described the new mark as a shift from "classic, American design to modern, sexy, cool."[8] Designed by Trey Laird of Laird+Partners in New York, the new identity abandoned nearly every aspect of the blue square signature that the brand had used for more than twenty years. The crisp, thin Americana typeface gave way to the generic utility of the Helvetica font. And the large blue box morphed into a faint exponent set to the right of the word mark. Most critics assumed that the offset square was a reference to the old logo and meant to imply that the brand was "thinking outside the box." Instead, the Gap faithful viewed the change as throwing the baby out with the bathwater. While Gap's managers believed they were simplifying the look and feel, the public thought it was signaling a change in the value it might provide. "New Gap logo looks as if it were done in Microsoft Word," said a viral Twitter post.[9] Was Gap going to start cutting corners?

Seven days later, Gap retired the new design and framed the debacle as a lesson in online culture. To remedy the situation, it announced that it would let its fans decide what its mark should look like. It invited customers to submit their own logo design ideas on the crowdsourcing site 99designs. While more than 1,000 amateur and professional designers accepted the challenge, submitting over 4,600 entries,[10] the move launched new controversy. The branding community objected to Gap's decision to resort to crowdsourcing to solve a strategic problem. Most experts thought it marginalized the link between strategy and design, and many consumers seemed to think that leaving the identity to the masses was a sacrilegious way to care for a beloved brand. Some just thought the move was as cheap as the first logo attempt. In a widely circulated blog post, veteran designer Mike Monteiro defended the design trade by delivering an analog to Gap. "Never in my experience has any of your employees offered me a free pair of pants because the ones I was wearing looked bad. I wouldn't expect them to. Their job is to sell me clothes. My job is to sell design."[11]

The contest came and went, and Gap awarded prizes to a few, but as of this writing the legacy logo lives on. Despite the intense public outcry about the changes in its brand identity, industry analysts estimate that Gap lifted its holiday store sales that year by approximately 5 percent.[12] (This led some to theorize that the whole controversy was a publicity stunt.) But the Gap logo experiment raises two interesting questions: *Why did ordinary consumers care so much about the proposed logo change?* And: *Should future brands pick their logos through a beauty contest?*

Questions that arise from the No Child Left Behind and Gap cases are difficult to answer today because we have all been conditioned to think about brands in a way we wouldn't have just fifty years ago. The concept of "brand" is now a strange and puzzling part of our cultural vernacular, and it's a far cry from its origin.

THE SIMPLICITY PRINCIPLE

Brands exist because we hate uncertainty. In our purchasing and consumption decisions, we rely on cues to predict what we should expect from products, services, and organizations. The cues often come from symbols like names and logos. Branding relies on the simplicity principle, which posits that we are inclined to choose the simplest hypothesis that is consistent with the data presented to us. Sometimes, the only data we have are meaningful symbols like a name or a logo. But here's an important reality check: Too many brands are heavy on symbolism and light on predictable outcomes. When they don't deliver on a promise, we have new data to factor into our hypothesis: our experience with the brand. Real brands simplify our understanding of what we should expect in the brand experience, and they focus their attention on delivering against that expectation again and again.

Your brain performs millions of functions every second. It is a remarkable computer—more powerful than any thinking machine we've yet designed. Part of your brain's power comes from its extraordinary efficiency. Your brain is designed to conserve energy through pattern recognition. Did you ever notice how little conscious thought is required for you to stop your car when you approach a stop sign? A stop sign is a cue that triggers a pattern of behavior. There was at least one time in your life when you invested a lot of mental energy to understand how stop signs, the rules of the road, and the motor function needed to drive a car related to one another. But after a while, your brain memorized the relationship of the required behavior (depth perception, muscular contractions, etc.) to the value associated with such behavior (you won't crash) and the cue that signaled this pattern to begin (a red, octagonal sign bearing the word *Stop*). The cue enables a shortcut. When you see it, you don't have to consciously think; you know what to expect and what to do. Because of this, you conserve mental energy that you can redirect to other activities such as changing the radio dial or conversing with a passenger. That's the same mental machinery that enables brands to work.

This link between a cue and an expected outcome is so ingrained in your mind that you are likely to associate red signs with a need to stop, even in nondriving contexts. You have been conditioned to *behave* in a specific way every time you are presented with that cue. That's why so many cancel and stop buttons are red. You expect that a red signal is a cue to stop, and you are so conditioned to behave this way that you would probably bring your car to a stop even if you encountered a red octagonal shape stamped with the word *Go*. It takes a lot of mental muscle to constantly study your environment for exceptions. Unless primed to do so, your brain doesn't anticipate the unexpected. It's simpler and more efficient to rely on cues to predict future outcomes. And that is precisely the reason we have populated our world with brands: to simplify understanding in order to influence behavior.

Brands provide symbolic cues that influence your expectations and behavior because they are linked to relevant benefits that you value. That link between cues, expectations, and experience is critical because we all favor brands that consistently meet or exceed our expectations, and we punish the ones that don't. It's that simple.

Framed in this context, my son was mostly right when he used my purchase of the first iPhone as evidence that I bought a brand instead of a product. I knew that first iPhone was functionally inferior to competitive devices. But, I had been purchasing first generations of Apple products since 1987, and for the most part Apple exceeded my expectations. I had many rational and purely emotional reasons to expect that the iPhone would satisfy me (and it did), but if the iPhone had been released by an unknown brand, I probably wouldn't have made the same decision. My behavioral choice was guided by the pattern of my experience with the Apple brand, not its logo.

Unfortunately, we live in an age when it is too easy for us to mistake brands for the critical cues of brand identity, and that makes us prone to discount the value of an exceptional branded experience. It doesn't help that we liberally use the word *brand* in everyday speech. A brand can be a traditional packaged good like Tide or Crest, but it can also be a person like Tiger Woods or Martha Stewart. It can be a story-based franchise like Harry Potter or Star Wars, or it can be a virtual service that isn't tied to a monetary transaction, like Facebook.

To make matters worse, we have fetishized brands by crediting too much of their success to the design of their brand identity. My son's request for Photoshop is telling. A lot of people believe they can create a great brand if they have the right creative tools. You might be tempted to believe that launching a great brand is as easy as buying Photoshop or holding a contest on 99designs. That's partially because the digital world we live in makes it easier and less costly to create a logo or design a beautiful piece of communication then ever before. We are saturated with creative expression, and that's why there are a lot of great names and stunning logos that stand for nothing. For the simplicity principle to work, a brand's identity has to link to real, value-producing behavior. That's when identity becomes a true cue to a cause-and-effect relationship. On its own, identity is to brand as sex is to parenting. You can spawn a great name or logo, but that doesn't guarantee you'll raise a great brand.

That's not to say that brand identity is irrelevant. Luc was again quite right when he observed that I select some wine by my reaction to the label. Unfortunately, his observation ignores an important modifier of the simplicity principle: context. In the same way that I might decide to run a stop sign if I were rushing someone to the emergency room, the context of my brand experience moderates my brand behavior. When I consume wine, I like variety. It's boring to drink wine from the same producer again and again. While I'm generally prone to brand loyalty, it doesn't serve me very well in this context. The trouble is that there are so many wines to choose from that I will often rely on the value signaled by the label. While it is certainly an imperfect cue, in the context of the relatively low-risk purchase behavior of buying a bottle of wine to try something new it's a cue that reliably moderates my expectations. I've certainly had great wines with terrible labels, and I've drunk plenty of bad wine packaged with a clever name and a beautiful logo. The purpose of this book is to convince you that the latter case isn't a sustainable strategy, and that you'll create long-term business value when you align the expectation cued by the label with the experience that's in the bottle.

THE FORGOTTEN DISCIPLINE
OF BRANDING

Branding is a strategic discipline. It should influence how people behave—both customers and employees. It's not magic. It's not happenstance. And it's certainly not guesswork. It requires purposeful conduct. Real branding is something managers do to create value by delivering branded experiences that meet or exceed people's expectations. It is an important act of business strategy. In fact, though branding is rarely described as such in business management curriculum, good brand strategies guide mission-critical decisions in capital investment, human resources, research, product development, and operations management.

Simplification is an important aspect of branding discipline. Brands excel when they simplify the way we think about value-producing behavior. But don't confuse simplification with being simplistic. It's simplistic to think you can create incremental customer value by changing a name or logo. Simplification, on the other hand, is a managerial process that creates stronger associations between a brand and its real benefits. It relies on two powerful mental processes: encapsulation and objectification. Through encapsulation we connect a lot of information about brand-related behavior and the value it produces, and through objectification we link that encapsulated value proposition to a brand identity. It is the simplicity of what the identity represents in our mind and how it influences our own behavior that makes real brands *contagious*. A brand identity should cue a subconscious thought process. Sometimes the cue is as simple as a color (IBM's "smarter" approach cued by the color of "Big Blue"), or a shape (the elegant design and functionality of the products represented by the bitten Apple), or a distinctive sound (the liberating fares and convenient service linked to the Southwest Airlines "bing"). The cue can be subtler still, like a scent (the sexiness of youth linked to the fragrant scent of an Abercrombie & Fitch retail store). But the cue is only a trigger, not the substance. Think of identity cues as the henchmen of the simplicity principle. They provide another data point that leads our minds naturally to the simplest hypothesis. Cues perform the kind of mental magic we would normally associate with telepathy. They make it possible to transfer information about value. Real branding uses the simplicity principle to harness this seemingly telepathic phenomenon. However, it works only when we exercise the management discipline to fulfill the promise that is expected by the cue.

A *brand promise* is not the same as a *brand position*. It is a common nugget of brandlore that the two phrases mean the same thing. They do not, though they are related to each other. A position asserts a line of argument (as in "what position shall we take in this message?") or it pinpoints a location in perceptual space (as in "which position do we or shall we occupy in the mind of the consumer?") Positioning thrives on "open space"—perceptual territory that your brand can claim because it is unclaimed by competitors. Imagine you operate a brand in an environment where every competitor uses a red logo. To effectively position your brand, you might choose to make your logo blue because that color is "ownable." This example is a gross oversimplification of positioning, but it illustrates one reason a position is different from a promise. You position to be different and to stand out. It's an essential activity, indeed, but it is possible to reposition a brand by focusing on purely cosmetic changes and not deliver any real, incremental value. In contrast, when you make a brand promise, you still stake a position, but you also create a covenant with consumers. You commit to deliver value.

Positioning is an artful and intelligent way to design messaging campaigns. One particularly useful application is to position in order to *de*position a competitor. Coupled with semantics, a position can help you cast doubt on your competitors and it can cause consumers to reconsider their current behavior. Used in this way, positioning is a powerful redirection tactic that transforms public opinion in a short period of time. Consider how Republican pollster Frank Luntz described the way he depositioned the estate tax in a matter of days. "It's not an estate tax," he said. "It's a death tax, because you're taxed at death. And suddenly something that isn't viable achieves the support

of 75 percent of the American people." It's compelling proof of why positioning is useful, but it also demonstrates the difference between a position and a
promise. Luntz's position didn't prescribe value-producing behavior.

A brand promise is the glue that aligns experience with expectations.
Without it, you may stake any number of positions, but they're little more
than marketing tactics. You don't *have* to promise anything to take a position.
You can change your look so people think you are something that you are not
(a beautiful wine label attached to an undrinkable vintage). You can send out
messages that appeal to distinct audiences and trends. You can use evocative
words, imagery, and experiences to create a perception of what you might aspire to be or what you want others to think of you. But that's not the same as
promising to deliver specific value and executing all of your business activities
to live up to that promise. Many brands have fallen into an endless cycle of
repositioning initiatives, constantly redefining the brand in an effort to satisfy
market trends and shifts in consumer tastes. This never-ending positioning
process actually destroys brand value over time because it confuses us and
makes us question what the brand really stands for. It weakens the brand's
credibility by eroding the link between our concept of the brand, what we
expect from it, and what we know of its reputation. Here's how it works.

If you lend me $5 and I promise to pay you tomorrow, on the next day
you will expect me to give you $5. If I do, you will find me to be a man of
my word. You'll be likely to lend me $5 again, and when someone men-
tions my name in a similar context you might vouch for me. Your experience with my brand helped me establish a good reputation. On the other
hand, if you show up the next day and I pay you only $2, you'll have doubts
about me the next time around. If someone asked you about me, you might
be inclined to warn them. My reputation is in danger because of your most
recent experience with my brand, which did not live up to the expectation
I set with my promise to you. It won't matter how I go about positioning
myself next time. I can dress differently. I can make claims about cleaning
up my act. I can try to convince you that I am financially stable or I could
tell you I aspire to lofty goals. None of that is likely to impress you because

I didn't fulfill my promise the last time. My positioning activities might convince *other* people to give me $5, but as soon as you log on to Twitter and squawk about your disappointing experience with my brand, I'd have what public relations experts call a "reputation problem."

In a 2004 study published in the *Journal of Consumer Research,* credibility was shown to be one of the strongest factors driving brand consideration and preference. We prefer brands that make credible promises. But the most interesting part of the study was the drivers that lead to brand credibility: trustworthiness and expertise, and trustworthiness trumps expertise.[13] You may be an expert, and I may associate your expertise with the delivery of value, but if I don't trust you, all the expertise in the world won't win my business.

When a brand behaves according to its promise, it develops a good reputation that leads to trust, which can make a brand more credible than competing alternatives.

Looking at a brand through the lens of a credible promise, it's understandable why renaming No Child Left Behind was folly. The policymakers hadn't promised to make any real change in the value delivered by the legislation. Instead, they hoped a name change would reposition public opinion about legislation people distrusted based on experience. In a similar way, Gap's logo debacle made consumers worry that the brand was being too simplistic, perhaps cheapening its value. The new logo made them question the brand's credibility.

A promise differentiates and positions a brand by defining what it is, what it does or doesn't do to create value, and why it matters. There's a subtle element in a brand promise that you often don't find in a brand positioning. A promise distinguishes what the brand is willing to *omit* as much as it defines what it will *deliver.* This distinction creates credibility. It's easy to misconstrue an omission as something negative, but omissions are an important part of behavior. They define what a brand explicitly doesn't do. If you think about it, people often define themselves and their behavior by what they aren't and what they don't do. "I don't drink. I don't smoke. And I don't play cards," was once a popular saying that defined an individual's valor. Brands are no different. Southwest Airlines has prospered by not doing some things that other airlines do: no assigned seats, no first-class cabin, no meal service. These omissions are not marketing gimmicks, they are fundamental service decisions that drive the business model and they contain memorable attributes that make the brand salient because they support the brand's promise to deliver great value through low fares and friendly service.

CHOOSE OR LOSE

Why Brands Must Link Promises to Tough Choices

Think about the brands that you admire the most. Chances are that you admire them for a few specific things they promise to do extraordinarily well. In order to do those things extraordinarily well, they choose to do other things in mediocre fashion or even poorly. Apple is famous for ignoring product features that competitors would describe as critical to success. Early versions of the MacBook had deplorable battery life. The iOS operating system does not allow mobile devices to use Adobe's popular Flash platform. And when it was first discovered that the iPhone 4 had a design flaw in its exterior antenna that caused the phone to drop calls just by holding it in your hand, Apple told customers to hold the phone differently. But you'd be hard-pressed to find someone who'll tell you that Apple delivers an experience that falls short of expectations. Apple carefully chooses the value its brand promises to deliver, and it also chooses what it's willing to sacrifice in order to fulfill that promise.

Brands rise when they make tough choices. Does your brand make tough choices? That's perhaps the most important reality check for modern brands. Sadly, most brands can't answer yes. In pursuit of growth, market share, stock performance, and countless other objectives, many brands try to be everything to everybody. In so doing, they fall into branding's "kitchen sink trap." This occurs when you claim to deliver any value that could conceivably appeal to the broadest possible audience. When you fall into this trap, you usually end up with an utterly complex idea that is guaranteed to either miss expectations or blend into the crowd. Consider the following promise statement for GoogSoft, a fictitious software company:

> GoogSoft develops affordable, scalable, and innovative tools, technologies, and mobile applications that enable people to be more productive, creative, and connected when they are using the Internet by developing solutions that are the most intuitive, feature-robust, and completely customizable in the industry.

At first blush, what's wrong with it? Put this book down and ask yourself what sticks in your mind about the GoogSoft brand. Maybe it was the affordable part, or the creative benefit, or the completely customizable solution. You might remember one part of this promise, and I might remember something else. If we polled hundreds of people and asked them what they remember about the GoogSoft brand, we'd have a distribution of results that reflected a statistical average for blandness. That's because GoogSoft isn't making choices. It's throwing everything that might matter to consumers into its brand promise. It is unlikely that it can deliver an experience that meets these expectations (cheap, scalable, feature-rich, innovative solutions that enhance productivity, creativity, and connectivity). Table 1.1 illustrates what I mean.

Imagine the data in this table is the result of a brand equity study we conducted. There are many ways to measure brand equity, but for our purposes I've chosen an approach that is inspired by EyeOpener, a research tool developed by my friend and colleague, Rolf Wolfsberg. The listed attributes correlate to the actual drivers of brand preference within GoogSoft's competitive category. They are shown in order of importance to consumers. The middle column lists which brand leads on each attribute, and the number to the right measures GoogSoft's performance on this attribute relative to the category leader. When the number to the right is negative, it indicates

TABLE 1.1

Attribute rank (in order of importance)	Attributes that are most important to customers	Brand that scores the highest on this attribute	GoogSoft's lead/ (gap) on the scorecard
1	Is easy to use	GoogSoft	+1.22
2	Makes me more productive	MicroGoog	-1.10
3	Has the lowest price	GoogSoft	+2.30
4	Has all the features that I need	MicroGoog	-1.00
5	Is easy for me to customize	GoogSoft	+0.15
6	Can scale to grow with my needs	MicroGoog	-0.04
7	Is innovative	iSoft	-0.50
8	Allows me to be more creative	iSoft	-0.12
9	Connects well with other applications or services	MicroGoog	-1.47

how far GoogSoft trails the category leader. When the number is positive, it tells us how much of a lead GoogSoft has on this attribute relative to the next nearest competitor. GoogSoft has the most leverage on three attributes: ease of use, customization, and affordable pricing. It lags significantly on feature-richness and connectivity. While it may frustrate us that people don't believe our brand is as feature-rich or connected as competitors, it's folly to make these attributes part of our promise unless we're choosing to deliver the value associated with those attributes. And choosing to win on those attributes might cost us the attributes with which we currently win—

being easy to use and inexpensive. We should think very carefully when we make that decision because, according to our study, being easy to use is very important to customers and we're the clear leader on this attribute. While we invest our time trying to add more and more features to win attribute number 4, we may cede ground to competitors on our most credible and relevant brand promise. If we decide that the future lies with the lagging attributes, we must be prepared to sacrifice the value we own in the leading attributes.

Unfortunately, a lot of brands want to own all the attributes. They don't want to sacrifice one set to gain another set. This is what leads to the kitchen sink trap.

But that's not the only strategic trap. Some brands fail because they live according to a *hollow promise* that mistakes the simplicity principle for haiku. Brands that define their value using the hollow promise fall in love with evocative words and artful expressions that are hard to translate into behavior. Here's an example of a hollow promise for GoogSoft:

GoogSoft is an emergent creativity enabler.

Read that promise again, close your eyes, and try to imagine an emergent creativity enabler. I suspect you might be left with a bit of a blank slate, and that's precisely the problem with the hollow promise. It's a head-scratcher. It is born of the best of intentions, but it fails to guide value-producing be-havior.

I come across the hollow promise a lot in my line of work. It's most often the product of the marketing team, not the business owners. They invest a lot of time to coin what they believe is a defining line. Perhaps they argue to themselves that mobility and connectivity are low-level expressions of a high-level need—the need to evolve with technology. They consult a thesaurus and decide the word *emerge* is the best choice to describe evolving technology. Eureka! GoogSoft is all about emergent solutions . . . solutions that make people creative! Maybe they consider the word *make* pedestrian, so they return to the thesaurus and they brainstorm and they settle on the word *enable*. It's just a matter of time before they transform that expressive verb into a compound object: *an emergent creativity enabler.* As proud as they are of this artful line, they're crestfallen when someone asks how to teach people inside to develop "emergent creativity enablers." What does *emergent* mean to the average person? And, more important, why on earth should I care about "emergent creativity enablers"? I don't recall ever adding one to my Christmas list. This is precisely the reason so many chief financial officers are suspicious of branding initiatives. But the hollow promise is not branding. It's wordsmithing. Real branding clarifies three fundamental questions:

- What is it?
- Why does it matter?
- How does it create value?

When we talk about value, it's important to be specific. Sometimes, in an effort to retain our options, we are tempted to overgeneralize about the value the brand delivers. Consider the following example:

> GoogSoft makes technology solutions that deliver superior value
> to customers and consistent financial returns for shareholders.

Promise statements like this one fall into a different kind of trap; they describe table stakes. If a brand doesn't deliver superior value to customers, it's not much of a brand. The questions are: What kind of value do you provide and how do you provide it? Likewise, if your brand is part of a for-profit operation, you'd better deliver consistent financial returns or you might not be in business tomorrow. There's nothing in a table-stakes promise that differentiates, nor does it define value-producing behavior.

Allow me to illustrate real branding in action—the type of branding that guides business decisions as much as it inspires creative expression.

A TALE OF TWO BRANDS

How Washington Federal and Washington Mutual Shared Only a Common State

"There's a lot people don't know about us."

Roy Whitehead looks more like an aviator than the CEO of one the nation's strongest banks. While he dresses every bit like a banker, there's something about him that suggests he might own a bomber jacket and you'd certainly trust him to pilot your plane. Canvas the halls of Washington Federal and you'll be hard-pressed to find someone who disagrees. But the story of the Washington Federal brand isn't about Roy Whitehead. He's just one of many examples that explain why the brand is one of banking's best, despite the fact that it isn't as well known as its national peers. Like many other brands, the team at Washington Federal contemplated a change to its brand identity. But unlike the people behind the No Child Left Behind and Gap changes, the Washington Federal team wanted to make sure that any change in its identity clarified and signaled the foundational values that made their business a success.

"We have never had a layoff. Not once. And we've been around for more than ninety years." When Roy says this, he's not engaging in recessionary grandstanding. His statement is a core tenet of Washington Federal's value-producing behavior. The bank believes it cannot deliver value to its customers if it doesn't treat its employees with fairness and respect. The average turnover at the front line is lower than industry average. It's staggeringly low among its more seasoned staff, and that sense of ownership among its staff has translated into personal service delivery and very high levels of customer satisfaction.

Discipline makes Washington Federal a strong brand. Its culture is driven by a passion for "commonsense banking." It is a value so critical that it has led it to smart but unusual choices. For example, the bank has not installed ATMs at its branches (though it has inherited a couple dozen in acquisitions) because it believes personal contact creates strong relationships with customers, and the cost of installing and operating ATMs would interfere with its capability to deliver this value.

If you think that Washington Federal is a small-time bank, think again. It maintains one of the highest capital levels of the nation's 100 largest financial institutions. In 2009, the year the recession punished most banks, Washington Federal generated more than $40 million in profit from 160 branches.

The bank is unapologetic about its profitability. In fact, Whitehead will tell you the bank has a "societal obligation to perform well." In his reasoning, if a bank isn't strong and profitable, it is a threat to its community. Throughout the Washington Federal culture you'll find a belief in commonsense banking because that approach allows the bank and the neighborhoods around it to flourish together.

It's ironic that for nearly a hundred years, Washington Federal competed against another Washington financial institution that professed to serve the community but failed in the end. Before its catastrophic demise, Washington Mutual was once known as a bank that focused on customers first. It established a credible reputation as a relationship-focused bank through a heritage of activities such as a school savings program that taught K–6 students how to handle money, with an emphasis on savings. Many customers grew up with a branch in their school, where they learned the value of disciplined financial practices.

Unlike Washington Federal, Washington Mutual pursued growth at the expense of this core brand value. It aggressively expanded toward a dream of being for banking what Walmart is to retail, through the heavy use of subprime mortgages that were often immediately sold to third parties and credit card programs that catered to customers with subprime credit. It did all of this by positioning itself as a bank that knew "the power of yes." Of course, this promise wasn't very credible or sustainable. At some point, a bank has to say no so that it can protect the interests of all of its stakeholders.[14] In the end, Washington Mutual failed because it set unrealistic expectations and made empty promises.

The people of Washington Federal believe they have an obligation to be candid with customers. "We're not afraid to say no so that we can protect a client's interests," Whitehead told me. "That's why we don't have commissioned salespeople. It's to protect the client's interest. And that's why we carry our mortgages. We want our borrowers to find a loan they can actually afford. Our goal is to see them own the paper one day. Yes, we sometimes say no. You can do that and preserve strong relationships with your clients. In fact, the best clients respect you for it."

Despite its reputation for consistently delivering on a promise of commonsense banking and a commitment to customer relationships that routinely exceeded expectations, Washington Federal did face a brand challenge. The bank's identity didn't send the right signals and in some ways limited its ability to develop relationships with new generations of customers. Because Washington Federal chose to keep costs low so that they could deliver good returns to customers and shareholders, its identity was dated and beginning to send the signal that the bank was underfunded and small. The original company name, Washington Federal Savings, mistakenly led some customers to think the bank only offered deposit accounts, when in fact it was a valued mortgage lender and growing commercial banker. It had also acquired two banks (First Mutual and First Federal), which it wished to consolidate under one brand. (See Figure 1.1.) When you looked at a Washington Federal branch, with its generic signage and its nonexistent ATMs, you might mistakenly have thought it was a dying brand, when in actuality it led most of the nation's banks in return on assets.

Washington Federal had a legitimate rebranding need. It delivered an exceptional experience, but it was having a hard time encapsulating the value-producing behavior that made it so credible. The answer to its branding challenge was a new identity that linked common sense to flourishing neighborhoods in the simplest of ways. (See Figure 1.2.) Its new identity didn't rely on an ornate logo. Instead, it's almost an antilogo: the words *Washington Federal* stacked and followed by a period. The identity also included the tagline "invested here," a less-than-subtle reminder that the bank

FIGURE 1.1

Washington Federal print collateral, website and signage

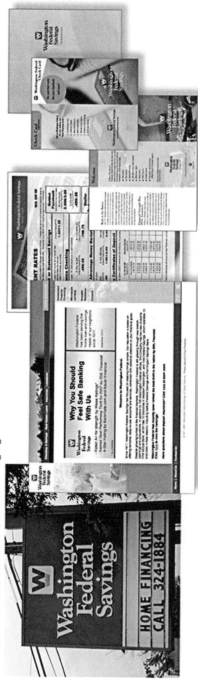

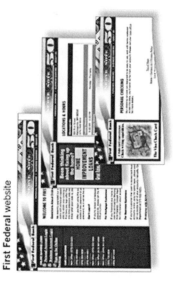

First Federal website

First Mutual branch exterior, website and print collateral

FIGURE I.2

measures its success by what Whitehead called "the greater good"—an investment in the local community through solid performance and adherence to strong values. "The greater good doesn't mean that we build ball fields and adopt stray puppies," Whitehead added. "It means that we understand people in the community rely on a bank as a financial foundation. When we fulfill that obligation, the community is stronger."

Everything about the new identity was designed to simplify the way people think about Washington Federal. It encapsulated the most important linked concepts: a simplified approach, a disciplined commitment to common sense, and an orientation to local interests. The bank is willing to sacrifice other attributes to deliver consistently on this promise.

In the chapters that follow, we'll look at brands that are bigger than Washington Federal. Some are global icons with spectacular awareness and loyalty. But I deliberately chose to finish the first chapter with the story of the bank because, unlike No Child Left Behind and Gap, it refreshed its identity for the right reasons. It didn't use identity as a reactive marketing tactic. Instead, it wanted its identity to accurately set the expectation that its brand lived up to every day. It aligned a credible and compelling expectation to a great experience. And it viewed brand as more than a marketing function. The business *was* the brand. Washington Federal succeeded because it made a meaningful promise to its customers that it knew it could fulfill again and again. Common sense, indeed.

....

CHAPTER TWO

WINNING THE MEMORY GAME

Despite my own best efforts and those of my colleagues in the branding trade to persuade you otherwise, there's no magic to branding. The "magic" we observe when branding is done well relies on basic principles most of us mastered in the games of our childhood. Branding is just another type of memory game.

Imagine you and I shuffle a deck of ten cards consisting of five unique pairs of matching pictures. We spread all the cards facedown on a table. Then we take turns flipping over two cards at a time. If the two cards you flip over match, you get to add the pair to your stack. But if the cards don't match, you have to turn them back over and it's my turn to play. We continue playing this way until all the cards are removed from the table. You win by remembering where cards are when you need to match a pair. In fact, the pairing process makes memorizing easier.

Branding works in a similar fashion. Every day we are exposed to many brands. Each tries to grab our attention by presenting us with a unique symbol or cue. To win this memory game, you have to help the consumer pair two separate ideas: what your brand is and why it matters. As simple as that may sound, many brands struggle in their efforts to help consumers match the two ideas.

The popular perception is that we remember brands with catchy names or logos. While a logo or a name might indeed catch consumers' attention, that's no guarantee they will remember it when choosing between your brand and a competitor's. In fact, if you don't anchor your brand to something concrete, consumers might not include you in their consideration set at all, even though they still think your logo is really cool.

I opened this book saying that a real brand makes a promise that is predictably fulfilled in each brand experience. To do this, your brand must consistently remind me why I should care about it at all. It has to take root in my memory as something specific. There shouldn't be any guesswork. In this chapter, we will explore what makes some brands easier to remember than others. We will also discuss why so many aspiring brands are ignored, denied entry, or downright evicted from our minds.

THE ROAD TO AND FROM MEMORY

Think of memory as a two-way street. First, memory is about storage. Your memory is a place to file away information for later use. Unfortunately, your brain can't remember everything. If you tried to store every experience, every idea, and every mundane piece of data that you encounter in your life, you would quickly exhaust your supply of brain cells. That's why your brain is selective. It filters through all the information that streams by you in a day, and it uses clever rules to decide which information is worth storing in memory. To win the memory game, a brand's first priority is to pass the brain's fitness test and earn a lease on some memory cells.

Storage is only half the battle, though. Each of us stores a lot of information in memory that we seldom retrieve. It's called forgetting. You know how it goes. Suppose you're casually rifling through your closet and you come across a shirt you'd totally forgotten. Now that it is in plain sight, maybe you remember when and where you bought it, or maybe you remember odd little details and emotions from the last time you wore it. These memories flow into your stream of consciousness with little effort. All it took was a simple reminder—a cue. Until you were cued, the shirt was out of sight and out of mind. But the cue unlocked memorized information about the shirt. How well a brand is retrieved from memory is a critically important factor when you play the memory game. We forget about a lot of brands we encounter, but that doesn't mean they don't get stored in memory. It just means they aren't top of mind. An effective brand is easy for us to store in memory and hard to forget.

If you want to win the memory game, you need to answer three important questions:

- What is it about my brand that will help me pass the brain filter?
- What can I do to ensure my brand sticks in a consumer's long-term memory?
- How do I encourage a consumer's brain to recall my brand at relevant moments in time?

Fortunately, there's good science to help you answer these questions. For starters, we know that associating a brand with a concrete idea makes it more likely to be understood and stored in someone's memory. Concrete ideas are specific. They connect to concepts we already know and understand. They are tangible, not abstract. We'll talk more about them in a moment.

Once you've defined your brand concretely, repeated exposure improves its chance of making its way into the consumer's long-term memory. Repetition plays an important role in making a brand top of mind.

Finally, the brands that are recalled most often are connected to a consistent system of cues. Variety might be the spice of life, but to ensure the highest rate of memory retrieval, real brands help us connect dots. Through consistency, they use cues that trigger a chain reaction of memory retrieval that reminds us why the brand really matters to us. Specificity, repetition, and consistency are the ingredients of brands that win the memory game. It may sound like common sense, but if you do a quick survey of the branding universe you'll find a lot of brands that ignore the rules and end up ignored.

REAL AND CONCRETE

Here's a simple question that frequently stumps a branding team: "What is it?"

"What is what?"

"What is the brand?"

"Oh, that's easy," the team says. And then they wax on with abstracts describing ways for me to think about the brand. They might say something like "the brand is all about *wonder*."

"Wonder?"

"Yes. That's what the brand makes you do. It makes you wonder."

I specifically chose this example because I found this one-word brand promise in a strategy document provided by a former client. Forget the fact that it isn't quite clear why "wonder" is a consumer benefit. I'm not sure I'd pay a dollar for the chance to wonder. My first question was what was a customer buying that provided the wonder in the first place?

"Is it a product?"

"Well, yes," said the client. "But the brand also represents the corporate brand. It's both. A product that makes you wonder built by a company that creates great products because they harness wonder."

I'm taking some liberties here, but it's not too far adrift from conversations I've actually had with clients and with very smart, passionately inspired strategists. Unfortunately, "harnessing wonder" probably won't win the memory game. It's too abstract.

You can tell me anything you want about your brand—how easy it is to use, how inexpensive it is, how good it will make you feel—but if I don't understand *what* it is, I probably won't remember anything about its "essence" or "personality." To understand the value of anything, your brain first attempts to classify it. It searches for a category of things to compare it with—a specific point of reference.

Embrace the Nouns

It's not a coincidence that a child's first words are almost always nouns. The way infants use their limited noun vocabulary is profoundly significant for brand strategists. An infant frequently uses one word as a complete sentence. She might say "Mama" to identify her mother when she enters a room. Later, when she's in need of comfort, she might say "Mama" as a signal that she wants to be held. And while she's playing with something that belongs to her mother, she might say the word *mama* to describe her activity. She's seen Mommy doing this. The child can use that one simple word to mean many different things—some purely functional and some wonderfully expressive. In branding, your goal is to provide customers with a similar anchor—a concrete subject matter upon which you can create multiple, relevant meanings.

If I tell you that Brand X is a new running shoe that's designed for a hip-hop lifestyle, you are more likely to remember that it is a shoe than you are to remember that it is positioned around a hip-hop lifestyle. A hip-hop lifestyle is more abstract than a shoe. We could debate what a hip-hop lifestyle means for hours. In fact, some consumers who like your shoe might not even know what "hip-hop lifestyle" means. But we would all agree pretty quickly on what a running shoe is. The challenge is that "running shoe" is a generic idea, and "hip-hop lifestyle" might define the essence and value of Brand X—the factor that differentiates it from competitors and gives it staying power. This paradox is what leads brands astray. The abstract idea is sexier and more proprietary than the concrete one, but the concrete idea sticks to memory with less effort. It does more than stick. Recent research suggests that concrete ideas are recognized faster, are recalled from memory with greater ease, and are perceived to be *more credible* than abstract ideas.[1] That's why a concrete association should always anchor your brand strategy.

Use Anchors for Abstraction

I know what you're thinking. Concrete associations are so boring. You study the big, rock-star brands around you and you say they are so much more than a noun. They have so much meaning. They seem abstract.

There's a strong relationship between abstract ideas and concrete anchors. Let's say that you love a good story. Do me a favor. Please point your finger at one. Maybe you just pointed at a book. A book is a concrete object that we use to anchor the abstract idea of a story. But a story isn't really a book. Stories have many forms. They can be movies, conversations, songs, and even pictures. The concept of story exists only in our minds. You can't really point your finger at a story, but you can point out some of the things that embody the idea of a story.

Suppose you're a sucker for romance. Draw me a picture of love. You might have drawn something that looked like a heart, but a heart is only a symbol—a symbol that represents the idea of love. This pairing of something abstract with something concrete is the essence of how a brand wins the memory game.

A lot of new brands and repositioned old brands fail because they purposefully avoid concrete anchors. They mistakenly fear that a concrete association limits their future options. Helio was a wireless carrier that launched in 2006 by defining itself as a mobile virtual network operator (MVNO). Forget the fact that few people know what a mobile virtual network operator is. When consumers wanted to know whether Helio was a type of phone or a type of phone service, Helio's response was that it was neither. In its advertising Helio advised customers, "Don't Call Us a Phone Company; Don't Call It a Phone." The brand was presented to consumers so abstractly that they didn't know what to think about it at all. It's no surprise that it lost

more than a half a billion dollars in its first three years. It was acquired by
Virgin Mobile in 2008 for $39 million in stock, a small fraction of the $440
million originally invested.

Rather than limit a brand's growth potential, a concrete anchor provides a foundation for growth. Remember, getting past the memory filter
is an important part of the battle. Brands are like viruses. Survival depends
upon their ability to latch onto a host. Once they do, they can mutate into
something bigger and they can spread within our memory. First, however,
they have to stick. We remember things that are easily understood better
than things that make us work to understand them. Concrete ideas stick.

Unfortunately, most managers fear them. "If people associate my brand
with a very specific thing," they reason, "I won't have license to expand." To
which I say, the average consumer still equates Nike with shoes and Amazon with books, but that hasn't stopped either of them from growing profit-
ably and extending their brands into lucrative new business segments with
great growth potential.

Consider two of the biggest and most abstract brands in the world:
Apple and Starbucks. Not long ago we thought of Apple as only a quirky
type of computer that less than 3 percent of us used. Starbucks was a convenient place to buy a decent cup of coffee. Each brand began life positioned very concretely—so concretely that the core idea behind the brand
was part of the brand name. It was Apple Computer and Starbucks Coffee.
But after years of brand evolution, these brands are variously described as
a way of life, a design philosophy, and a culture. Each company dropped
the originating category word from its brand name. It wasn't relevant anymore. In fact, you probably know each of these brands so well that you
could easily imagine what they would do in completely unrelated product
categories such as an airline operated by Apple or a Starbucks collection
of office furniture. But if we were to do a random poll of consumers, I
wager you'd hear them often use the words *computer* and *coffee* as points of
reference for Apple and Starbucks, respectively. Since I'm not a gambler,

I'd wager only because I've conducted the polls and found this frequent association to be true.

THE FIVE BRAND TYPES

Consumers tend to categorize brands into five dominant types: cultures, destinations, products, services, and ingredients. Of course, these types are not mutually exclusive. Many brands could be categorized as any and all of the five types combined. It doesn't matter whether you can logically place a brand into one bucket and one bucket alone. It matters which bucket people tend to put the brand into most readily, and whether or not that bucket best serves your strategy.

Starbucks is good example. Starbucks is a unique *culture* of people, it's a *destination*, a *product* (coffee-based beverages), a *service* (it prepares coffee so you don't have to), and it is an *ingredient* (you can buy ice cream from your grocer that contains Starbucks coffee). That multiplicity is part of why Starbucks is such a powerful brand. However, if you study the history and strategy behind Starbucks, you'll quickly find that its managers purposefully defined it as a destination. They wanted Starbucks to stick in people's memory as "a third place between work and home."[2] They believed this memory root would lead to the most profit and that it would create a competitive position they could defend and leverage.

By defining Starbucks as a place, its executives made decisions they might not have made if they had wanted Starbucks to be known first and foremost as an ingredient. For example, they invested for years in building thousands—some say too many thousands—of Starbucks locations around the world. After decades of exposure and familiarity, we think about Starbucks in many ways, but the "place" metaphor lingers and differentiates it. *Where shall we meet? Let's find a Starbucks.* But first, let's consider the five types of brands and how they differ from one another.

Cultures

Trader Joe's, Southwest Airlines, and IBM are all brands that succeed because when we think of them we think of their "people." We might also think of each one as a place, a service, or a provider of technology products, but it's very hard for us to separate their respective cultures from what they are or what they do. When culture is our mental anchor, we easily and naturally associate the brand with values—values that matter to us and values we expect to experience when we do business with these brands. Values are the reason it's hard for us to place these brands into other buckets. You can say that Trader Joe's is a retail destination, but most consumers attach the brand to the friendly culture that makes its stores work well. You can say Southwest Airlines is a low-fare airline service, but its most loyal customers think of it as an extension of family. You can say IBM makes some of the world's most powerful computers, but it has become a powerhouse of industry.

A culture-focused brand behaves according to values that matter to employees, customers, partners, communities, and investors. This type is most common in large, diversified companies—where no single product or service defines the brand. It is also the dominant brand type that defines organizations that own and operate brands that are seemingly disconnected from the corporate brands. For example, consumers know Tide and Post-it Notes as product brands. They don't typically think of them as cultures. But Tide and Post-it Notes are products of two corporate cultures, Procter & Gamble and 3M, respectively. These cultures behave according to a value system that influences the design, manufacturing, distribution, marketing, and customer support behind the product brands. While the attributes of the Tide and Post-it Notes product brands probably matter most to consumers, the value systems of Procter & Gamble and 3M matter more to their employees, retailers, investors, and suppliers.

A lot of professional service companies (law firms, advertising agencies, consultancies, etc.) define and differentiate themselves as particular culture brand types because it's hard to discern the differences among the services they provide. With no disrespect to the legal trade, it's hard to evaluate the service quality of different firms. It all looks the same to the layperson. However, a layperson can easily evaluate the *cultural* differences among firms. I can meet with several law firms and decide which one seems like it's the best fit.

In fact, the link between cultural values and the individual consumer's values is becoming far more important in nearly every context. In a 2010 study by Young & Rubicam, 71 percent of U.S. consumers agreed with the statement "I make it a point to buy brands from companies whose values are similar to my own." Nowhere is this sentiment more strongly felt than in the hearts and minds of the Millennial Generation (people born in the mid-1970s through the mid-1990s). A 2011 study of more than seven thousand Millennials worldwide advised, "In order to achieve a more authentic role, it's helpful for brands to understand what young people value in their REAL friends." These consumers favored brands that could credibly demonstrate authenticity, fairness, and social contribution. [3]

Destinations

It isn't always the *who* but the *where* that makes a brand stick in our minds. I previously described how Starbucks used this strategy to stand out and develop legions of followers around the world, but many countries and tourism organizations obviously leverage the same strategy. When you focus your brand on the destination type, you complete the sentence "Where do you go to . . . ?" Our lives are dominated by a sense of place. Cognitive linguist George Lakoff argues that orientation is a metaphor we frequently use in our language and understanding. We connect so many parts of our lives to destinations on a journey. We talk about going uptown or downtown as easily as our moods go up and down. We relate the concept of "home" to many more places than where we live. It can be the place where we're born or the default website to which we point our browsers. Among concrete brand types, a destination has some of the deepest symbolic roots and a bounty of opportunities for attaching meaningful abstract ideas.

Naturally, nations, cities, and tourist destinations tend to brand around the destination type, though some of these places prefer to brand around culture. Where a culture brand aligns values, a destination brand promises a change in orientation. We favor these brands because they deliver an experience we can find only when we go there and nowhere else. Starbucks "third place" promised a comforting, socially oriented experience that you couldn't find at home or at work. This is just as true when you think about most geographically focused destination brands; whether Ireland or the State of Hawaii, the brand promises a change in orientation you can experience only by going there.

But destination brands aren't limited to physical places. Television networks have focused their branding around "destination programming" for many years. A television network is a virtual place where you can change the orientation of your viewing experience. Now that a majority of U.S. households have access to cable or satellite television, offering hundreds of channel options, the focused networks like ESPN have enjoyed explosive growth and popularity because they have positioned themselves as destinations with distinctive and predictable orientations. The same is true for many online brands. Facebook has thrived and become one of the world's most successful online brands because of the way its members think of it as a place to go to connect with friends. In 2011, Google declared that Facebook was its chief rival. I found the distinction interesting because, from a branding perspective, Google is defined in most people's minds in a very different way. Google sticks as a service (which we'll explore in a moment). When you consider that distinction, you can understand why it has invested so much money to create new, socially oriented services and features that aim to define Google as more of a destination, like Facebook. In fact, Facebook is perceived so strongly as a place that *AdAge*'s Simon Dumenico compared it to a bar where "[y]ou're used to a certain amount of advertising in the bar—all those neon signs you've learned to ignore—so you're basically accepting, while also a little wary. But the truth is, you mostly just come here to kick back and hang out with your friends—to kill a little time and shoot the breeze."[4]

While most people think of Sony PlayStation as a product brand, when it relaunched Home, a service that allowed gamers to play downloadable games, they defined it explicitly as a place—a "game park," to be exact. Like a real-world theme park, PlayStation wanted people to think of Home as a place you went to on your console to explore hundreds and hundreds of downloadable games in a very social, playful way. Gamers responded by spending an average of seventy-two minutes on Home during a typical session. Home stood for more than a service. It was a different way of seeing and experiencing games, and it was anchored to the very concrete idea of a destination—a place to hang out with other gamers.

Products and Services

In some ways, product and service brands are very much alike. We are predisposed to think of each in terms of price, function, and quality. When you are defining the strategy for a product or service brand, you are concocting a recipe. It's the benefit derived from the mix of features and functions that you string together that anchors the brand to our memory. For example, if Brand X is an automobile, it might offer superior road handling at a premium price. Meanwhile, Brand Y might offer lesser handling while being priced for affordable luxury.

Product brands are easy for our minds to conceptualize. They are physical things. We can see and touch them. Some of the best product brands are top of mind solely because all of the branding is contained in the product. Dyson vacuum cleaners are a perfect example. People who use them swear by them, and the product design is so iconic that it sticks in our minds and is inseparable from our understanding of the brand.

Where it gets tricky is in product categories where every product has basically the same features. Coca-Cola is a good example. In taste test after taste test, consumers cannot discern any real difference between Coke and

Pepsi. Because they are so competitive, there is very rarely a significant difference in price. That's why Coke and Pepsi spend billions of dollars in advertising and promotion to try to link their brands to cultural values. And research suggests that consumers do associate Coke and Pepsi with values more than price, function, or quality. However, it's deceptive to reflect on these two legendary brands and assume that your product or service brand should take the same path. Coke and Pepsi have the benefit of scale and time on their side. When they launched in the late nineteenth century, they began by differentiating themselves with functional and qualitative attributes. Early on, Coke had trouble convincing customers that "the real thing" tasted better than the products of its imitators. That's part of the reason we have the legendary contour bottle. It was introduced in 1916 to help people differentiate Coke from other soft drink brands. But when Coke and Pepsi capitalized on the then-untapped soft drink market in every corner of the globe, they ran out of opportunities to differentiate on the basis of price, quality, and function. So each switched the emphasis of its brand promise to a set of cultural values. It doesn't change the fact that the brands first stuck in the cultural consciousness as a type of product.

Lately, sustainability has become an important focus of many product brands. "Green" brands have surfaced in product categories as diverse as laundry detergent and paper towels. It's reasonable to assume that consumers who have strong feelings about the environment and the sustainability movement would always prefer brands that are aligned with these values. But a 2010 study in the *Journal of Marketing* proved how strongly our brain connects product brands with functionality. Respondents were exposed to two private-label hand sanitizer brands. One was called Up & Up Green (Eco Friendly) and one was called Up & Up White. The products were featured side by side on a table at the entrance to a college cafeteria. Above the table was a sign reading, "Swine Flu Alert. Use Hand Sanitizers As Often As Possible." In one leg of the study, the respondents were clearly being observed, with a researcher in plain sight making note of which sanitizer people used. In the other leg, the observer could not be detected. When respondents could tell they were being observed, they gravitated toward the green brand, perhaps thinking it was the socially acceptable choice. But when they didn't know they were being observed, the majority chose Up & Up White. The moral of the story is that when functionality really matters (such as when you're worried you might catch swine flu), values often take a backseat.

With service brands, we run into a different challenge. We can't really see or touch a service brand. A service isn't a concrete thing; it's a means to an end. A service brand relieves us of the burden of labor, often by having other people do it for us. For this reason, it's hard to separate a lot of service brands from the people who deliver the service. It creates a challenge that is the reverse of a product brand's challenge. A lot of product brands would like to differentiate themselves based on the values of their culture, but consumers are prone to think about them in terms of price, quality, and functionality. In contrast, many service brands would love to be conceptualized purely on the basis of their price, quality, and functionality, but consumers tend to judge them based on the culture that delivers the service.

Let's say I run a dry cleaning service. I work hard to get your shirts cleaner and better pressed than any other brand. I have a competitive price point. And I offer additional services that other cleaners don't. But to deliver that service, I underpay my employees. Consequently, I've bred a toxic company culture. When you come in to pick up your dry cleaning, a sour, overworked cashier greets you and provides an unpleasant experience. You will probably judge my brand on that cultural fact more than on the quality, price, and features of my service because you are predisposed to think of my people and the service interchangeably.

A technology service such as Google can avoid some of this confusion. It is evaluated more like a product in that people tend to categorize it according to its function more than its culture. Search is a service that helps you find what you want on the Web. Gmail helps you send and receive e-mails. Your brain thinks about this brand first as a technological solution that is a means to an end and then maybe as a culture with certain values. In fairness to Google, it has invested considerably to draw attention to its culture. Insiders know that it allows employees to spend 20 percent of their time working on personal projects and that its code of conduct is "Don't be evil." While those values may strike a chord with employees and investors, the average consumer views Google as a type of service.

On a separate note, I find it interesting that in an interview with the *New York Times,* Amazon CEO Jeff Bezos defined the Kindle Fire, a tablet device, by saying, "I think of it as a service. Part of the Kindle Fire is of course the hardware, but really, it's the software, the content, it's the seamless integration of those things."[5]

Ingredients

The ingredient brand is the most misunderstood, misused, and abused type of brand. A lot of people think ingredient brands are a new phenomenon, popularized by Intel's successful "Intel Inside" brand campaign of the 1990s. That's hogwash. We've had ingredient brands for as long as we've had brands. Shoppers have looked for orange juice made with Sunkist oranges. We've attended blockbuster motion pictures filmed in Technicolor and searched for exercise gear made with genuine Lycra. And then there are all the culturally significant and staunchly protected ingredient brands. The French government vigorously pursues sparkling wines that falsely claim to be Champagne. Italy has established a standard that must be followed in order to claim that a suit is "made in Italy." And until the ascension of Starbucks, the best restaurants made sure you knew that the coffee they served was 100 percent Columbian. Ingredient brands have always had an important position in the brand landscape.

An ingredient brand is something that a host brand includes to make itself more valuable. When the ingredient brand is very powerful, it can claim a significant share of the premium a consumer might be willing to pay. For example, if I offered you two generic-brand chocolate chip cookies, one made with Nestle Toll House Morsels and the other with generic chocolate chips, you'd probably be willing to pay a few cents more for the cookie containing Toll House Morsels. The ingredient brand adds value. I tell students and clients that an ingredient brand lives to "bless" other brands—like a laundry detergent that contains Clorox bleach.

Contagion theory is one of the more fascinating strains of consumer research. In ways that often appear to be completely irrational, consumers perceive that one brand can rub off on another brand and make it better or worse. In one study, consumers were observed keeping certain products and brands on different sides of their shopping carts, presumably because close proximity lessened the value. Similarly, consumers have often developed a more positive point of view about a previously uninteresting brand because it included a valuable branded ingredient. For an ingredient brand to work, it has to be contagious. The quality that it provides has to rub off on the brand that hosts it. When ingredient-branding strategies fail, it is usually because the branded ingredient is irrelevant to consumers.

I once had a client that manufactured components for mobile phones. This client's products were valuable ingredient brands. Customers were willing to pay a premium for the technology because it made the products better. However, the client spent millions of dollars branding specific features that were incorporated into the core component. It created distinctive names and logos and went through costly processes to trademark and protect these features within the ingredient brand. They were ingredients of the ingredient. Customers cared about those ingredient ingredients about as much as you might care about the brand of cocoa that went into a Toll House Morsel found in a Mrs. Fields cookie. When we studied the market, we found that customers were familiar with few of these "feature" ingredient brands. In some cases, the customer had heard of the feature but didn't know what it really did or how it contributed to the value of the core ingredient. It was clear that the features didn't need to be branded at all. They didn't make the core ingredient brand any more valuable. When we pressed the client, we learned that it was impossible to separate featured ingredient brands from the core component brand. In other words, these featured ingredients were included by default and they never appeared elsewhere. What's the point of branding an ingredient that doesn't tip the scale for the host and can't be leveraged broadly? There is none.

To create a successful ingredient brand, you must satisfy three criteria. First, the brand must make a distinct contribution to the brands that include it. Ideally, the brand is associated with a single attribute. Toll House Morsels taste better. Clorox bleach promises whiter whites. Narrow, focused associations work better for ingredient brands than broad, fuzzy associations.

However, the narrowness with which we think about ingredient brands is also a potential hazard that is best illustrated by "Intel Inside." Back in the 1990s, consumers had been conditioned to believe that the best computers had the fastest processors. As an ingredient brand, Intel guaranteed speed, and consumers were willing to pay a premium for it. More recently, however, devices have changed. PC sales have tapered off significantly as consumers rely more on their smartphones and tablet devices. The relationship between performance and processor speed is a lot less clear. Instead, consumers are drawn to connectivity, battery life, and product design. This explains why Intel has invested heavily to reposition its brand. When it launched its "sponsors of tomorrow" campaign, it seemed almost as if Intel wanted consumers to think of the brand as a culture. But the values associated with a culture are less persuasive in an ingredient context, and they are often in conflict with the values and attributes the host brand may want to own in the consumer's mind. Intel is still the dominant semiconductor brand in the world. Only time will tell whether or not they can use their market position to reframe the way that consumers think of them, and whether or not that really matters to the corporate brand's long-term success at all.

Second, an ingredient brand must be perceived as additive. While you might be able to buy and consume an ingredient brand off the shelf on its own (I confess, I have snacked a time or two on a bag of Toll House Morsels), ingredient brands are at their best when they are incorporated into the formulas of other brand types, predominantly products and services. If they can't be added to something else, they're not ingredient brands. That may seem obvious, but I've been pitched by too many brands that claim to be ingredients but are destined for death because they will live most of their lives going it alone. An ingredient brand is a beneficial parasite. It cannot exist without a host.

Third, ingredient brands should provide their owners with sizable leverage. They do this in one of two ways. Sometimes, they provide leverage to the owner by offering an exclusive advantage between product or service life cycles. You can find Apple's iOS operating system only on Apple branded devices. iOS is an ingredient brand that provides Apple with a constant source of value as the company introduces newer and newer generations of iPhones and iPads. If Apple introduces a new type of device—for example, an iCar—it can use the iOS ingredient brand as a true selling advantage for the new platform. It creates leverage by ensuring compatibility and ease of use. This differs from ingredient brands that provide leverage by getting themselves included in the broadest possible mix of third-party products and services, where an ingredient brand like Bluetooth creates a positive network effect. This mode of leverage can spawn lucrative licensing deals, whereby companies sometimes compete for the right to include the ingredient brand in their own product or service formulation.

If you intend to launch an ingredient brand, make sure you satisfy all three conditions. Your brand should be narrowly linked to a specific value. It should be additive in nature. And it should provide you with uncommon leverage. If it doesn't do all three, it's probably not an ingredient brand and you'd be better off getting people to think of it as one of the other brand types.

THE BRAND STACK

When I tell clients that they need to clarify the type of brand they want to be, I often get a lot of resistance. They argue that it's not practical to think of a brand in one narrow dimension. They're surprised when I agree with them. When I ask them to clarify the type of brand they want to be, I'm not asking them to limit their options. I'm asking them to tell me which type of brand will give them the most competitive advantage.

To demonstrate what I mean, I draw a brand stack (see Figure 2.1). Let's say that we surveyed all of your customers and a large sample of prospective customers. We played a sorting game in which we asked customers to put your brand into one of the five buckets. We keep track of three metrics. First, we record the bucket they were forced to put your brand into. Did they sort it into the "culture" bucket or did they sort it into the "product" bucket? The second metric we measure is how long it took them to choose a bucket. If they did it right away, we can assume that it was pretty easy for them to categorize you the way they did. If it took them a long time, we can assume that they were conflicted by the choice. Last, we asked them to do the exercise three more times, each time removing the buckets they chose before. This helps us choose their picking order.

FIGURE 2.1

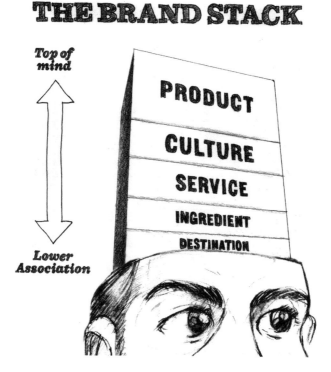

After we analyze our three metrics, we draw a stack that shows how people are likely to categorize you. The top bar is "top of mind." That's the way most people think of you right away. One layer down is the secondary way people think of you. The size of the bar gives you a sense of frequency compared to the other associations. It's possible that consumers indeed think of your brand along all five of the typologies, but the brand stack shows us the type into which people are predisposed to sort you. We can use the brand stack in two ways. First, we can get a good sense of what people think today. Second, we can decide whether or not the way people think is aligned with our strategic goals. If your brand stack reveals that people think of you as a product and your long-term growth strategy requires that you be thought of as a culture, we can take steps to reposition the brand so that values are emphasized over product attributes. Conversely, if you believe your future lies in becoming the necessary ingredient behind other brands and the world views you as a product with many attributes, you're going to have to scope down to succeed.

The beauty of the brand stack is that it reveals the multiple dimensions of a brand and doesn't assume that it's all or nothing. It can be used over time to compare shifts in associations. There are many different ways you could design a study to capture a brand stack. It could be a purely qualitative exercise or a rigorously quantitative endeavor. Your goal is to map the relative strength of each type and the ease with which your audience links it to the brand.

BEFORE YOU BUILD A BRAND . . .

In this chapter I've outlined the differences among the five dominant brand types. Specifically, I've tried to persuade you that, despite all the exceptions to the rules, the average consumer sorts brands into one of these five types and that the concreteness of that type is the foundation of why and how consumers memorize the brand. I've also tried to convey that you shouldn't fear concreteness because focusing on a specific brand type creates a vital anchor—a way to stick in the mind of the consumer. It does not limit the brand's ability to grow more abstract over time, nor does it limit a brand's potential to infiltrate new markets, new product or service categories, or new brand extensions. Brand types are obviously not the whole story. In the next chapter I'll present the other half of the equation: the way in which a brand delivers value. But before we go there, allow me to suggest that you not brand at all. That's right. If you are thinking about launching a new brand or if you are considering whether or not to invest in a lagging brand, I want you to reconsider.

I told you that branding is a memory game. It makes sense to invest in a brand only if you can make it easy to memorize and hard to forget. But our commercial landscape is littered with brands that are hard to memorize and easy to forget.

If you find yourself struggling to anchor your brand to one of the five brand types, that's a warning sign that your brand may be destined for failure. This is true particularly if you are launching a new brand. You're asking too much if you want consumers to immediately link your brand to more than one type. Either they will choose a dominant type on their own or they'll pass you by. Similarly, if you're trying to reposition a lagging brand, you need to focus your brand on a dominant type in order to change direction. Otherwise, you'll be like the driver who gets stuck in the mud and keeps spinning his wheels, hoping that eventually something will take hold. It's better to throw something under the tire and try for some traction.

You also must consider two factors that I mentioned at the beginning of this chapter. Repetition is essential. If you cannot ensure that your brand idea will be repeatedly exposed to your audience, your brand is not going to stick in long-term memory. Let me make it clearer for you. Do you have the resources to associate your brand repeatedly with multiple brand types? Resources = time and money. Lots of managers have told me that "brand" will be the key to their business's success. Then they show me all the different ways consumers should think about their brand. When I ask them how much they plan to spend to launch and maintain so many fronts for their brand, I often have to suppress a laugh. You don't have to have a billion-dollar marketing budget to create a brand, but it gets more and more expensive to secure the required repetitions when your brand has multiple definitions.

Furthermore, you have to be prepared to spend beyond the act of creation. Do you have sufficient budget to remind people what your brand is and why it matters at every relevant touch point with your audience? Too many companies position their brand, create a brand identity, and then wait to update packaging, build signage, or develop corporate identity materials. Every one of your brand's touch points has the potential to increase the repetition of brand exposure and categorization. You need those repetitions to make your brand stick the right way in someone's memory.

The breadth of touch points also provides you with the third essential element. You have to consistently apply the brand for people to cue it up in memory. If you aren't prepared to align all the relevant pieces of your brand so that they loop back to the brand promise and the core idea that will solidify your place in a consumer's memory, don't brand. If yours is a culture brand, are you prepared to invest the considerable time it takes to educate, inform, and inspire the people within your organization so that they behave in a branded way? If yours is an ingredient brand, are you prepared to invest the time with your partners or internal product teams to ensure that they think about the value of the ingredient in a consistent way that creates the most leverage for your brand? Consistency is essential, and if you aren't prepared to ensure that consistency, then I beg you, please, don't brand.

However, if you are ready to commit your brand to a life of concreteness, repetition, and consistency, onward!

CHAPTER THREE

....

THE BENEFIT
OF YOUR BRAND

I t's the moment of choice. Maybe I'm not even aware I'm choosing. Maybe
I'm sitting in traffic and I am only aware that I'm hungry. My mind drifts
to dinner. For reasons I certainly can't explain, I want pizza. It takes me
a fraction of a second to have a preference. A half hour later I'm savoring
the flavors of the local pizzeria that popped into my head. Even though my
mind probably weighed many options, my choice felt pretty effortless. Several known benefits could have factored into my selection, such as a particular flavor of sauce I might have been craving or a price point, or the speed
of service, or positive emotions associated with my past experience at the
restaurant, or a need for a little variety. But I didn't sit in my car considering each of these one by one in a thoughtful conversation with myself. I just
knew what I wanted.

Our brains go through this process of weighing the benefits of different
options many times a day, every day. But we're consciously aware of it only
some of the time. Brands are meant to influence this decision process. They
succeed only when they stand for a relevant benefit—something that matters to the person making the choice.

When marketers say that you must "sell the sizzle and not the steak,"
they're referring to the benefit of your brand. In Chapter 2, I told you that

your brand has to represent something specific; if not, it will have a slim chance of being remembered. I also said that we memorize brands as pairings, matching a specific type of thing to a relevant benefit. This chapter covers the six common strategic themes that serve as benefits for a brand. We're going to focus on the sizzle, or, more specifically, the benefits of a brand's promise.

Figure 3.1 shows the six themes along a spectrum. Think of it as a bridge between your left brain and your right brain because the themes to the left are a little more rational, while the themes to the right are a little more aspirational. That doesn't mean the benefits on the left are any less valuable than the benefits on the right. The two ends are different, and the spectrum is meant to show the degrees of differentiation.

By narrowing the benefits to six common themes, I'm obviously generalizing. Don't misunderstand my intention. You won't succeed if you reduce the discipline of branding to a formulaic process of picking a generic brand type and matching it to a generic brand benefit. Every brand has its own DNA, with subtle genetic differences that factor into our preference for it over another. I only want to draw your attention to the common bloodlines. The six brand themes we are about to explore represent strategic directions that surface over and over again in branding. More important, they guide strategic decisions. When a brand is managed well, it is focused around

FIGURE 3.1

some variation of one of these six themes in order to create a significant and distinctive benefit for consumers. This benefit provides the reason for the brand. When you strip off all the cool design and buzz factors, pull back the manicured layers of creative communications tactics, it is always one of these six strategic themes that answers these two questions: Why does this brand exist at all? Why should anyone care?

ACCESSIBILITY

Benefits of Scale

Though we are often counseled to adopt a mentality of abundance, a fear of scarcity drives a lot of human behavior. That's why it should be no surprise that access is one of the most prevalent branding themes. It is also a promise that rewards organizations that are willing to scale. When a brand matters because it has the most locations or the lowest prices, or because it is always open, you can be sure the brand strategy revolves around accessibility.

Visa has long focused its brand promise around the benefits of complete access. For decades, the brand told us that it was "everywhere you want to be." Even after the brand repositioned itself to appeal more to lifestyles, it continued to promise us that "Life takes Visa." It's more than a tagline. Visa has invested more in its network of merchants and card issuers than any other payment card brand. It's safe to say that if you go to any merchant in North America that accepts a payment card, Visa is accepted. The same is not true for American Express. Visa promises that you'll never have to worry about whether your card will work. This is compelling because people do worry about it. No one wants to be the character from the movie who ends up washing dishes because he couldn't pay for his meal. As more and more people move to cashless transactions, the benefit of Visa's promise will only grow more relevant, especially if the brand invests to maintain its acceptance leadership.

The accessibility theme also lies at the root of low-price brand leaders. Walmart matters to consumers because of its low-price guarantee. It is a brand that promises a better quality of life by providing more access to the necessities of life. Everything Walmart does as a brand is designed around its promise of accessible prices. Internally, Walmart executives have characterized the brand as the "Robin Hood that worked to bring the 'American Dream' to people in rural America."

For a brief period of time, Walmart tried to change its brand direction, and it learned a hard lesson. Looking over its shoulder at the sexy, pop-culture campaigns of Target, its largest competitor, Walmart tried to convince shoppers that it was a lifestyle brand. When store sales fell flat, it didn't take long for Walmart to realize that "lifestyle" wasn't what shoppers valued from Walmart. They valued accessibility. Even though prices didn't change during the failed repositioning attempt, consumers worried that Walmart might become less accessible in order to become more hip.

Walmart commits to its promise in compelling and innovative ways. It is truly a filter for strategic decisions. For example, many brands have pursued "green," or environmentally sensitive, initiatives. Most decide to go green because they presume it will make them look like good corporate citizens, which will encourage consumers to give them their business. Walmart adopted a green strategy, but it didn't decide to go green as a ploy to prove that it could be politically correct, as some observers suspected. Walmart went green because energy is a significant component of its cost structure. Reducing energy costs lowered Walmart's operating costs, which helped it keep prices low for customers.

I'm often asked if price shouldn't be a theme in its own right on the brand spectrum. There's a good reason why it's not. Consumers relate to price in two distinct ways. Sometimes they use price as an indicator of quality ("this wine costs more, so it must be better"). At other times, they perceive price as an indicator of personal sacrifice ("how much will this wine set me back?").[1] When price is perceived more as a sacrifice rather than an indicator of quality, the benefit of the brand is usually *access*. By minimizing the amount of sacrifice required, low-price brands provide consumers with better access.

FEATURE FOCUS

Benefits of Functionality

Access is fine, but what if I'm willing to pay more for a brand that does more—either in one specific way or in more ways altogether? When I link my promise to the features of my brand, I'm promising you the benefit of superior functionality. An access brand might bank on the notion that "beggars can't be choosers," and you'd be willing to sacrifice features for a lower price or for improved access to my product, service, or company. A feature brand, on the other hand, banks on the fact that there are profitable markets for brands that work better.

If we could zoom in on the thematic spectrum I showed you earlier in the chapter, we might see a mini-spectrum that bridges the gap between an access brand and a feature brand (see Figure 3.2). In the overlap between

FIGURE 3.2

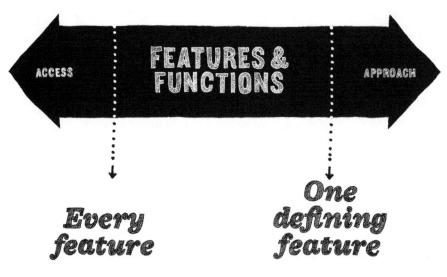

an access brand and a feature brand you might find brands that win because they promise the greatest number of features (the left-hand side of our mini-spectrum). Historically, Microsoft and its portfolio of product brands have focused their attention on this end of the spectrum. The Microsoft brand often promises the most features and the most robust functionality. Microsoft is a feature brand, but the benefit of all those features gets close to the benefit of an access brand. By having features that suit the needs of anybody, Microsoft has aimed to be the brand for everybody.

As you move from left to right across the mini-spectrum, access becomes less important. In this range, a brand offers fewer features, but those that it does offer it tends to do very well. In fact, these features are a source of competitive advantage and they provide the core benefit for the brand.

Headphone maker Skullcandy leveraged the features strategic theme to capture a sizable share of the personal audio market. From its inception, the brand has focused on young consumers and action-sports enthusiasts. That's why its colorful earbuds and headsets are often found dangling around the necks of snowboarders and skateboarders in more than seventy countries. Founded in 2003, Skullcandy went public on the NASDAQ exchange in July 2011. In eight short years it went from nothing to a leading brand by promising that its products would consistently deliver on three key features:

- The "Skullcandy sound"—high-quality audio engineered for the type of music its audience listens to most
- Cool product design—bold colors, loud patterns, and creative materials
- Reasonable prices

Though the brand rarely advertises its price points, Skullcandy earbuds and headphones have historically been priced much lower than competitive products, making them a perfect fit for younger audiences. Skullcandy products don't offer every feature, and they won't appeal to all audiences. Durability is a deliberately missing feature that has occasionally earned the brand some bad press. However, because the brand is priced lower and connected to the cyclical whims of fashion, it can afford to ignore durability. That is not the core benefit of its promise. As long as it consistently delivers the Skullcandy sound through designs that appeal to active listeners, the brand fulfills its promise.

APPROACH

Benefits of Philosophy

The biggest difference between an access brand and a features brand is a shift from quantity to quality, but as we move further and further toward the left of the spectrum, quality becomes more prominent. Many brands win our hearts because of *how* they deliver quality, rather than *what* quality they deliver. Imagine I present you with two pairs of jeans. On inspection, they look and feel identical. However, I tell you that one pair was made from denim that was milled in the United States and hand-sewn by workers who received full benefits and a living wage. The other pair was made from comparable materials sourced elsewhere and mass-produced in Malaysia. If research were a reliable indicator (and it usually is), you'd probably be willing to pay more for the first pair of jeans. In fact, you might be willing to pay considerably more. Why? Before I told you where and how the jeans were made, you could tell no noticeable difference between the two pairs. They looked and felt identical. But now you know that the manufacturers had different approaches—and approach matters!

American Apparel vaulted into the commoditized garments category in part because it leveraged just such an approach-driven brand strategy. All of the company's merchandise is manufactured in the United States. And American Apparel employees receive above-average pay for the industry and an impressive array of employee benefits. While you might not be able to tell the difference between an American Apparel T-shirt and a generic brand, you might prefer it to the generic because you know that it supports the U.S. economy and that people who were paid fairly for their work made it.

Approach can be a powerful form of attachment between a consumer and a brand, but it can also pose a significant challenge. An approach-driven brand strategy works only when your audience actually cares about how benefits are created.

Let me provide you with a real-life illustration. My father engineered software during the early days of the defense industry. He had a passion for the poetic logic of code. While he was one of the most easygoing people I've ever met, he was a stickler for efficient and elegant code. I know this because when I was twelve years old he bought me a Commodore Vic 20, a dinosaur of personal computing that came without any software. I remember the first time he turned it on. The cursor blinked at me on the blank, black television screen. It didn't do anything. This lame contraption didn't interest me until I learned that I could play games on it—games that I had to program myself.

I learned to program because I wanted to play games. I got good at it, even writing a few from scratch rather than plugging in a recipe. Every so often, my father would inspect my coding style, and he would offer me a challenge. "Change this section and see if you can achieve the same result with fewer lines of code," he would say. This seemed silly to me. The code I wrote worked perfectly well. Why did I need to shorten it? But it was no use bargaining. Dad made my life miserable unless I tried again.

On one occasion, I spent a full summer day fiddling with my code, trying to make it shorter. When I finally surrendered, my father sat in front of my computer. He replaced several lines of my code with one brief, elegant statement. The program ran exactly the same as it had before. While Dad was quite proud of himself, I sarcastically added, "Big deal. It does the same thing."

It took the old man only a moment to reply.

"Yes, but my approach was better."

Now, try to imagine yourself as a twelve-year-old boy with a limited attention span. I didn't care the least bit about the efficiency of my code. I just wanted to play games. Sure, Dad was right. Efficient code was better because it enabled the computer to work faster and accomplished all kinds of technical things that made my game a better product of engineering. But I couldn't see any real difference in the two constructions, and his approach made my life needlessly difficult. Other than making my dad proud, I didn't place much value on approach.

The moral of the story: If you opt to follow a strategy of building your brand on the benefit of an approach, be sure that approach is relevant to your audience. In fact, it must be so relevant that they are willing to forgo more accessible options, more functional options, or higher-quality options. They have to care so much about *how* you do what you do for them that they'll pay for that benefit more than any other.

Make no mistake: An approach can create an intrinsic benefit that matters to consumers. In fact, there's a growing body of research suggesting that how a goal is achieved is as important or more important than simply achieving the goal. In the academic literature, fitness brands are offered as an example. There is one segment of consumers who care about one benefit and one benefit alone: losing weight. They hate going to the gym. They go only because they have to. Perhaps their doctor told them to go, or they can't stand the way they look in the mirror. Whatever their reason, if they could take a pill and magically make the weight go away, they'd never set foot in a gym again. All that matters to this segment is the goal itself. In contrast, there's another sizable segment of gym members who go because they believe an active lifestyle is essential. For this segment, it isn't the goal of being fit that matters, but the act of maintaining fitness. They talk about exercise as though it is a way of life, a motivational force, and a driver of positive self-esteem. They talk about challenging themselves and proving their strength. If a magic pill could enable these people to maintain their ideal weight for the rest of their lives, they'd still go to the gym because they value the approach to achieving their goals over the outcome of the goals themselves.[2]

When my team worked with McAfee, one of the world's largest digital security companies, we quickly observed this same preference for an approach that leads to results. Every competitor in the category basically offered the same complement of features and functionality that was baked into McAfee technologies. When McAfee was preferred, however, it was because its audience perceived that the company was relentless about uncovering and thwarting the most daunting security threats. Customers hailed the brand's rigorous approach. That's why we worked with McAfee to create a new articulation of its brand promise: tackling the toughest challenges to overcome security threats and liberate customers. We focused everyone inside the organization around this promise. The McAfee way would make the brand more compelling to consumers than the competitors' way. It worked. Shortly after the rebranding, McAfee made some impressive share gains, and the company was soon bought by Intel for $7.6 billion in cash.

PERSONALITY

Benefits of a Relationship

Personality is a hallmark of nearly every great brand. Indeed, in later chapters we'll explore how to evoke your brand's unique voice and how to tailor a distinctive look and feel that projects your brand's personality. But there's a dimension of personality that cuts much deeper than the way we might describe the brand. Sometimes, the personality of a brand provides its main source of value. When we think of a brand as *someone* in our life instead of *something,* the benefit the brand provides is a heightened sense of personal relationship.

Relationships matter. It's not uncommon to find a situation where the brand relationship with the consumer trumps access, functionality, and perceptions of quality. I worked on a project some time ago during which I spent a lot of time in fields talking to farmers about seed brands. Lest you should think *fields* and *seed brands* are marketing buzzwords, my project was for a company that literally develops and sells the seeds that farmers plant in their fields. Farmers are a tough audience to study. It's tempting to think of them as homespun traditionalists—perhaps even unsophisticated—but don't fall prey to this misperception. In today's high-stakes, ultracompetitive global agriculture market, farmers are among the most technologically savvy and results-oriented consumers I've ever met.

Farmers value yield more than anything else. How much will they reap when it's time to harvest? That's what they want to know. If you can prove to them that your seed will yield more bushels per acre than a competitive brand, you stand a great chance of winning their business. Except . . .

A substantial segment of farmers stick with a brand year after year even when it consistently fails to win the yield game. Bob, one of the farmers I interviewed in Illinois, was part of this segment. He told me a story about a recent harvest that didn't go so well. Dave, his sales representative, sat beside him on his combine as the numbers came in. Bob's crop yield was less than 70 percent of what Dave had told him to expect. Before the night was over, Dave wrote Bob a check for the difference. Bob told me that as long as Dave worked for the brand, the brand would have his business, and if Dave went somewhere else, Bob said he would follow him. Relationships were critically important to Bob.

People commit to other people all the time because of relationships. Ever have a friend who makes irritating mistakes but whom you love and are willing to forgive because he or she is a part of your life? This same orientation toward lasting relationships can exist between a consumer and a brand, and it usually occurs when we think of the brand as a personality rather than a faceless company.

Zappos, the online shoe retailer, has built just such a brand. William Taylor, author and cofounder of *Fast Company* magazine, describes Zappos as "a company that's bursting with personality." In fact, the personality of the brand is so critical that it adheres to the principle of hiring for attitude, training for skill. Its managers place more value on hiring someone who will sustain the culture that customers adore than finding people with above-average skills who require less training. Tellingly, compared to other companies, the Zappos application for employment is unconventional. Prospective employees must complete a crossword puzzle that contains shoe-related clues. The purpose: assess whether or not applicants are problem solvers and, more important, see how much they love shoes. Applicants are also asked open-ended questions in which they are encouraged to share their personal experiences with shoes and the brand. After they pass this initial screening, an immersive four-week training period begins, during which they receive full wages. All candidates are also offered a $1,000 bonus if they choose to quit. That's right. If a candidate decides that Zappos isn't for him or her, Zappos will pay the candidate $1,000 to quit the program! While this may seem a very strange proposition, it's one of the many clever ways that Zappos ensures every employee is invested in the personality of the brand and the relationship Zappos promises to its customers. Only the employees who truly care about customers and service stay the course. They're the ones who talk to customers over the phone or connect with them via e-mail. Though loyal Zappos customers will concede that its prices aren't always the lowest nor their selection the broadest, these customers wouldn't shop anywhere else. They describe how much they love the brand's personality, which makes them enjoy every shopping experience. Some say they get excited about shopping on Zappos website. They describe how much they feel they have a relationship with the brand. It's a personality they want to live with.

There's another variety of personality-driven brand—one that is much more literal in its translation of brand to person. It occurs when the brand is truly an extension of a real-life human being. Calvin Klein is an extension of Calvin Klein's personality and fashion sensibility. So is Kate Spade. Actually, Kate's husband, Jack Spade, is one of my favorite examples of how a personality extends into the world of a popular brand. Walk into a Jack Spade store and you're immersed in a world of Jack. The stores are filled with a balanced mix of core goods—the line of bags he designs for men, for example. But you'll also find a seemingly random collection of things that inspire

Jack: vintage jazz albums, books on documentary filmmaking, journals, and "odds and ends." Everything in a Jack Spade store is essentially stuff that Jack finds cool. It creates a deeper sense of relationship with his customers, who are drawn to Jack's curatorial style. We like him, and we like the things that interest him. By default, we like his brand.

Of course, the Jack Spade brand is a niche example. If you want scale, turn your attention to Oprah Winfrey and Martha Stewart. Both have built empires that bear their name and extend their personality to a wide assortment of products, services, and media. These brand moguls have high standards, and everything they brand must satisfy a consumer's needs for functionality and quality. But when a consumer attaches to the Oprah or Martha Stewart brand, they're really buying a piece of the curator's personality to relate to in their everyday lives.

CAUSE

Benefits of Moral Purpose

Some cynics doubt the merits of altruism, but many brands provide benefit to their audiences by leveraging the strategic theme of a cause. A cause-driven brand wins your respect and loyalty because it taps deep into your belief system and aligns itself with moral issues that are bigger than a singular personality. These are societal issues. The Body Shop was one of the earliest brands to successfully leverage a cause as the reason people favored the brand. Sourcing her cosmetic ingredients from third-world countries that needed economic stimulus to satisfy basic human needs, Dame Anita Roddick founded The Body Shop with a dual purpose in mind: sell women quality products that help them feel beautiful and support people and places that have few resources. She prohibited the use of ingredients that had been tested on animals and used her advertising communications to promote "ethical consumerism." Women certainly gravitated toward The Body Shop brand because they loved the quality of the products it offered, but they received the benefit of feeling good about their occasional vanities because they knew that their consumption of the product supported a higher cause.

Perhaps the best illustration of a modern cause brand is from another personal care company. When it launched in 1955, Dove made a functional brand promise: to be gentle to your skin because it contained one-quarter moisturizing cream. But by 2006, grocers' shelves were filled with products that contained special moisturizers and innovative ingredients. A feature/function positioning could no longer differentiate Dove from competitors. To reposition the brand, Dove looked to a cause. During a round of global market research, Dove executives noticed that only 2 percent of women around the world described themselves as beautiful. More than two-thirds of those women blamed the media. Said Dove's agency planner, Olivia Johnson, "You feel deflated when you see the gap between these images of perfection and your own physical reality." So Dove decided to embrace the cause of "real beauty." In close consultation with feminist experts, social psychologists, and opinion leaders, the Dove team repositioned the brand with the aim of making more women feel beautiful. Success would be achieved when new rounds of research revealed that more than 2 percent of women around the world would describe themselves as beautiful. "We wanted to democratize beauty and make more women feel more included in its definition rather than excluded," said Johnson.

The campaign for real beauty has been considered one of the best advertising campaigns of the past decade. Featuring real women with very little makeup and un-retouched images, the campaign redefined beauty and made it larger than life. One advertisement featured a close-up of an older woman in a scarf, shot against a white background. Next to her face were two check boxes. One said "wrinkled" and the other said "wonderful." Next to it was a question: "Will society ever accept 'old' can be beautiful?" Then a call to action: "Join the beauty debate" and a link to the campaign website. The Dove brand became the centerpiece of a cause, and everyone who worked on the brand took great pains to put the cause front and center.

Philippe Harousseau, the head of brand development for Dove at Unilever, put it bluntly: "If you are not crystal clear what the brand's mission is, you cannot control what happens when people amplify it. Everyone working on Dove knows . . . the mission statement does not say Dove is about women feeling more beautiful, but about more women feeling beautiful. Our notion of beauty is not elitist. It is celebratory, inclusive, and democratic."[3]

If you plan to use the cause-positioning pattern, exercise caution. It requires great discipline and a lasting commitment from everyone in your organization. The discipline required is putting the cause first. What happens all too frequently is that the brand launches with an emphasis on the cause, but within a short period of time the cause is pushed aside to pursue tactical objectives such as sales quotas, earnings pressure, or partner satisfaction. You certainly have to run a good business, but if you promise to serve a cause, you risk alienating your audience whenever you set it aside for the sake of commerce. The winning "cause brands" find a way to serve both masters: the cause *and* the return on investment. Arianna Huffington, the editor-in-chief of *The Huffington Post*, emphasized, " . . . [M]ore and more brands want to identify with causes. It's not just good for the brand, it's good for the bottom line."[4]

LIFESTYLE

Benefits of Belonging

Lifestyle brands fascinate us because of their capacity to connect us with a desirable story. There aren't a lot of brands that you could legitimately categorize as legendary, but lifestyle brands dominate the field. That's because the lifestyle brand promises to activate a desirable story that lives in consumers' minds and aspirations. Every time consumers search for, purchase, and/or use a lifestyle brand, they connect themselves with the story that gives it strength and they gain the benefit of belonging to its culture. Lifestyle brands are necessarily irrational. They don't gain their strength from rational benefits such as access, features or the pursuit of a societal cause. They are strong because they connect to desirable emotional states and self-expressive benefits.

Ralph Lauren was born Ralph Lifshitz in the Bronx, the son of European Jewish immigrants. His life couldn't have started farther away from polo grounds, but when he launched his own line of short-sleeve knit shirts, he emblazoned his collection with a now famous logo that captures the essence of the "king of sports." In short order, he began designing clothes and fashion products that drew inspiration from the equestrian set. Polo has become one of the world's most powerful lifestyle brands, and therein lies a story. The Polo brand isn't just about clothes. It is about a way of life that is masculine and refined. It conveys a sense of heritage and success. It's a brand that matches a lifestyle to which many people aspire, and that's the secret of its success.

Lifestyle brands enable a brand mythology cycle (Figure 3.3). In our mind, each of us adheres to a set of beliefs and values that really matter to us. That worldview leads us to hold some parts of our life as sacred. It might be our family, our intellect, or our professional life. It's different for each of

FIGURE 3.3

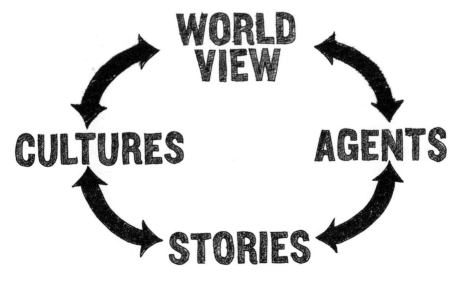

us, but we each, in our own way, have a value system that serves as a kind of script for our behavior. In the same way that our value system leads us to hold some parts of life as sacred, we also find some things in life to be profane—the opposite of what we value. If you value industriousness as a sacred virtue, you might find indulgence disgusting. Las Vegas might seem the antithesis of what is important to you—hard work, practical investment, and an aversion to risk. That same belief system predisposes you to value some brands and despise others. That's why people who adore Whole Foods might be predisposed to hate Taco Bell.

You validate your brand beliefs with agents. Agents prove that your belief makes a difference. For example, if you value creative thinking, you might view an Apple iPad as tangible proof. You might also look at the life and accomplishments Apple's cofounder, the late Steve Jobs, as the work of an agent who proved that creative thinking can lead to innovative products. You might also link these beliefs and proof points to a narrative about yourself. Psychologists try to uncover these narratives when they analyze their patients. Who do you think you are? What has happened in your life? How do you see yourself versus your reality? What do you aspire to? We can piece all of these questions together through a narrative that represents you.

But we rarely have one narrative that defines our life. We usually have many. We live in a society where we have to shift our identity from time to time. You may start the morning as a mom. That mental script is guided by one set of values. After you drop the kids off at school, you may drive to work and switch your life narrative to that of a manager. If I asked you to talk about your work life, it's very likely that another set of values would surface. For most of us, the values that respectively underpin these two lives aren't drastically different, but the script that governs each story often has a life and meaning that is all its own. Brands come into the picture when you need help activating one of your life stories. It is likely that the brands that help you live up to your aspiration of being a great mother are different from the brands that validate your aspiration to be a great businesswoman. Each narrative leans toward a set of brands that activate, validate, and fulfill your expectations. Each narrative describes a different lifestyle. You value the brands that make that lifestyle feel real.

Let's take it one step further. Imagine that we discuss what you like to do in your personal time when you are playing neither of those roles. When you're not in the mom role and you're not in the businesswoman role, you might tell me about your love of food. You love to cook. You love to eat out. You love to watch programs on the Food Network. You tell me how often you go to Williams-Sonoma. You describe your last vacation alone with your husband in Tuscany. You tell me that you plan to go to a culinary school for a week next year. A new narrative unfolds. Again, it may share some similarities with the parent and businesswoman stories, but it has its own distinct characteristics and an entirely different set of brands. This is the dynamic of lifestyles and lifestyle brands. When they are performing at their best, they bring these narratives to life. And in some respects, they help us shift gears between the many selves we maintain on a daily basis.

Every brand must ultimately be true to itself. Brands that pretend to be something they are not ultimately fail to create experiences that match the expectations they falsely set. But lifestyle brands operate by creating an experience that is often at odds with reality. This may shock you, but most of the consumers who buy Polo apparel do not own or ride a horse. They probably know very little about the game of polo. And an awful lot of them aren't affluent. Polo is one of many brands that its consumers choose to escape one narrative and conjure another. The brand helps them fulfill a lifestyle goal to which they aspire and makes that lifestyle more a part of their everyday reality.

TAKING A STAND, CHOOSING A BENEFIT

Branding is rarely about absolutes. It isn't necessary for a brand to select one strategic theme to the exclusion of all others. Nor should you interpret the oversimplification of the themes in this chapter as the boilerplate for a brand strategy. These themes represent bedrock sources of value that we find time and time again when we study consumer behavior and attempt to answer the question: Why does this brand matter?

To put the themes to work in your own brand endeavors, you first have to decide where you stand today. Do consumers already associate your brand with one of the dominant strategic themes, or do you find a hodgepodge of associations? If it's the latter, your best course of action is to clarify what the brand stands for and why it matters. You'll also have to consider some tough choices. As you focus your brand around a strategic theme, you may lessen the value that it provides to existing market segments. How do you choose one market over another? Is it advisable to choose based solely on market value?

The answer to these questions depends on two other questions. First, what strategic themes do your competitors leverage? Is the value of their brands as diffuse as your own, or do they seem more focused on one strategic theme? How well does that theme resonate with the market? Do you have a real opportunity to serve that value better than the competitor? We'll see in later chapters that real positioning is about just such an evaluation of your competitors. You have to consider how your brand relates to others in the category as much as how well it attracts consumers.

Perhaps the most important question you have to answer is: What do the people inside your company value? Real brands begin on the inside. They aren't manufactured as tricks to lure customers; they reflect the values of the people who provide them. You should study your market research and you should study your competitors, but if you don't take a hard look at what motivates and inspires the people inside your company, you will miss the opportunity to create a compelling brand. You'll find your strategic theme when you can answer these questions:

- Why do people show up for work here every day?
- What do we think we're doing to create value for our customers?
- If this brand evaporated tomorrow, what would be lost? Would anyone care? Why?

Of course, you have more to think about than what benefit you should provide. You have to ensure you can deliver that benefit consistently. Remember, a brand's value is directly proportional to its ability to deliver experiences that meet or exceed expectations. The strategic theme you select must be operationally sound. That means you have to be able to create the core benefit of that strategic direction every day, in every experience, without fail.

....

CHAPTER FOUR

LEVERAGING PORTFOLIO VALUE

confess that I liked "The Human Network," Cisco's short-lived consumer brand campaign. I also confess that I liked the campaign mostly because I have a nerdy fondness for actress Ellen Page. There. I said it. You know. My wife knows. And if Ellen ever reads this . . . well, a guy can dream. But aside from my schoolboy crush on the Oscar-nominated actress, I'll admit that it was hard to understand how she fit as a face and personality for the Cisco brand. It seemed Cisco hoped Ellen would show us how the brand was integral to everyday life, but to most consumers Cisco was a brand stamped on a box sitting on a rack tucked away somewhere in an IT closet. When "The Human Network" debuted, you weren't likely to find Cisco on things in your home or in your pocket, which is why a lot of people were confused about Page's presence in the brand's advertising campaign. "This isn't a product we'd expect her to use in real life," wrote Seth Stevenson for *Slate*. Indeed, when Cisco's Martin Hardee unveiled the new campaign on the company's blog, one customer wrote, "I am in awe of Cisco and its accomplishments but totally turned off by Ellen's role in these commercials."

Cisco may have launched the campaign precisely because it wanted consumers to get accustomed to seeing its brand on products they used in everyday life. Perhaps Cisco wanted to become relevant to consumers to resolve challenges that were growing within its brand portfolio. Cisco needed to address its *brand architecture*—the organizing structure that determines how brands in a portfolio are related to and differentiated from one another. Cisco had acquired a few consumer-facing brands that were quite different from its business-to-business heritage. These new brands did indeed live in our homes and in our pockets. The company had recently purchased the Scientific Atlanta brand of cable set-top boxes, the Linksys brand of home networking devices, and the Flip family of pocket-sized video cameras. At the time of the campaign, the acquired product brands were more relevant to consumers than the Cisco brand. Maybe Cisco's mission was to elevate the Cisco brand so that these product brands were so subservient that one day Cisco could retire them all, if it wished.

Cisco was famous for a disciplined adherence to a *master brand strategy*—when a company prefers to use one brand across its entire portfolio rather than own and operate several independent brands. In Silicon Valley, tales abound of entrepreneurs who sold their companies to Cisco and found teams changing the signs on their building before the ink was dry on the agreement. These stories may be exaggerated, but the essence is true. Once Cisco bought a company, it generally erased any trace of the acquired brand. Cisco leveraged its brand as much as it possibly could, and it was hard to argue with the strategy. For many years, Cisco soared to the top of the Interbrand and Millward-Brown rankings of the top one hundred brands, while most of the brands it had acquired didn't rank at all.

Yet it wasn't so easy to apply the Cisco master brand strategy to Linksys and Flip. While Linksys was in a product category very similar to that of Cisco's core platform of products, it didn't provide the same value. Linksys made affordable routers that people bought at retailers like Best Buy to provide Internet access in their homes or to connect their computers and printers. Linksys thrived because it was cheap and easy to use. Unfortunately, it wasn't generally perceived to make the highest-quality components. That was actually okay, because consumers valued accessibility over quality in this case. If your home wireless router failed and the price was low, it wasn't too disruptive to replace it. But if Cisco was the brand on these routers, it could have eroded the value of its core business with IT customers who paid a premium for Cisco gear because "nobody ever got fired for buying Cisco." Before Cisco could retire the Linksys brand, it had to reengineer the Linksys brand experience or develop a brand architecture that resolved the two conflicting experiences.

Flip provided a different challenge. Its devices seemed completely out of Cisco's traditional product category. Flip was targeted at consumers, not business customers. And it was a kind of video camera, not a kind of network switch. It turned heads in its category because it was innovative, affordable, and cool. For a low price, you could buy a video camera that was about the size of your cell phone, and you could transfer your video to your computer with ease. A lot of consumers loved Flip, but few of them connected Flip to the Cisco brand. In fact, most of Flip's consumers weren't very familiar with the Cisco brand at all. That may be one reason Cisco opted to reposition its master brand so that its brand architecture could be more consumer-relevant, and perhaps this was why Cisco chose a hip, young, and culturally accessible actress like Ellen Page to make the case. You could certainly picture Ellen using a Flip.

Unfortunately, the campaign did not work. About a year after launch, "The Human Network" quietly disappeared from the airwaves and from the company's website. Cisco refocused its branding efforts on the routers, switches, and network gear that had made it famous in the first place. The biggest casualty of the repositioning experiment was Flip. Cisco shuttered the brand in 2011, much to the outcry of loyalists and the business press, who thought a promising brand had suffered a premature death.

In this chapter, we'll explore the tricky business of managing a brand portfolio. We'll introduce the concept of brand architecture and see how it helps you organize and define relationships among brands inside your portfolio. We'll also see why some brands in a portfolio do well on their own, while others need a little help from a relationship with a parent brand. Finally, we'll explore the way consumers categorize brands, because this is the most important consideration when you design a brand architecture.

Brand architecture matters because, when it is applied well, it provides your brand with a good offense and a good defense. As an offense, it helps you exploit new opportunities that allow your brand to grow. As a defense, it provides a systematic way to prevent brand dilution, portfolio conflicts, and encroachment from competitive brands. Like many of the concepts we've explored thus far, the mechanics of brand architecture are often misunderstood and misapplied. Cisco is a great example of the challenge before you. Understanding the fundamental concepts that drive successful brand architecture strategies helps you create an approach that ensures that all of your brands thrive.

BRAND ARCHITECTURE

A Portfolio Approach to Brand Management

Brand architecture defines relationships among brands in a portfolio by providing an intuitive organizing structure. The word *portfolio* is important. If you have only one brand and that brand is never extended, never subbranded or paired in any way with another brand, you probably don't need to worry about brand architecture. Consider yourself lucky. Most brands exist in a world of variations. Brand X might have six flavors, while Brand Y has five product configurations. Or maybe Brand X is tailored to serve one market segment, while Brand Y meets the needs of the general market. Figure 4.1 illustrates a conventional view of brand architecture using the General Motors (GM) brand as an example. The GM master brand extends into several "family" brands such as Chevrolet, Buick, and Cadillac. Each family brand is further divided into subbrands that correspond to product lines—in this case, specific models of the Chevy brand family such as the Malibu, Volt, and Corvette. Each model is offered in different variations such as coupe, sedan, and wagon. And it's pos-

FIGURE 4.1

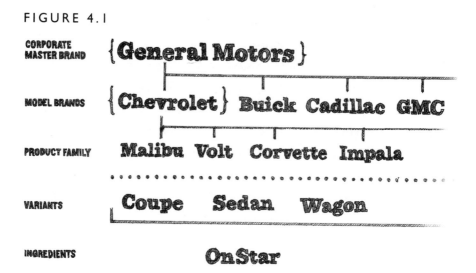

sible that all of these makes, models, and variants can be configured with GM's OnStar roadside assistance service, an ingredient brand that spans the entire portfolio. Brand architecture helps you consider how all of these brands and variations relate to one another (if at all) within your portfolio.

Many people think brand architecture focuses on rules for naming and identity—a structure that dictates what kind of names to use when creating a new brand or how to place two or more names and logos together. While a good architecture indeed influences these decisions, nomenclature guidelines and identity lockups are only *outcomes,* and if you focus too much on names and logos you'll miss the real value brand architecture can provide.

LET EQUITY FLOW

When you have a portfolio of brands, you often have the potential to leverage equity flows. An equity flow is just what it sounds like: Equity in one brand transfers to another brand in the portfolio and creates economies and marketing advantages. Equity flows are really just another example of contagion theory, which has influenced human behavior for centuries through a belief that "qualities can be transferred from a source to a target and that proximity to the source enhances feelings of contagion."[1] The NCLB case in Chapter 1 illustrates how our beliefs about contagion affect branding decisions. Those who advocated a name change for this legislation believed that the brand equity of George W. Bush tainted the NCLB brand because President Bush and NCLB were too closely associated with one another. But brand contagion isn't always bad. In fact, with brand architecture we try to encourage the spread of favorable brand equities as much as we try to control and contain the risk of infection posed by less favorable associations.

To illustrate, imagine that I launch Vincent's Cyclery, a fine maker of quality bicycles. My promise: casually stylish bicycles that offer a smooth ride and durable construction. I launch two models, a beach cruiser that I call the Vincent *Beachcomber* and a mountain bike that I call the Vincent *Trailblazer*. Both models sell very well, and my little brand becomes the darling of active lifestyle enthusiasts. Sensing an opportunity to sell those enthusiasts a line of apparel that is as stylish as my bikes, I launch *Ridewise* by Vincent, a collection of cycling jerseys, shorts, and accessories. If my apparel line succeeds, it will have done so with a lot of help from its siblings. Equity probably flowed from the Vincent master brand to the Ridewise subbrand.

In fact, equity could have flowed up, down, and across my brand portfolio, as Figure 4.2 illustrates. The association with quality and casual style that guides every product bearing the Vincent master brand influences how the Vincent Beachcomber and the Vincent Trailblazer are evaluated. These product models developed their own brand equities, and, because they were extensions of the Vincent master brand, their equities flowed up to make the Vincent master brand stronger. When I launched my apparel line, I "borrowed" equity from the master brand and its extensions. People know my brand because of my bicycles, so it wasn't too much of a stretch to find the brand on cycling apparel. I earned the consumer's permission to launch an apparel line because I had equity in related brands. If my line of apparel succeeds, it should transfer equity back to my master brand and its extensions.

FIGURE 4.2

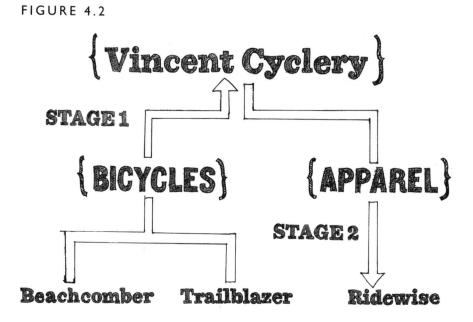

That's how it repays its debt. It makes the master brand stronger and often broader. Each brand in my portfolio has to earn its own equity by delivering an experience that lives up to a brand promise. But every brand in the portfolio has an additional obligation to support the equity of the master brand. The system creates and transfers value.

THE CLASSIC PORTFOLIO STRUCTURES

My hypothetical example used a portfolio structure that relied on a strong master brand in order to create a base of common equity all of the sibling brands could leverage. Brand strategists refer to this model as the *branded house*. It is one of the most popular organizing structures in all of branding because it is fairly simple and it is usually the most cost-effective approach. But it doesn't work well when brands in the portfolio are extremely diverse or when the promised experiences of the brands in the portfolio conflict with one another. In these cases, many brands opt for a *house-of-brands* approach, in which each brand in the portfolio operates as if it were a master brand, with no relationship to siblings or to a parent.

Procter & Gamble (P&G) is perhaps the most famous example of a company that profits from deliberate use of the house-of-brands portfolio strategy. The average consumer is unlikely to sense much of an association between P&G's product brands and its corporate brand, and that's just the way P&G wants it. The only way consumers would know that a product such as Tide was manufactured by P&G would be to look on the back panel, where they would find a small, conservative endorsement. The product isn't branded as "P&G Tide," nor is it "Tide by P&G." It's just Tide. Every P&G product is branded this way. The P&G brand doesn't mean much to end consumers. It means something only to employees, investors, and P&G's network of suppliers and distributors.

The reason P&G chose this model is that it allows the company to introduce more than one product within the same category without creating confusion or conflicts. P&G is also the maker of Cheer, a detergent that competes against Tide. The two products have slightly different promises. Tide is a premium brand that promises tough cleaning capacity, and Cheer is an economy offering that promises fresh scents. There's little value in connecting the equity between these brands. In fact, if both Tide and Cheer were P&G branded, consumers might get confused about the value propositions and forgo both products in favor of a competitor. Tide and Cheer compete on their value propositions alone. The arrangement allows P&G to own a large share of the total market because it can credibly appeal to multiple market segments and fight competitors head-on.

The house-of-brands model surfaces a lot in consumer packaged goods. Johnson Wax, Sara Lee, and VF Brands are all companies that employ this approach to create strong market leverage. But it comes at a price. Because each product or family brand within a house-of-brands portfolio acts as though it were a master brand, it has to furnish its own marketing budget. You can't take advantage of many shared resources and investments. This means that the amount of resources required to sustain these brands is much greater than what is required for product brands contained within a branded-house portfolio, where the master brand is kept strong so that product brands can benefit without as much incremental investment.

Cost is only one factor that favors a branded house. Many managers also prefer the branded-house approach because it creates a greater sense of cohesion throughout an organization. With a strong branded house, your employees rally around a common purpose, rather than dividing into factions of independent brand cultures.

In truth, the two brand architecture approaches lie at opposite ends of a spectrum. Many brand portfolios lie somewhere in between the two extremes of that spectrum. We call them *hybrids*. Toyota is a great example. Toyota is a master brand that defines a whole corporate culture, but it is also a family brand of cars. You can buy a Toyota Camry, a Toyota 4Runner, or a Toyota Prius. In each instance there is a tight relationship between the company brand and the product brands. You know a Toyota vehicle includes Toyota service, Toyota engineering, and the backing of the Toyota Motor Corporation. But when Toyota goes to market with Lexus, it deliberately severs all of those associations. The Lexus brand operates as if it were a member of a house of brands. When Lexus was first introduced to the market, some parts of the car had Toyota branding—the engine block, for example. Customers didn't like it. Given the premium price they were paying and the value they expected to receive from a luxury car, they did not want to believe any part of the car was as ordinary as a Toyota. Even though these parts were manufactured at the same plants as ordinary Toyota parts, customers were willing to pay more only if they perceived that every component in a Lexus was different, even the service organization. More value would be created than destroyed if Lexus was an extension of the Toyota master brand, which is why Lexus serves as its own master brand. To Lexus customers, the Toyota brand lives in the shadows.

There are many instances when a hybrid approach makes the most sense. In fact, a hybrid approach to brand architecture can help you leverage a parent brand where it can add considerable value, while allowing you the flexibility to pursue unrelated business strategies without jeopardizing your core brand equity. The trouble with hybrid approaches is that they create the proverbial slippery slope, whereby brand extension decisions you made in the past become precedents for future portfolio management decisions. These precedents either lead to brand extensions that fail to leverage relevant master brand equities or force a master brand extension when an independent brand would have created greater advantage. Before you know it, your brand architecture is chaotic and doesn't make sense. It becomes hard for anyone to make smart decisions about where and how your brand equity should flow and where it shouldn't.

In brand architecture, the rules matter less than the relationships they're designed to promote and protect. While there's nothing wrong with deciding whether your brand architecture should look more like a house of brands or a branded house or something in between, that's usually a decision you make as your portfolio evolves and you reevaluate. Too much time is wasted trying to preserve the purity of one approach over the other. The reality is that most of the arguments fail to consider the key question a brand architecture should answer, which is how your target audience sorts through your brand portfolio.

THINKING OUTSIDE THE BRAND

Have you ever struggled to find a file in someone else's filing cabinet? Perhaps you're trying to find a receipt for tax purposes. You look for a file named "receipts," but it doesn't exist. Next you look for "taxes." Still no luck. Maybe it's a receipt for a doctor's visit, so you check for "doctor," "health care," and "medical." Nothing. Finally, you find the receipt you're after in a file labeled "accounting." It didn't make much intuitive sense to you, but it did mean something to the person who filed it. This is the challenge customers frequently face when sorting out a brand's architecture: It makes a lot of sense to the people inside the brand, but not so much sense to the people outside.

This challenge is especially true in a master brand approach to architecture. The two key goals of the master brand approach are to create a free flow of equity among the brands connected in the portfolio and to leverage the equity of the master brand whenever possible. To achieve these goals, customers must sense a natural order to the members of the portfolio and they should sense that the master brand adds value to all of the subbrands it blesses. I use the word *bless* purposefully. When a master brand is extended haphazardly, it can curse its extensions. In fact, the connectivity of a master brand can help or hinder your business results. When brand architecture fails, it is most often because the master brand is forced onto the subbrands with very little intuitive connection. I've found that this happens most often in the wake of a merger or an acquisition. The management team mandates a branded-house approach and aims to create cost savings by consolidating the combined brand portfolios. The branding team does the best it can to create a forced logic that rationalizes why certain brands live together, but it's completely contrived and it confuses people inside and outside of the brand organization.

When brands in a master brand portfolio aren't organized to make it easy for customers to sort out relationships on their own, you face two formidable risks. The first is that equity doesn't flow at all because it isn't easy to understand how one brand relates to another. When this is the case, you may just as well have opted for a house-of-brands approach. Each brand must fend for itself. If that isn't bad enough, the second risk is worse. When your brand architecture doesn't make sense to customers, you may damage your brand equity because customers often react negatively to irrelevant or confusing brand associations. To understand why this is so, you need to understand how much categorizing influences the way we make judgments about nearly everything in our world.

We human beings are natural categorizers. We introduced our planet to the Dewey decimal system, the periodic table of elements, and an onerous set of entertainment awards. We can't help ourselves. We even sort people into types. Conservative or liberal. Lover or fighter. Pisces, Sagittarius, or Virgo. These categorizations do more than create order for us. They create meaning. When we learn someone is a Pisces, we might assume that the person is moody, creative, and quiet, even though the person could just as easily be loud and analytical. Though we are often counseled to avoid stereotypes, stereotyping is an example of our natural human instinct to understand something and attach meaning to it as a result of the category to which we think it belongs. Brand architecture relies on this categorization instinct. It preserves and creates value for brands in a portfolio by suggesting how people should categorize them.

There are various ways brand architecture can influence how we categorize a brand in a portfolio. The most frequent sorting approach is to relate subbrands by the degree to which they are typical of their master brand. If we think back to my Vincent Cyclery example, I clustered the bicycles together and clustered the apparel together. Both clusters are related to my master brand, but the bicycle cluster is more typical of my master brand than my line of apparel. The name of my master brand alone provides a strong cue about what you should expect from the bicycle product family. You expect a brand with *cyclery* in the name to offer bicycles. The name also provides a link to the apparel brand, but it is one step removed. The apparel brand name has the word *ride* in it, which naturally relates to a master brand that is focused on cyclery. We have to do a little interpretation, but the link is there. We separate the two families of brands within the portfolio because the types of products they represent are somewhat dissimilar. If we laid out all the products associated with Beachcomber or Trailblazer, we'd find a lot of commonality between them. Every part of that product line would look like bicycles or bicycle parts. If we then laid out all the Ridewise products, however, we'd begin to find many differences. Lycra shorts have few attributes in common with carbon bicycle frames. In my make-believe brand portfolio I have created an architecture that relies upon product fit.

The things that share the most attributes are clustered together. But a strong brand architecture that allows for significant equity flow can be created even when the product lines in the portfolio are very dissimilar. When consumers can't discern a link between one product and another, they'll rely on brand-specific associations. Let's explore how these work.

Our brains typically use a two-step categorization process. The first step is to look for the common characteristics of something we're evaluating. We try to match those characteristics against a checklist of sorting criteria in our minds. If we observe that the object has wheels, pedals, a handlebar, and a seat, we'll sort it into the bicycle category. But we don't just look for things a bicycle must have to get sorted that way. We also look for criteria that would make it most definitely not a part of the category. If I added wings to the list of characteristics in my example, you would doubt whether it was a bicycle. Members of a category have very typical characteristics—and very atypical characteristics as well.[2]

The challenge is that a brand portfolio can't always be sorted out with such obvious criteria. For example, if I asked you to draw me a picture of a chair, you might draw something with four legs and a back. That's the most typical way we think of a chair. However, I bet you and I would agree that a beanbag is a kind of chair, even though it has neither legs nor a back. There are degrees to which something is typical of a category. The trick for the brand manager is to determine how far something can stray from the most prototypical example and still be considered part of the category at all.

Thinking back to the Cisco example that opened this chapter, Flip devices were not very typical of Cisco's historic brand category. That's a big reason that Cisco would have found it difficult to rebrand Flip using the Cisco master brand. Since a video camera and a network switch don't seem to have many common sorting characteristics, Cisco would probably have had to resort to a different method to help consumers categorize. It would have had to connect Flip to a strong brand association.

Consumers can be quite accepting of brands that have a broad portfolio of subbrands—portfolios in which there is a lot of variety and it's hard to think of one subbrand that is most typical of the master brand. Consider Virgin. Its portfolio includes a couple of airlines, recorded music, mobile phone service, banking, and wine. These product and service categories seemingly have nothing in common, yet there's a sizable audience of consumers who are willing to consider Virgin across all of its subbranded businesses. Despite a lack of typicality, equity flows quite well throughout the Virgin portfolio. Why?

Virgin's equity flows because the Virgin master brand has strong *brand-specific associations*. These associations conjure favorable attitudes, opinions, and emotional responses that can override our surface evaluation of how typical the brand is within a product or service category. The first step in our sorting process is to assess the degree of typicality, but if that fails, our second step is to assess the degree to which the offering looks, feels, and behaves like the Virgin brand. As long as Virgin demonstrates that the emotional benefits of its brand-specific associations make dissimilar subbranded offerings better, we'll grant it permission to offer an increasingly broader brand portfolio. In fact, we begin to see Virgin as its own category.

It's easy to covet a brand architecture that relies on brand-specific associations rather than category typicality, but take heed: The principles of real branding still apply, regardless of how broad or narrow we might consider the master brand. The brand that anchors an architecture has to deliver an experience that matches audience expectations. In fact, you should stretch a master brand only as far as your ability to deliver consistently satisfying experiences that live up to our expectations of a typical offering in a category or our attachment to brand-specific associations. Sometimes those experiences relate to easily observable category characteristics (e.g., everything branded by Gillette promises the benefit of better skin care for men), and sometimes they relate to benefits that live purely through our emotions (e.g., Virgin makes you feel like a rock star). Regardless, every extension in the portfolio has to live up to the benefit promised by the master brand. If a Virgin brand extension delivered an experience that didn't have the usual Wow! factor, consumers would be let down as much as if Gillette delivered a body care experience that caused a rash.

You might be tempted to think that a broad brand like Virgin is better than a narrow brand like Gillette. But the narrowly focused Gillette brand is worth billions of dollars. It has proven to be very relevant to consumers, and there are many extensions of the Gillette brand, though they are narrowly focused on the typicality of the skin care category. What differentiates a broadly categorized brand from a narrowly categorized one is this: The value that it delivers tends to fall more to the right of the spectrum we discussed in Chapter 3 than a narrow brand. A broad brand is usually attached to a promise and an experience that is typical of a lifestyle, a personality, or a cause. A narrow brand is usually attached to function and access.

I'm often asked if a narrow brand is fated to stay a narrow brand. The answer is no. With time and money, most brands can be broadened. But I usually follow up with this question: Why would you want to broaden? Sure, you can argue that Virgin's breadth makes it easier for it to enter the men's skin care category than it would be for Gillette to enter the airline category. But Gillette would probably have more leverage in the skin care category. I said earlier that we attach meaning to things through the act of categorization. I also said that our brains use a two-step process. First, we evaluate the typicality of something before we categorize it. If that doesn't work well, we move on to brand-specific associations. What I didn't tell you is that there's ample research to show that most consumers stop evaluating when they can complete the first step.[3] In other words, if I determine that your product or service is typical of a certain category, I usually stop searching for why you're relevant to my decision. Because of this relevance, Gillette would probably have much more leverage to exploit all the angles of the skin care category than Virgin would, even though Virgin might have much stronger emotional attachments.

These two processes are not mutually exclusive. Although positive brand associations give Virgin permission and advantage to be active in many atypical categories, when you study Virgin's brand architecture you can't help but notice that each subbrand within the portfolio uses typicality as an organizing principle. Virgin America services are clustered together and separated from Virgin Money offerings. This is evident in the way the brand is expressed (the name and use of the Virgin logo differ slightly) and in the way that value is delivered (Virgin America organizes offerings around the availability of fares and schedules, while Virgin Money organizes around specific financial objectives such as savings, mortgages, and credit cards).

Context should play an important role in your architecture decisions. In some contexts, a consumer is persuaded by the typicality of a brand in a product or service category. Often in these contexts the consumer uses *analytical thinking,* whereby our prototypical example of what to expect from the category matters more than our attitudes toward a brand. You find this mode of thinking when consumers don't want to invest a lot of time in the decision-making process or when they are less inclined to care about how a product or service makes them feel. At other times, the same consumer may prefer *holistic thinking,* whereby they're willing to consider brands that are atypical of a product or service category because their values and their emotions matter more. This mode of thinking is typical when they are more focused on what the brand says about their identity and their values. Broader brand portfolios rely on holistic thinking more than narrow brand portfolios. Because of this, you should think twice before you assume that one of your brands can be stretched to cover all of your subbrands.[4]

I've had many clients who brought me in to clean up their architecture after they finished a spate of acquisitions. There are almost always solid business reasons for their acquisitions—access to shared technologies, bigger distribution channels, economies of scale—but quite often it turns out that the brands they acquired have little in common. Out of a desire to minimize total marketing costs, these clients mistakenly believe that the answer to their architecture challenge is to build or stretch one brand that can unify them all. They have been told that this will be less costly than managing a portfolio of independent brands. But none of their brands invite holistic thinking. In order to move to the egalitarian branded-house approach they want, they would have to invest a lot to create brand associations that encouraged customers to choose based on favorable emotional states or attitudes rather than category typicality. I suspect this was Cisco's intent when it launched "The Human Network" campaign. They were probably hoping to strengthen brand-specific associations so that consumers began to view extensions like Flip and Linksys as having a certain Cisco-ness that unified the portfolio. An endeavor such as that can be very expensive and, in some cases, practically unsound. It is often more effective to consolidate brands by typicality and manage a smaller house of brands than it is to build one unified branded house.

To this end, you should also consider your audience's dominant mode of thinking. Some people are predisposed to be analytical most of the time; others are predisposed to think holistically most of the time. You may be more "show me the money," and I may be more "show me the love." It makes no sense at all to develop a brand architecture that organizes a portfolio based on holistic attitudes and emotional attachments when the bulk of your audience skews to the analytical mode of thought.

I worked with a business-to-business brand that sold highly specialized instruments and chemical products to scientists. The company's branding team wanted to transform the architecture to feel more like a lifestyle brand. They wanted to connect customers with the emotional benefits of the brand because they thought that would differentiate it and provide a competitive advantage. It was an inspiring idea, but when we studied the customer base we learned quickly that the scientists the client was targeting didn't trust decisions that were based on attitudes and emotions. This audience responded better to analytical reasoning. Typicality carried more influence than brand associations. For that reason, this client had to develop a brand architecture that relied more on the typicality of independent subbrands than on a unifying corporate master brand.

I often encounter a lot of resistance when I suggest a brand architecture model that feels more hybrid or house of brands than a pure branded house.

Unless the clients are makers of packaged goods, the house-of-brands model feels wrong to them. I certainly sympathize with the noble pursuit of building one strong master brand, but that strategy won't work when there are insufficient brand equities to support a diverse portfolio, or when the clients are limited in what they can spend to build those equities, or when the clients market to an audience that is biased away from making decisions based on attitudes and opinions. I'm asked, "What's the risk of trying to stretch a brand that isn't very elastic, anyway?" There's quite a lot of risk in stretching such a brand, actually. Those beautiful equity flows that everyone covets can transfer contaminated equity as easily as they transfer the nourishing kind.

When customers don't understand why you categorized a brand the way you did, they often think less of the brand.[5] An independent brand toward which they might have been neutral or inclined to consider because of its typicality can easily be dismissed because it is attached to a master brand that is considered perfectly atypical. That's why it's not surprising that so many faithful Cisco brand advocates reacted negatively to Ellen Page's presence in a brand campaign. She was atypical of their categorization of the brand. This backlash can be worse when a popular subbrand that is typical of one specific product or market category sends unfavorable brand associations to a perfectly strong master brand because the subbrand creates an atypical image for the master brand.

Consider the case of Dell. When Dell burst into the computer category, it offered a game-changing brand concept: a computer built to order with a customer's specifications. Michael Dell's direct-to-customer PC approach was so powerful that it won over both consumer and business audiences. However, in the late 1990s Dell focused its brand associations on economy. Dell dominated the college market as a result of a significant campaign that had young people proclaiming, "Dude, I got a Dell." Dell's positioning related to a strong master brand architecture. That became a problem when it tried to make gains in the profitable business server market. Few chief information officers wanted to trust their mission-critical network computing to a brand that had become synonymous with the cheap PCs populating dorm rooms everywhere. In reality, Dell servers were very durable. Many of them outperformed competitors. That didn't matter. One part of the brand architecture contaminated the other parts.

There's a reason contagion theory has fascinated scientists for hundreds of years. It often seems so irrational. For example, many consumers who prefer to buy secondhand clothing will never buy secondhand undergarments. You could wash those undergarments in boiling water loaded with bleach and they will still seem contaminated to these consumers, even though they might not think twice about wearing a secondhand shirt with little more than a rinse. Contagion theory applies to more than things we touch. Go to Las Vegas and see how close people sit to the guy with the hot hand at the craps table. We think his luck will rub off. Conversely, the employee that is about to be laid off sits alone in the cafeteria. Our minds connect proximity to contamination, and they do it in a predictable way. When we believe something increases our chances for gain, we prefer that it be as close as possible. If we think something creates a risk, we want it far away. This phenomenon should factor into your brand architecture decisions. Organize your portfolio to create leverage through relevant proximity. In this context, Cisco might not want to do away with the Linksys brand but it might want to create the perception of distance between it and the Cisco master brand (as of this writing, the Linksys brand lives on, though it is now a clear sub-brand of Cisco).

Contagion and proximity can also be used quite effectively when you specifically want to broaden your brand. Brands like Apple, Virgin, and Nike have used this strategy quite well. Apple was once thought of very narrowly. It was a computer company. In early 2001 it introduced iTunes, software developed to make it easier to play music on a computer and sync it with digital music devices. Although tightly connected to the Apple master brand, iTunes worked on PCs, too. When Apple launched the iPod later that year, the equity established by iTunes allowed Apple to broaden its brand. Very soon, Apple became more than a computer company, and it developed strong brand-specific associations. Elegant, easy-to-use design became a more potent way for people to categorize Apple-branded products. That made it easier for Apple to launch iPhone, Apple TV, and iPad. Each extension benefited from close proximity to other extensions and from proximity to the Apple brand. And each extension broadened Apple's brand architecture.

THREE COMMON ARCHITECTURE MISTAKES

I suppose the only thing worse than a lack of brand architecture is a bad architecture. When the reasoning is flawed, the cost can be substantial. Your brand architecture usually determines how you present your brand to the world, which means that every time you change it, you may have to change names, logos, and a plethora of branded materials such as packaging, retail environments, and signage. Even more costly than these material things, investments in your infrastructure may be required by your new architecture. I worked with an agricultural client who acquired a very successful family brand of seed products. It kept the acquired brand name, but it didn't keep the sales and service organization that created the brand's value. Within a few years, the entire share it gained from the acquisition had eroded. Brand architecture is not simply about names, logos, and degrees of corporate endorsement. It's about the system of relationships you want to link to the brands in your portfolios. There are three great ways to miss this point: sorting by history, sorting by internal organization, and sorting by competitive organization.

Sorting by History

You have a track record. You've learned a lot about your customers and your markets. So why wouldn't you use history as the foundation for rationalizing your brand portfolio?

The answer is that, of course, you should incorporate what you've learned from the past. But history is not a great guide to the future. You need to use caution when you rely too heavily on historical performance. Markets evolve and brands adapt. While history may give you plenty of cues to how your customers categorized brands in the past, it may not reflect how they will do so today and in the future. It takes only one competitor to introduce a new way to categorize before your way feels outdated.

Sorting by Internal Organization

Your brand portfolio doesn't have to reflect your organizational structure. It has to reflect the system of relationships you want people to connect with the brand. Sometimes, the way you deliver value to customers is directly related to the way you have structured your teams on the inside. But just as often, it isn't.

I worked with an amazing research and development firm that was responsible for some of the most remarkable innovations in our time. By necessity, its organizational structure was highly matrixed. Some research teams served multiple product teams. Some product teams served multiple markets. There was a lot of overlap in how people reported to one another, which was perfectly fine for the way this corporate culture worked. But it wasn't fine for helping customers sort out the company's portfolio of brands. Customers were most interested in products and market solutions, not labs and research centers. It took a while for my client to see its brand through the customers' eyes. To win, this client had to forget about whether the brand architecture reflected the internal organization.

Sorting by Competitive Organization

It's said that imitation is the greatest form of flattery, but when you organize your brand portfolio based on a model established by your competitors, you often miss the opportunity to differentiate yourself. Sometimes when I show clients a new model for their brand architecture they tell me, "Our competitors don't organize their brands that way." That's when I thank them. Don't misread this. I'm not suggesting that you should organize differently for the sake of being different. That can lead to unnecessary customer confusion and all the downside risk that comes from being atypical. But when your strategy is to change the way customers think about the category, a break from the competitive brand architecture model may drive home the point you want to make. When vitaminwater organized its brand according to "formulas" and not "flavors," it sent the signal that its products were not ordinary soft drinks. The company influenced *how* consumers evaluated the product line. Instead of selecting by taste, the architecture encouraged consumers to select by benefit, whether it was an energy boost from tropical citrus or the supposed XXX benefits from acai, blueberries, and pomegranate.

WHEN TO FOCUS ON BRAND ARCHITECTURE

Your brand architecture should evolve with your brands, helping each brand adapt to changes in its market environment. In a perfect world, you're always thinking about the architecture and you frequently use it to develop a stronger competitive position. While you don't want to create more confusion by constantly shuffling the deck, you do want to constantly improve your portfolio. You may add brands, retire brands, or make subtle changes in the way individual brands are presented to the world, but you need a system that develops and preserves value over time. You should use your brand architecture to create leverage across the portfolio. To do this, you have to answer important questions about each brand in your portfolio, including the master brand:

- How typical is this brand of its product or service category?
- How much does this subbrand rely upon brand-specific associations of a parent brand? Are those brand-specific associations strong enough to provide competitive advantage for this subbrand?

- How broad or narrow is the total brand portfolio?
- Who is the target audience for the brand, and what is their dominant mode of thinking about brands in this category (i.e. analytic versus holistic)?
- How typical or atypical is this brand in comparison to other brands within the portfolio?
- How well can audiences outside the organization relate brands within the portfolio to one another? Is it intuitive? If not, how much effort does it take to sort it correctly?

These are the critical questions managers should ask when analyzing their brand architecture, but sadly few of these questions are ever seriously considered. Instead, decisions are made haphazardly or according to the mistakes I have already shared. There are very specific moments in time when you should pay particular attention to brand architecture and focus on these questions. They are:

- *Mergers and acquisitions.* Anytime you combine two brand portfolios that were not originally designed to work together, you need to re-evaluate your brand architecture. In most merger-and-acquisition situations, your portfolio will contain a number of redundancies. You will undoubtedly have to address operational issues related to those redundancies, but don't confuse the operational characteristics with the brand characteristics. You have to evaluate each redundant brand based on its overall strength and fitness for the new portfolio.
- *Cost-cutting.* When times are lean, many companies decide to reduce the size of the brand portfolio. Every brand in the portfolio requires some level of investment to sustain its equity. In my experience, brands multiply in the boom years only to face the chopping block when resources are scarce. Before retiring a brand or consolidating its associated products and services under another brand in the portfolio, it's worth your

time to consider the aforementioned key questions. Retiring brands is often one of the most emotional and political decisions an organization contemplates. I am consistently surprised by the passion that surfaces when managers are asked to let go of their brand. Your job should be to focus on the true drivers of brand architecture success rather than succumb to separation anxiety.

• *Crisis.* You won't really understand the meaning of contagion theory until one of your brands is caught in a crisis. When Windows Vista began facing serious consumer criticism in the marketplace, all of Microsoft's close subbrands were tainted by the experience. Unfortunately, when one of your brands is involved in a negative reputation event, it's usually too late to use architecture to lessen the spreading infection. However, brand architecture is often the means by which companies rebuild and restructure once the controversy subsides. Some companies adopt hybrid architecture approaches to create perceptual firewalls between high-risk brands and the rest of the brand portfolio. A high-risk brand isn't necessarily a brand that will fail to fulfill its promise. It may just be a brand that is subject to different brand-specific associations and a more fickle target audience.

• *Hygiene.* Especially in rapidly growing organizations, a brand portfolio can reach a tipping point where it just doesn't seem to make any sense anymore. This is especially true in rapidly growing organizations, where brands have been added or changed ad hoc to resolve short-term growth objectives. When hygiene creates the demand for a refined brand architecture, it's usually because the architecture is impeding future growth. Conflicts within the portfolio are confusing the marketplace or tying up resources that could be deployed on activities with higher returns. Hygiene is the most common reason clients hire my team for a brand architecture assignment. The client wants an objective, outside expert to determine how to structure the brand portfolio. What they don't usually expect are the tough decisions that result from the exercise. We often find that many tiers of the portfolio shouldn't be branded at all because they don't help customers assess typicality, nor do they leverage or create a brand-specific association.

* *Diversification.* Brand architecture can be a powerful means to achieve a diversification strategy. When organizations sense that future success will emanate from competitive fields that are very different from the current field of competition, you can use brand architecture to chart your brand's evolution. For example, Google created the Android platform brand to help it diversify into the consumer devices marketplace. It recognized that smartphones, tablets, and other mobile technologies would transform cloud computing. Most people thought of Google first and foremost as a service that facilitates search, even though the company developed a suite of applications and services that did much more. To retain the equity that made Google Google, Android was introduced as a means to reflect where the company was going.

HOW TO EFFECT CHANGE

Think Prototypes and Exemplars

Throughout this chapter I've discussed the importance of leverage. It's one thing to draw up a hierarchical chart on paper indicating how your brands should relate to one another. It's quite another to put that plan into action. Most brand architecture strategies leave out the most important detail: How do we generate the desired equity flows? The answer to the question concerns leverage.

Within any brand portfolio some brands invariably have more strength than others. A good brand architecture strategy determines how to leverage the strength of brands within a portfolio. Recent research has supported two compelling approaches. The first is a top-down approach that relies on a strong master brand *prototype.* Think of a prototype as a mental model for

FIGURE 4.3

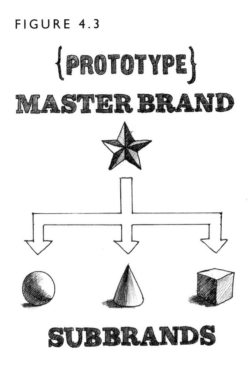

{PROTOTYPE}
MASTER BRAND

SUBBRANDS

the whole portfolio rather than any one of its brand extensions. (See Figure 4.3.) The Virgin brand we have discussed frequently in this chapter relies on a powerful prototype. Whenever Virgin extends its brand, we are likely to assess how well the extension fits the prototype and less likely to evaluate how well the extension fits its product or service category. As long as a Virgin subbrand doesn't contradict the mental imagery of the prototype, the prototype can transfer favorable attitudes to it.

The second approach is more bottom-up or, at the very least, parallel. It relies on *exemplars*. An exemplar is a subbrand that creates uncommon value for the entire portfolio. It is either the best-in-class example of a product/service in its category or it is a star performer in the portfolio compared to its peers. (See Figure 4.4.) Many people didn't know much about the Qualcomm brand, one of the world's largest manufacturers of semiconductors for mobile devices. In fact, a lot of people thought Qualcomm was in the sports industry because it owned the naming rights to Qualcomm Stadium, which the San Diego Chargers NFL franchise called home. When Qual-

FIGURE 4.4

comm launched Snapdragon, a subbrand attached to an innovative chipset platform for smartphones and other smart devices, it created an exemplar with powerful leverage—leverage to transfer equity throughout the entire portfolio, including up to the master brand. It's the equivalent of saying, "from the company that brought you Snapdragon."

The two approaches are not mutually exclusive. In fact, you may use both simultaneously to create different points of leverage. In perhaps the best study to document the mechanics and the potential of prototypes and exemplars within a brand architecture, the Nike brand was used to illustrate how the two approaches can work together to influence consideration and preference.

Assume that Nike is introducing two extensions: kneepads and car audio systems. While kneepads do not closely resemble any existing product of Nike, the kneepad extension fits with the brand's "athletic" prototype. The car audio extension is inconsistent with the prototype, but it shares many features with a specific Nike exemplar (i.e., sports audio). Thus, the Nike kneepad extension has a high prototype fit but a low exemplar fit, and the Nike care audio extension has a high exemplar fit but a low prototype fit.[6]

In this context, I find it curious that Cisco didn't use more specific exemplars to validate the brand-specific associations it wished to create. Instead of having Ellen Page discover how classrooms were connected by telepresence technologies or how a police department could conduct innovative surveillance, it might have been more useful to show how Flip and Linksys connected to The Human Network. Those exemplars had the power to create new brand-specific associations.

For the purposes of organizing your portfolio and determining how to leverage the equities it contains, look to prototypes and exemplars as starting points. Many new or emerging brands can benefit from a strategy that leverages exemplars to transfer equity to a master brand. Over time, the equity in the master brand can become a prototype that makes future brand extension easier and the resulting brand portfolio broader. There is also evidence to suggest that a migration toward a prototype-driven brand portfolio can significantly change the behavior of your customer base. When a prototype brand becomes favored by consumers, it often "influences extension evaluations even when the extension and the core are very dissimilar."[7]

PUTTING ARCHITECTURE TO WORK

A good architecture blueprint begins with a framework—a framework that is simple and easy to understand. Aim for one page, and *show,* don't just tell, how the pieces fit together. Your framework should focus on the value propositions of each brand in the portfolio, its degree of typicality, and the brand associations it relies upon to succeed. There are many ways to do this, but instead of showing you one approach I'd rather emphasize how important it is that your framework be actionable within your organization and capable of being revised. You need to chart the way your brands can create leverage and understanding.

Your framework should inform a system that guides future brand decisions. When your organization is thinking about creating a new brand, people should be able to use your framework to decide whether that's wise. Your decision system should help them decide whether the brand they want to create is typical or atypical of an existing brand category. This helps them determine what needs to change.

Although many companies obsess over decision systems, the truth is that a decision system itself is merely a skirmish in the larger battle. The success of your brand architecture depends on your ability to make it real in practice. How well do you train people to apply it? How well is it understood throughout your organization? How can you use research to calibrate and validate it? How effectively do external stakeholders recognize it? Does it change the way people on the outside of the brand think about the brand, its value, and its promises? Do you have the resources to support this architecture over time?

A good framework clarifies how the portfolio migrates from one state to the next. Your migration plan doesn't have to occur slowly. In some cases, the only thing that's worse than no migration plan is an overly conservative plan. Many of my clients make a bold move to change their brand architecture only to let that architecture crumble because they're too afraid to pull the trigger and make the required changes. Instead, they design a migration plan that has the brand portfolio change over a long, slow period of time—five years or more. Here's what happens: People forget about it, new decisions are made that interfere with the original plan, and the change is so slow that the external audiences you wish to influence don't comprehend that anything has changed or is changing at all.

When the architecture requires a significant change from the status quo, most companies resist a "light-switch" migration—one in which the architecture looks one way today but completely different tomorrow. Most opt for a phased approach, and most of the time that's wise. However, sometimes the best approach is absolutely to flip the switch. In fact, a lot of my clients who initially opted for a measured and phased approach ended up flipping the switch and accelerating the reorganization of the brand portfolio in the end. The truth is that customers rarely run to the hills, vowing never to return because a brand architecture has changed. Even if they do, they can usually be wooed back into the valley when you stick to your promise and deliver a consistently compelling experience.

....

CHAPTER FIVE

POSITIONING BRANDS FOR CONTEXT

There's an old consulting story that illustrates the nuances of context. Three friends hit the golf course together. One is a priest, the other a doctor, and the third a business consultant. It's a perfectly beautiful day. The three men are driving the ball well and having a great game until they start the back nine. There, they find themselves waiting for a long time behind a slow-playing foursome in front of them. At one point, the priest waves down a ranger. He asks what's holding things up. The ranger explains that the foursome is a group of firefighters who lost their sight saving the historic clubhouse from a nasty blaze. He said the club is so grateful for the firefighters' heroism that it allows them to play the course for free whenever they want.

After the ranger left, the three men stood quietly for a bit until the priest said, "That's very sad. I think I shall add those men to prayers in my next mass." The doctor said, "I know an ophthalmologist who is doing some really great research on sight restoration. This might be a good case for him." After a moment, the business consultant asked, "Why can't they play at night?"

You could say that each of the three men in the anecdote viewed the same situation in a different context. The priest wanted to help the firefighters. The doctor saw an opportunity to help a colleague. And the business consultant saw a way to help himself. Three different tactics to resolve a common dilemma.

YOUR MOMENT IN TIME

Markets will change. That's a law, not a theory. Some markets change daily, while others make slow, steady progressions over a period of many years. Whether the gears of your market turn fast or slow, turn they will. At the beginning of this book, I told you that a position is different from a promise. A promise relates to your brand's purpose—its reason for existence—and defines the benefits you'll deliver in a brand experience. A brand's position differentiates it in its marketplace. You position to be different and relevant. As a market evolves, and as other market participants advance their positions in the market, your task is to determine the position that serves your business needs and provides you with unique advantage while living up to your brand promise and delivering compelling brand experiences. Not an easy feat.

When we think about positions and marketplaces, we're interested in one specific moment in time: your position tomorrow. We are interested in where you are today only as it relates to the gap between where you are positioned today versus where you want to be positioned tomorrow. We have limited use for where you were yesterday, yet far too many brands make the mistake of dwelling on their historic accomplishments. We'll see later in this chapter that there is indeed a competitive context in which past behavior lends you positioning credibility. But historic credibility makes you relevant only if it relates to a differentiating benefit today.

SIZING MARKETS

Perhaps the trickiest part of establishing context is determining the scale of the market you wish to apply it to. It's easy to run in circles getting too granular or negating your logic by trying to think too big. Imagine that you are a luxury watchmaker. Do you want to be the dominant luxury brand, or do you aspire to dominate the broader watch market? Either aspiration is valid, assuming that it aligns with your promise and you have the means to deliver an experience that supports that future position. The size of the market you want to own dictates the necessary breadth of your brand architecture. It determines whether you want to be perfectly typical of a luxury watch brand or a perfect prototype for a brand that is relevant across many kinds of timepieces.

Size matters. Through advertising and promotion, you'll translate your positioning into claims that attempt to get customers to try, buy, and apply. Those claims have to stand out from competitive claims. If you size your market too narrowly, your positioning may pigeonhole your brand into a niche. Conversely, if you size your market too broadly, your positioning may eliminate any noticeable point of differentiation. When brands get stuck and find it hard to gain ground, the problem is often that their positions serve one market while hoping to gain a position in another.

LOOKING SIDEWAYS

Differentiation is one of the most important aspects of positioning. Up until now, we've focused on how a brand remains true to what it really is. On occasion, we've explored how one or more unique characteristics of a brand can be leveraged to differentiate it in the marketplace. But I've counseled you to avoid putting too much emphasis on making your promise different just for the sake of being different. Indeed, because every brand can ultimately be reduced to one of the six common themes, your promise might not sound all that different from competitive promises. However, the way in which you deliver on your promise can be very different. This is where positioning helps. Do you deliver like a noble leader or like an aggressive challenger? Positioning adds context that separates your brand from the alternatives.

Differentiation is a moving target. If you differentiate successfully, be prepared for a competitor to copy you and render that differentiation irrelevant. Markets are crowded with brands that make identical claims, replicate the same activities, and follow one another's strategies in the search for new customers. These markets look like the soccer games my children played when they were very young. All the kids piled onto the ball, rather than spreading out and creating opportunities to advance the ball down the field without competitor interference. *Differentiation is an ongoing process.* That's why positioning flows from your brand promise, and not the other way around.

When you're positioning, you'll often find the most value by looking sideways—thinking about contexts that are out of your category. Such contexts can provide you with a rich point of differentiation because they frame your market challenge through an unconventional lens. For example, when the team at Virgin designed its airline, it looked outside its category for context. Instead of thinking like other airlines, Virgin thought of its service in the context of a disco club. It would be a place where people would be willing to line up for the experience. They asked themselves, "If this airline were a trendy club, what would it look like?" Perhaps this context explains why we board a darkened Virgin plane that glows with mood lighting, pulses with house music, and stocks premium liquor. Virgin looked sideways.

THE FOUR CATEGORY CONTEXTS

It helps to think of positioning contexts by thinking of two different variables: growth orientation versus conventionality. Figure 5.1 illustrates typical

FIGURE 5.1

ESTABLISHMENT BRANDS The status quo; biggest, oldest, cheapest, etc.	**CHALLENGER BRANDS** Champions of a "better way" to serve the market
PUBLIC BRANDS Noncompetitive; here for everyone	**ADVOCATE BRANDS** Serve a narrow, specific market need

positioning contexts using these variables. In the upper left are establishment brands. They're dominant, and they intend to keep growing by providing a known quantity to the broadest possible audience. They're different from the challenger brands that occupy the upper right. Challenger brands want to disrupt the conventional status quo in order to take power. As we move to the lower quadrants, the quest for power and growth is less important. The public brands on the lower left position themselves as the most accessible and least competitive brands. Their purpose is more important than achieving an advantage over a peer or a competitor. In fact, they often encourage competitive activity because it benefits the category as a whole. In contrast, the advocate brands on the lower right position themselves to serve narrow audiences with highly differentiated benefits. They are unapologetic about serving a discrete audience.

Establishment Brands

Imagine that you are one of about one hundred people suddenly stranded on an island. After a few miserable months waiting for a rescue, you and your fellow castaways decide to make the best of your situation by building a functional island community.

Let's say that you have a gift for cooking, so you decide to open the island's first restaurant. Before long, your fellow castaways fall in love with your food and you enjoy a monopoly position. For a brief period of time, yours is the only restaurant that people come to when they don't want to cook for themselves back in their huts. But as the island population grows over time, a few other restaurants inevitably emerge to provide a little variety. However, none of them have your reputation or history. You are positioned in a unique context. You are the establishment brand.

Establishment brands are leaders. They are the biggest brand in the category by any number of measures (sales, employees, retail locations, customers served, etc.). Sometimes, they lead because they have the most prestige. Perhaps they are the oldest, or they pioneered the basis by which every competitor competes. Whatever their basis of leadership, an establishment brand is the brand to beat. They are the most imitated, the most feared, and the brand people think of most when they think of the category: Kleenex for facial tissue, Xerox for copies, and Google for search.

If you're lucky enough to occupy the establishment position, congratulations! I also send my sympathy. Establishment brands have a lot to live up to. Because you're the brand to beat, all competitive guns are aimed at you. To make matters tougher, customers expect more from you than from anyone else. They think that you should set the standard for every brand in the category. That makes it hard to respond to competitive attacks. When competitors flood the market with discounts and promotional gimmicks, you have to think twice before matching their tactics because you have more to lose. It's your obligation to maintain the integrity of your brand to keep customers loyal, and that can make you feel you have limited options.

Establishment brands are not all alike, and knowing which of the three establishment positions you currently occupy is important to your future positioning strategy.

Establishment Position #1: The Imperialist

The imperialist position is the gold standard. You're the eight-hundred-pound gorilla that controls the category. You have uncommon leverage because your nearest competitor has a long way to go to catch up. Think of Google in search, Facebook in social media, Intel in semiconductors, and the New York Stock Exchange (NYSE) in stock markets. All of these brands are imperialists. They dwarf the competition, and they're synonymous with their category. The price they pay for this privileged position is massive responsibility. So much is expected of them that they can rarely keep all of their audiences happy.

Imperialists attract a lot of unwanted attention. They're labeled as arrogant, anticompetitive, bureaucratic, and domineering. Of course, the people who work inside an imperialist brand reject these criticisms. They feel tremendous pressure to sustain the order they've brought to the category. They're overachievers. Imperialist cultures are sometimes stoic, are often noble, and frequently consist of perpetual martyrs. They're saving the world, and it's killing them. I've had the privilege of working for a lot of establishment brands, and I'm always surprised by how seriously they view their responsibility to serve something bigger than themselves. They don't consider themselves arrogant; they're proud servants of the brand. They don't consider themselves anticompetitive; they're making their brand more accessible to a broader, underserved audience. They don't see themselves as bureaucratic; they're preserving the integrity of the brand. And they certainly don't see themselves as domineering. They'll tell you that they're exerting influence only because customers, employees, and investors expect them to lead. There's truth in that. When an imperialist stops leading, customers defect, employee morale plummets, and investors lose confidence.

To position an imperialist brand, you have to balance leadership with benevolence. While Machiavelli advised that it is better to be feared than loved, imperialists sustain their position when they demonstrate their self-lessness. The most effective imperialist positioning strategies introduce broad societal themes. It's no surprise that more and more imperialists are talking about corporate social responsibility (CSR) initiatives. These initiatives aim to sustain the market's confidence by demonstrating that the brand is a good citizen and that it contributes to the market, the community, and the world at large. Unfortunately, a lot of companies launch these initiatives as a quick-fix tactic. In the same way that a brand promise won't work if it isn't validated by people's experiences with the brand, a CSR program that merely gains press attention today without any tangible investment or action by the brand tomorrow will fail. In fact, so many imperialist brands have launched phantom CSR initiatives that many consumers are skeptical.

Google positioned itself as a good corporate citizen when it reminded its employees, "Don't be evil." It supported this notion by encouraging employees to dedicate 20 percent of their time to personal causes, regardless of their profit potential. However, when Google became an undisputed imperialist in its category, many became suspicious of the brand's true motives. Amnesty International questioned Google's commitment not to do evil when it noted the brand's tolerance of human rights abuses in China. The U.S. Department of Justice questioned Google's unfair competitive practices. And privacy advocates wondered what Google CEO Eric Schmidt meant when he responded to concerns about Google's search practices by saying, "If you have something that you don't want anyone to know, maybe you shouldn't be doing it in the first place." If Google isn't careful, it will become the most hated brand, as Microsoft was for a time in its history. In fact, many observers consider Google the new Microsoft—a characterization that is not meant in a flattering way.

General Electric is an imperialist brand that only competes in categories where it can be number one. When GE launched its "ecoimagination initiative," it brought the same competitive mentality to a public interest. Rather than talk about environmental issues and occasionally sponsor environmental causes, GE wove "green innovation" into every single business unit. It wasn't enough to make token gestures to appear to support an environmental cause. GE positioned itself as a company that innovated by making greener technology a necessary ingredient. It proved that its societal contribution was perfectly aligned with its brand promise. Greening led to technology for "better living."

Establishment Position #2: The Unwilling Coalition
Many establishment brands share power in their category. You're in the parity position when you sit close to another establishment brand. You're part of an unwilling coalition—unwilling because each brand would love to rule the empire. In many categories, this will never happen because there isn't enough ground to truly differentiate.

Coke and Pepsi have shared leadership of the soft drink category for more than a century. If there was a silver positioning bullet that would allow one of these two fierce competitors the opportunity to reign supreme, it would have been fired years ago. Instead, each brand shifts its positioning frequently. Each relies more on advertising and engineered brand associations to achieve marginal and impermanent gains in consumer preference.

Parity brands compete in a nuclear arms race, wherein big dramatic changes in positioning can escalate into a price war. To avoid that, parity brands generally resort to one of two positioning options. First, they may hunt for what's trending in an audience's life and find relevant ways to connect with it. Trends are fickle, and this tactic works well only when the brand is grounded by its promise and nimble in its activities. For example, Southwest Airlines only sponsors activities that are connected to its travel destinations. When it decided that American football was a valuable way to position itself against competitors, it pursued a completely brand-appropriate approach. It provided fares and promotions aimed at college football fans, knowing that many of these fans would be interested in traveling to away games if they had access to reasonable fares. Southwest also leveraged its much-loved corporate culture to position itself as the brand of airline you would naturally expect to include football fans themselves among its employees. Advertising programs focused on the destinations for football flights as much as they did the sport itself. While any one of the U.S. airlines could have followed the trend and found a surface way to position its brand around American's love of football, Southwest found a way that was perfectly aligned with its brand promise—a way that could be defended and leveraged.

The second option is the least pursued. You can go "all in." Brands that position around one differentiating theme take great risk. Instead of hedging their bets, like a lot of their establishment peers, they don't align their equity with a portfolio of options, the majority of which are too underfunded to make much of an impact. The "all in" position requires a singular focus around one compelling positioning idea.

When MasterCard launched the "Priceless" campaign in 1997 during the World Series, it followed the "all in" positioning strategy. Everything the brand did from that moment on was focused on the idea that "there are some things money can't buy; for everything else there's MasterCard." It supported this notion by highlighting the things that really matter to us in life. In fact, that special something that you can't buy with money was always the unexpected payoff of every MasterCard television advertisement. It was an award-winning positioning idea that became the filter for brand activities. That's what made it so compelling. The brand wasn't distracted by anything that couldn't tie back to the "Priceless" positioning. What made "Priceless" so effective? Its resonance. Consumers adopted the campaign into their vernacular, many of them making their own "Priceless" ads to mark major events in their own lives. And "Priceless" was completely aligned with MasterCard's brand promise to be the best way to pay for everything that matters. Sadly, this effort wasn't sustained. Within a few years, the priceless campaign became little more than a tagline that appeared in promotional programs—programs that usually had no connection at all to the things in life that mattered most. The brand returned to an opportunistic portfolio strategy of positioning around what was hot at the moment.

Establishment Position #3: The Dowager Brand

The dowager brand is perceived to be the market leader, but it is also perceived to be losing ground. First defined by Dennis Rook and Sidney J. Levy in a 1999 research study, dowager brands resemble the widowed empresses of history. They command respect and they have prestige, but they're fading and becoming less relevant. New entrants challenge a dowager for prestige, and low-price competitors whittle away at the dowager's market share.[1]

The dowager nearly always has a rich, authentic history that makes it the brand that is synonymous with the category. Nonetheless, many people think the brand is "old news." It doesn't help that the dowager tends to rest on its past laurels. To regain its glory, the dowager must establish contemporary relevance.

Microsoft has become a dowager brand. It's still dominant in some markets, notably with the Windows operating system and the Office suite of productivity tools. It is the brand most people think of first when they consider these categories. Yet in recent years Microsoft has been overshadowed by Google in the growing market for software-as-a-service, and it's lost ground to its old rival Apple in the prestige-technologies market. Microsoft has faced a slow, steady decline in relevance that has been underscored by notable product failures (Windows Vista, the Zune digital entertainment device, and the short-lived Kin mobile phone). Meanwhile, technology has changed and made the brand's core equity less compelling. As consumers move toward cloud computing and light operating systems that work on tablet devices and smartphones, the need for a robust operating system that lives on a desktop PC or a powerful laptop computer is becoming less relevant. A lot of Microsoft's problems can be solved through acquisitions and through more focused investment in its product technologies. However, it is odd that Microsoft hasn't invested more of its brand energy on associating with its legacy. With its original promise of putting a computer on every desktop, Microsoft changed the way the world thought about computers and technology. In recent years, it has increasingly distanced itself from its past. Smart dowagers embrace the part of their past that demonstrates how unique experience and a cultural legacy leads to a better future.

When Lou Gerstner arrived at IBM in 1993, IBM was a dowager. It was losing billions of dollars, and it was cementing a reputation as the last of a dying species. I find the story behind Gerstner's historic turnaround of the IBM brand interesting because his strategy relied on two critical assumptions. First, Gerstner realized that IBM had to become relevant again. "Customers wanted solutions. They didn't want to know what their equipment ran on."[2] Yet he also realized that IBM's legacy and reputation were linked to its culture, which was the root of why it became a giant in the first place. When IBM revived its brand, it didn't ignore this brand equity. In fact, it reminded customers that it was the most natural place to find smarter solutions because of its track record and because of the culture it attracted.

In recent years, the *New York Times* was a dowager brand that has embraced digital media to reinstate its relevance. The *New York Times* faced the same fate as many newspapers—declining subscription revenue and declining interest in print advertising. When most newspapers were merely using the Web to repurpose print edition content, the *New York Times* invested in its online presence to reemerge as one of the most important sources for news on the Internet. In fact, it won numerous design awards for its thoughtful information architecture and reader-friendly display options. It also received renewed interest by being one of the first publications to develop formats specifically for the iPhone and iPad. The *New York Times* leveraged new media to reestablish the relevance of its dowager equity.

Challenger Brands

Challenger brands don't care if you're an imperialist, a parity brand, or a dowager. They just want to unseat you. A challenger brand is on a mission to take down the establishment. Ever since Adam Morgan popularized the context of the challenger brand in his book *Eating the Big Fish,* a lot of managers have been inspired to think like a pirate instead of like the navy. A challenger brand is truly a state of mind. It views existing market shares and the establishment's leadership position as consequences of birth, not of merit.

A lot of brands that claim to be challenger brands aren't challengers at all; they're just number two or three in their category. To understand what I mean, imagine our hypothetical island scenario once more. After a few years, your castaway restaurant has reached maturity. Everyone refers to your brand as though it were the category. People don't say, "Let's eat at the restaurant." They say, "Let's eat at Murray's." Operationally, you developed a very practical model of food preparation built around the coconut as the staple ingredient, which is good because you have abundant supply. You use a simple, open-fire food preparation method, and you uphold certain traditions from the mainland, such as serving all plates at once and in three courses. Over the years, others have tried to do what you do, but their businesses failed because you'd already mastered the concept. Though they can technically replicate what you do, everyone agrees that it is never as good as "the real thing."

Then a challenger comes along. Meet Linda, one of your fellow castaways, who opened a restaurant where coconuts are not on the menu. Linda hates coconuts, and she reasoned that just because they're everywhere doesn't mean we have to eat them. She innovates, using root vegetables and fresh seafood when she can catch it. Her menu is seasonal and varies by what's fresh now. Because she has to work with what she can find, she closes as soon as she runs out of dishes, making her place a destination people flock to "before the good stuff runs out." Linda doesn't think islanders want to be reminded of the traditions they'd find on the distant mainland. She thinks it's painful. Instead, she wants to embrace the island culture in which she lives. She abandons all dining formalities to create a scene in which people can socialize while they eat. She serves her food as soon as it's off the fire. Her dining environment is loud, frenetic, and a bit of a theatrical experience. Because it is all about a new island food tradition, she has expanded in interesting ways. She ingeniously created a "pop-up" food concept whereby she can serve lighter variations of her menu close to where islanders work during the day. Linda has introduced street food to the island.

If you try to match Linda's model, you'll probably fail. She developed a service concept that relies on a completely different approach to market—an approach that Linda thinks is better than yours. Though she's really quite a friendly lady, she's determined to beat you by playing a different game. That's how challenger brands think. They're the brands that stick out and draw attention because they make us wonder why nobody thought of doing it like that before!

A challenger brand thumbs its nose at the establishment. Whether it's the brand's graphic identity or the service elements of the customer experience, a challenger brand infuses everything it does with a strong point of view that usually revolves around contrarian logic. You think soft drinks are bad for you? Vitaminwater lets you drink your vitamins. You think a vacuum cleaner is low-tech and boring? Dyson gives you a space-age design that uses the most advanced suction technology. You think finding things on the Web means sifting through tables of links? Google gives you a simple search box.

Challenger brands reframe our expectations, usually by focusing all of the brand's energy on our pain points. At the core of every great challenger brand is a fundamental belief that the establishment gets it wrong. The challenger is usually right. Challenger brands address the most frustrating parts of using an establishment brand's products or services, and they transform those parts into awesome, differentiating brand experiences. They also make those points of differentiation look effortless, which is part of the magic. When JetBlue debuted with an entertainment system built into every seat, a lot of people wondered why the established brands hadn't thought of it first.

While a dowager brand can leverage the past to retain our loyalty, challenger brands never look back. If you're opting to position yourself as a true challenger, you are necessarily breaking with the past. You're defining new rules, changing the perspective of the category (in some cases, defining a new category altogether), and driving forward until you have changed the status quo.

Advocate Brands

Establishment brands and challenger brands compete for share in a war to rule the category. But many brands in a category don't care about leadership. An advocate brand is more focused on specialization than leadership. Instead of being president of the United States, these brands aspire to be a ranking senator, or maybe an influential lobbyist, or perhaps just a great dentist. It's often assumed that every brand wants to grow and become number one, but growth might not be the primary objective of an advocate brand. First and foremost, it wants to be the best at serving the needs of a very specific audience. In fact, many advocate brands are very happy to be labeled "niche." You can tell this is true when an advocate brand turns irrelevant audiences away. Warren Buffett's investment firm Berkshire Hathaway became known on Wall Street as the company with the most expensive stock price. You would have to pay more than $100,000 a share to become an investor in the company. The pricing strategy is deliberate. Berkshire Hathaway is a brand for serious, long-term investors only.

It's hard to find large sizes at Abercrombie & Fitch. That's intentional. Nothing ruins the sex appeal of the brand's clothing more than seeing it on a plus-sized customer. In 2011, it took the unprecedented step of paying a high-profile customer to stop wearing its clothes. Michael "The Situation" Sorrentino was a popular, albeit controversial, cast member on *Jersey Shore,* an MTV reality show. He was frequently seen on camera wearing Abercrombie & Fitch products. In fact, he had a habit of lifting his shirt to reveal his sculpted abdominal muscles before flipping the waistband of his underwear to reveal the Abercrombie & Fitch logo. Abercrombie & Fitch decided that The Situation's voluntary endorsement of its brand was "contrary to the aspirational nature of our brand," so it paid him an undisclosed amount to stop.[3]

When you position your brand as an advocate, you're promising exclusivity. Yours is the brand for a discriminating audience that values specialization so much that it will sacrifice features and characteristics that would appeal to a broader audience. Advocate brands can be very profitable and they can have a very long legacy, but they survive and thrive only when they position themselves as a voice for a specific crowd. They're not for everyone.

Public Brands

Where the advocate brand makes it clear that it is only for the chosen few, the public brand is most definitely for the world. It isn't on a mission to dominate the category. In fact, a public brand isn't very competitive in the usual sense. Public brands position themselves on common ground that includes competitors. In a sense, they are advocates for the category. It shouldn't surprise you that nearly all nonprofit organizations are essentially public brands. The American Red Cross is not very concerned about defending its position against a competing humanitarian brand. The brand is delighted when more organizations enlist to provide emergency response. It serves the purpose of the brand.

Public brands are not restricted to nonprofit organizations, however. Commercial brands such as Bluetooth position themselves as neutral on most fronts. The Bluetooth brand succeeds when more and more products developed by competing organizations incorporate Bluetooth wireless technology. Bluetooth would stray from its public position only when a rival platform surfaced that would make Bluetooth an obsolete standard.

For many years, MasterCard and Visa operated as virtual nonprofit organizations. The two brands were technically owned by member banks that invested in the payment clearing networks to avoid the cost of building a proprietary infrastructure that allowed card members to swipe a card and make a purchase at participating merchants. When the two brands launched in the 1960s, they were competitive because they had exclusive relationships with specific member banks. However, as they grew, it became increasingly common for the relationships to overlap. Many banks allowed their customers to choose a Visa or a MasterCard. Predictably, the two platforms became less competitive and more focused on convincing consumers to use payment cards instead of cash and casting doubt on American Express, which remained a private transaction network. The situation changed again in the 1990s when banks returned to exclusive deals with one payment network or the other. The competitive positioning further intensified when both companies became public corporations in 2006 and 2007.

SHIFTING CONTEXTS

As the MasterCard and Visa examples demonstrate, positions often change. The context of a brand strategy is too often overlooked, or so much emphasis is placed on context that the positioning is mistaken for a value proposition. Yes, there is value in being the established brand, and, yes, there may be value in challenging the status quo. But these are never the value propositions per se. I might be very impressed that you have been doing what you do longer than anybody else, or that you serve more people, but those facts just reinforce my decision to select whatever you do over alternative options. It differentiates you but doesn't change your promise.

Context provides a critical ingredient for a strong brand strategy, and it completes the recipe. Every good strategy clarifies the subject of the brand, the value it provides, and the context within which it provides this value. Figure 5.2 illustrates using all of the brand strategy concepts we have discussed so far. The brand type defines the subject. Your promise should define the brand's benefit through its value proposition. The context differentiates the brand by positioning it against competitive offerings in the category. Put together, you answer the questions that every brand must address in order to stand the test of time and create real equity. What is it? Why does it matter? How is it different?

FIGURE 5.2

{ BRAND }

TYPE + BENEFIT + CONTEXT

CULTURE	ACCESS	ESTABLISHMENT
PRODUCT	FEATURES & FUNCTION	CHALLENGER
SERVICE	APPROACH	ADVOCATE
DESTINATION	PERSONALITY	PUBLIC
INGREDIENT	CAUSE	
	LIFESTYLE	

Positioning plays an important role in your brand strategy because it guides the context of your communications and the execution of your brand experience. The beauty and the ugliness of a context are that it can and will change as a result of forces beyond your control. You can count on disruptions in your market: new technologies, changing regulations, shifts in customer demand, consolidation, expansion, macroeconomic shocks, and so on. When these forces make it necessary for you to change your strategy, your positioning is the dial you should consider changing first. Your audience expects your brand to make slight shifts from time to time in order to stay relevant in a changing marketplace. As long as your brand lives up to its promise, consumers are perfectly willing to consider your approach to demonstrating how you're different. When brands run into trouble, it's usually because they keep changing the promise instead of the position. When that happens, your consumers may become skeptical about your continued relevance.

Positioning is an ongoing challenge. You will likely lose a lot of sleep if you're managing a brand that was once the great establishment brand but is now being pushed into a dowager position. Differentiating and changing your position in that context is a high-stakes game. Many brands, like Yahoo!, have been in this awkward position, where they must decide whether or not to invest in the only sustainable sources of revenue (display advertising in Yahoo!'s case) even though those sources of revenue continue to cement the brand's declining dowager status. You're just as likely to lose sleep moving your brand from a challenger position to an advocate position because you're certain to sacrifice some customers, and that nearly always launches an endless process of second-guessing your decision.

Positioning is also a challenge when you can think of your market in multiple contexts. The Microsoft master brand could be considered a dowager, but its Xbox subbrand has been a strong challenger that shook up Sony PlayStation. Situations like these warrant a holistic approach whereby brands need to be considered in relation to the total brand architecture rather than as isolated occurrences.

Finally, remember that the goal of positioning is to determine your future stance. It's a two-pronged strategic exercise. First, you assess your current market position. You analyze where you sit against competitors to gauge how much you're differentiated. Then, you determine what position you want to occupy. Throughout this exercise, you're using your brand promise as a guide. You'll think of a lot of creative ways to change your position, but your promise and your experience must serve as a reality check.

····································

CHAPTER SIX

BRAND ATTACHMENT

The Barefoot Bandit and Our Sense of Self

You'd never guess that the green-eyed teenager in the photo was a fugitive. The boy in the self-portrait that buzzed around the world's media that day in 2009 stared up at you wearing Apple earbuds, resting his head on a knapsack in a patch of brush. You could have easily mistaken him for a Boy Scout. This was Colton Harris-Moore, an eighteen-year-old runaway who eluded authorities for over two years when he embarked on an adventurous crime spree that resulted in over one hundred cases of theft, burglary, and criminal trespassing. The world knew him as "the Barefoot Bandit," a name he earned after a surveillance video caught him pilfering without shoes. He must have approved of the brand name because he began drawing chalk footprints on the floors of his victims.

Like many people, I became fascinated with the Barefoot Bandit because his story seemed like something only Hollywood could invent. He ran away from home, survived on his own in the woods for weeks at a time, burglarized affluent communities, flaunted legal authorities using a catchy alter ego, and stole a few planes to venture from the remotest corner of the Pacific Northwest to a tropical island in the Caribbean. But not everyone loved Harris-Moore. The residents of the towns and communities where he committed his crimes despised him. One said he wanted him dead. Harris-Moore damaged property, robbed people of their valuables, and violated a lot of people's sense of security. Some who knew him when he was young pitied him, describing him as a socially challenged kid from a battered home who loved animals and was infatuated with airplanes. Then there were the millions of people around the world who made the Barefoot Bandit into a folk hero. They romanticized his run from the law through a frenzy of social media activity. A Facebook fan page created about him attracted more than thirty thousand followers, with fans likening him to a modern-day Jesse James. "He's the right criminal at the right time," said Zack Sestak, the self-appointed head of Harris-Moore's fan club. "Executives are getting billion-dollar bonuses, and . . . the normal people, everyday people, people who are struggling to pay their bills—they see someone like Colton taking on the system, and they say 'All right!' "[1]

I found it a little odd that so many people identified with Harris-Moore. A cottage business developed with entrepreneurs selling T-shirts and novelty items bearing his likeness. Music videos appeared on YouTube celebrating his adventure and urging him to "fly on." It seemed especially odd because there was no indication that Harris-Moore would have approved of any of it. After he was captured, he refused to grant interviews, appeared shy in front of news cameras, and frequently asked the media to go away. He is said to have sold the rights to his life story only as a means to repay his victims.

It struck me that the Barefoot Bandit was an interesting example of a force that gives branding so much potential power: attachment. When people become attached to brands, their attachment changes their behavior. Though I can't say for sure that Colton Harris-Moore began his life of crime because he was attached to brands, his story is littered with some of the most prestigious brands in our culture. There's more to it than that, however. The story of the Barefoot Bandit provides a compelling glimpse at why there's a growing backlash against brands. Looking at Harris-Moore and the people who were drawn to his story during his run from the law, it's tempting to suggest that branding has led us completely astray from moral values. Indeed, this has been the central argument of Adbusters, the anticonsumerist organization of activists who stage demonstrations and mount campaigns to convince the public to reject advertising and media because they lead people to focus too much on using external rewards to develop a sense of personal identity. I believe there is ample truth in their argument. Branding, marketing, and media are often misused in irresponsible and unsustainable ways— ways that overpromise on the value that can actually be delivered; ways that manipulate by appealing to our most shallow, image-driven vulnerabilities; and ways that define brands as substitutes for human relationships.

That said, I believe that brands can play a valuable role in our culture and that those of us who have the privilege of guiding brands have a responsibility to understand the impact they can exert on a consumer's individual identity. We've studied the way brands make a promise, the way they stand for real benefits, and the way they relate to their category. In this chapter we're going to look at a connection that people have with brands that seems positively unreal; yet it is the force that has driven some of the most successful brands to extreme heights, and the force that has rallied antibrand activists to cry foul. In this chapter, you'll see how consumers use brands to validate their sense of self.

BRANDS AND THE SELF-CONCEPT

Brand attachment measures how much consumers (or any members of a brand audience, for that matter) view the brand as an extension of themselves. This differs quite a bit from measures of brand attitudes. When we measure attitudes, we mostly aim to gage how much people like a brand. In contrast, attachment measures how much people will say that a brand is like them—they identify with a brand because it reflects their values and resembles the way they see themselves.

In a 2010 study published in the *Journal of Marketing,* researchers found that by measuring the strength of a consumer's attachment to a brand, they were able to predict actual behavior better than when they measured the strength of a consumer's attitudes about a brand. They measured attachment by asking consumers questions such as "To what extent is [brand name] part of you and who you are?" and "To what extent does [brand name] say something to other people about you?"[2] The deepest brand loyalties coincided with brands that reflected or extended a person's self-concept.

We perceive who we are through our self-concept. It's not a single variable. Instead, it's a complex collection of many characteristics that may include our gender roles, ancestral heritage, educational background, racial identity, religious beliefs, and political persuasions, among other factors. We're aware of some of these factors, while others are deeply ingrained in our subconscious. But they all add up to our sense of identity. Our self-concept begins to develop the day we're born, and it evolves until we take our last breath. Some of us are bound to self-concepts we defined long ago, while others are tweaking our lives one day at a time in a constant journey to change. In either case, we often enlist brands to help us validate and realize our self-concept.

Hard-core Harley-Davidson loyalists wouldn't be caught dead on another bike. While they'll certainly tell you they like the Harley brand, their loyalty runs deeper than their attitudes. They're loyal because Harley is as much a part of their identity as their body—maybe more so.

I've known Hollywood agents who don't feel they're legitimate until they own a genuine Armani suit and drive a luxury German car. There are guitar players who will sacrifice all their worldly possessions in pursuit of becoming a rock star, except for one: their Gibson Les Paul solid-body guitar. I've met auto mechanics who don't feel they can do their job as well without access to Snap-on tools, and chefs who carry their own Wüsthof knives from job to job. In each instance, the possessions and the brands that make them special are part of the consumer's self-concept.

When consumers intertwine a brand with their self-concept, it's an act of sacralization. Very often when I speak about the sacred dimension of brands at conferences I am stopped by a few attendees who are deeply troubled by this notion. They find it distasteful to compare brands to other sacred dimensions of life. I always tell them that I'm not encouraging people to worship brands. In fact, I find that kind of shallow materialism troubling. Yet the sacralization I'm talking about is very real and increasingly prominent. It's part of a phenomenon that social researchers have traced back to the industrial revolution, but it became more pronounced after television changed the way we consume media and relate to the rest of the world. In that new media world, we shifted our orientation away from traditionally sacred institutions—such as religion, the arts, and civic culture—to a new orientation that glorifies the individual. The reason brands are increasingly sacralized is because consumers, especially in Western culture, are on a quest to realize the blissful nirvana of themselves.

A landmark study on the link between consumer behavior and sacralization found that "the rise of individualism has made it possible to define the sacred as that which brings secular ecstasy to the individual." Famed mythologist and writer Joseph Campbell said it more profoundly: "Heaven in such a doctrine is the fulfillment of self."[3] There are many ways in which we achieve this goal. Brands are only one contributor. It helps to understand how people make things *sacred*. First, the kinds of things we sacralize are not coincidentally related to the types of things we brand: places, times, things (tangible and intangible), persons, and experiences. But what I find more interesting is the way in which we transform ordinary things into sacred objects that become attached to our identity. We do this through rituals (e.g., an organized Vespa ride), pilgrimages (e.g., family vacations to Walt Disney World), gift giving (e.g., sending a Hallmark card), collecting (e.g., Beanie Babies and Pokémon cards), and inheritance (e.g., handing down a genuine Rolex watch).[4] Each act of brand sacralization says something about us and reinforces our self-concept. Once the brand reaches that sacred status, it's indelibly attached to who we are—not because of its specific form or function but because of how it relates to our identity.

In this context, you can measure brand attachment in two ways. First, we can measure the degree to which a brand reflects a person's self-concept. Imagine a default point in the center of a line that most of us would choose for brands that are neither an extension of our self-concept nor the polar opposite of our self-concept. On this scale (pictured in Figure 6.1), we want to know at what degree from the center a brand would fall. When it's to the right, we'd say that the brand is "like me," and when it's to the left we'd say it's "the opposite of me."

You have to measure more than self-concept, though. After all, even though a particular brand skews toward my sense of self, it might not be relevant to me at this moment in time. For example, I might tell you that a TAG Heuer watch is a lot like me, but I don't think about TAG Heuer watches much. I don't own one, and I don't intend to buy one anytime soon. Although I find the watches beautiful and I'm inspired by their craftsmanship, I'm in no hurry to spend that much money on a timepiece. It's not sacred to me because it's not really as relevant as other needs. That's why you need to add another axis to the scale: relevance. Relevance determines

FIGURE 6.1

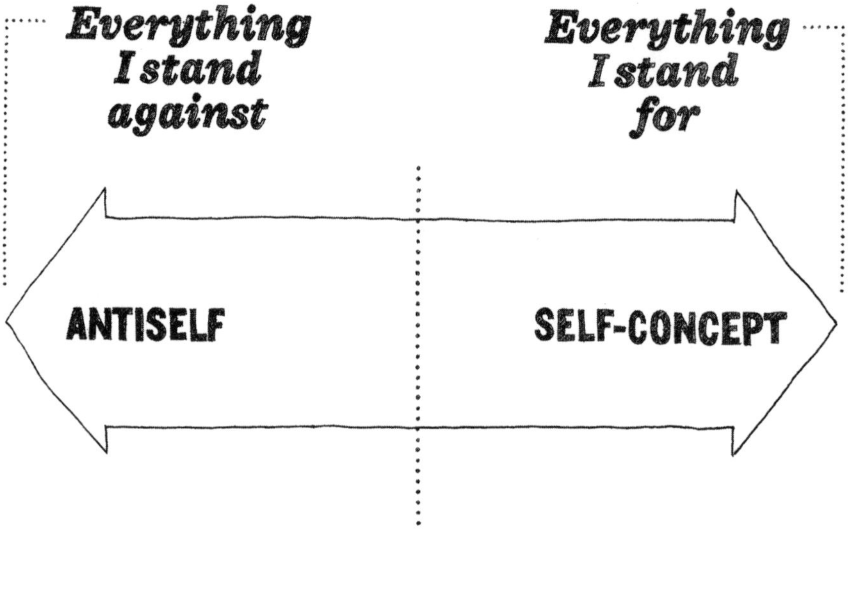

Everything I stand against — Everything I stand for

ANTISELF — SELF-CONCEPT

FIGURE 6.2

how much your audience actually has use for your brand. It determines how prominent the brand is in daily life (Figure 6.2). At the low end of this axis are brands that we don't think about all that much. Either we don't have many occasions to recall them or we don't use them enough for them to be relevant to our identity. On the other end of the spectrum are brands that we think about all the time or brands that are prominent on the landscape of options. On the upper part of the grid are the ones that we frequently use as points of reference. When you hear someone say, "I want to look very J.Crew tomorrow," the brand is being employed in speech in a way that makes it useful and instrumental to our thinking. These are the prominent brands.

When you cross these two axes, we can sort out the attached brands from the detached brands. The ones that are truly extensions of us scale out in the upper right quadrant. They are preferred because they are the most relevant and the most connected to our self-concept. We go to great lengths to keep them in our lives. In contrast, we have nothing but disdain for the brands in the upper left corner. We find it hard to ignore them because of how prominent they are, but they tend to repulse us rather than attract us. Instead of being sacred, these brands are profane. I had a colleague who could not stand the Ed Hardy brand of apparel. What I found ironic about his behavior was how often he referenced Ed Hardy in his conversations. If we met someone on the street who seemed a little too flashy, my friend would say something like "Can you believe that Ed Hardy hipster?" The Ed Hardy brand even showed up in a presentation he gave to some clients about what not to do with their brand. The Ed Hardy brand was so prominent in my friend's thoughts that he introduced it as a point of reference even though it was the antithesis of his identity.

On the lower portion of our scale are brands that aren't very prominent. Brands that you might find in a traditional brand attitude study are located in the lower right quadrant. We might say we like them, but they aren't top of mind or they just don't factor into our decision process much. In the lower left quadrant are brands that are the opposite of our self-concept and they rarely pass through our thoughts. Truthfully, if you drew a big circle right in the middle of the four quadrants, you'd probably find many of the brands we come across daily. We neither think of them all that much nor do we really see them as a reflection of ourselves. The brands that land smack in the center on or around the crosshairs are mundane, not sacred. Our behavior around them is mostly a force of habit, a consequence of price sensitivities, or a matter of convenience.

It's worth our time to understand how consumers collectively attach a brand to their self-concept because that attachment proves to be one of the best drivers of relevance. Relevance is strongly correlated to brand preference. While it's commonplace for companies to measure preference—how much consumers prefer their brand to competitive alternatives—they should invest as much energy explaining *why* consumers prefer their brand. In the research I've studied over the years doing strategy work for my clients, it's evident to me that preference is an outcome that is derived from brand relevance. We prefer a particular brand because it is more relevant to us than competitive options. And the brands that are often most relevant to us are those that we have sacralized and attached to our self-concept.

WHEN BRANDS CONNECT US WITH OUR ROOTS

When I had the privilege of working with Southwest Airlines, I spent a lot of time on Southwest flights. I made a habit of doing something I rarely do: I talked to the stranger sitting in the seat next to me. This was extra credit for me. I didn't have to talk to them, but I wanted to hear as many points of view as I could. Without letting people know that I was on assignment for the airline, I'd strike up a casual conversation and find a way to turn it toward the airline. On one of my flights I started a conversation with a well-dressed man flying back to Los Angeles from San Francisco. He told me he was a partner in a law firm and that he could fly first class on any carrier he preferred. I thought it interesting that he voluntarily disclosed this information, so I asked why he chose to fly Southwest when the other options sounded better. He told me he flew Southwest as much as he could "out of principle." He said that the luxury trappings of other airlines had insulated a lot of his colleagues, and they'd forgotten what it was like when "it was a level playing field and we all had to work like hell to get ahead." He was proud of that time in his life and fearful that he'd be less authentic if he began "flying another airline like all the other phonies." While he rattled off some practical reasons for flying Southwest—plenty of flights to choose from, low fares, friendly crew—he was most passionate about the brand because he said traveling with Southwest made him feel he hadn't turned his back on his roots. While I wouldn't say that he was at all typical of a Southwest customer, he definitely linked the brand to his own identity. His choice validated his self-concept.

The history in our self-concept can create astonishing attachments to

brands. G. Clotaire Rapaille is a French-born anthropologist and brand consultant. He is also a disciple of Jean Piaget, one of the early giants in the psychology of childhood development. Rapaille has made a name for himself by
helping brand managers probe childhood memories to find ways to create
strong brand attachments in adults. Procter & Gamble hired him to recharge
the equity in the Folgers brand of coffee. Rapaille is said to have discovered
that many adult coffee drinkers associated their mother with the smell of
brewing coffee. Though his techniques are a carefully guarded secret, it appears his insight was applied to advertising and promotion in order to create
a strong connection between Folgers and its consumers' self-concepts. By
connecting the brand to their memories from the past, it became a greater
part of who they were now—as inseparable from their sense of self as their
memories of childhood and their attachment to their mothers.[5]

Many advertisers consider nostalgia a dangerous "third rail." Brands
like Coca-Cola and Ford have more than one hundred years of rich history
that can provoke strong affections and positive feelings. The danger is that
a consumer will think the brand is dated if it is too closely associated with
the past. Would an association with Ford's Model T really help more consumers create a stronger attachment to the Ford Mustang today? Probably
not. However, Chrysler launched a very effective rebranding campaign in
2011 that struck a great balance. When "Imported from Detroit" debuted
during the Super Bowl, with rapper Eminem (a Detroit native) driving a
newly designed Chrysler 200 against images of the Motor City, the brand
tapped its history and its present day to create strong, authentic attachment.
In fact, Chrysler reported that "Imported from Detroit" contributed $116
million in first-quarter profit, compared to a $197 million loss the year be-
fore.[6] Automotive information publisher Edmunds.com reported that the
campaign boosted consideration for the brand by 267 percent within hours
of its first airing, and one week later that consideration remained 87 percent
higher than it had been before the campaign. For the many American auto
consumers who are proud of their heritage and looking for reasons to buy
American, Chrysler created a foundation for strong attachment.

ASPIRATIONS AND SENSE OF SELF

While our history undoubtedly influences our sense of self, most of us are predisposed to look forward, not back. Nearly two out of three people say they think about themselves "in the future a great deal of the time or all the time." And when thinking of themselves in the future, people say that they more often imagine a positive outcome than a negative one by a ratio of four to one.[7] Our hopes and dreams live in the domain of our possible selves. Fewer of us believe that we are destined to remain in our current station of life, and most of us believe we can become whoever we want to be.

The trouble starts when we allow nagging probabilities to temper our aspirations. The dreamer inside us constantly wrestles with the realist. That gap between what we *aspire* to be and what we think we'll *probably* be influences our brand behavior. In fact, we become so attached to many of our possessions and brands because they create the illusion that our aspirations are one step closer to reality.

Let me illustrate with a puzzling phenomenon. When economic times are tough, why would consumers skimp on staples like diapers and spend a little more on brand-name cosmetics? That was the question the *New York Times* asked in a revealing article on consumer behavior published in September 2011. Despite widespread fear of a looming double-dip recession, many makers of luxury goods such as handbags, shoes, and cosmetics were posting record sales while consumer staples such as batteries, bleach, and diapers were suffering staggering declines. The article noted that Estée Lauder had recorded its strongest fiscal year in a decade. The statistics showed that consumers were willing to splurge on little luxuries at the expense of some basic needs, and many observers rationalized that the behavior reflected a broad consumer need to indulge their urges.[8] I think that the trend actually revealed the influential power of our possible selves. We want to have brands in our life that connect us with our aspirations in spite of the probabilities. We might never be able to afford a $10,000 necklace from Tiffany, but for $175 we can carry a Tiffany keychain with us everywhere we go, which is probably why it is said to be one of the luxury jeweler's best-selling items.

INVESTING IN BRANDS THAT HELP US ACHIEVE ASPIRATIONAL GOALS

According to his mother, when Colton Harris-Moore was about 15, he made collages of things he wished to be or to have. One of these collages was shown in a 2010 CBS profile of the Barefoot Bandit.[9] Prominent brand names filled the poster board—along with images of airplanes. Though the brands must have seemed out of reach when he sat in his mother's dilapidated trailer on the outskirts of town, Harris-Moore's poster board was filled with dominant names: Cadillac, Giorgio Armani, Discover Card. These brands must have occupied the boy's imagination as much as the airplanes. When he was growing up, Colton Harris-Moore said that he wanted to be a pilot. He got his wish, although in a very unusual way.

During his time as a fugitive, the Barefoot Bandit stole and piloted five planes. The remarkable part is that he had no formal flight training. Investigators believe he learned how to fly by watching an instructional DVD that he purchased with a stolen credit card and by studying a flight manual that he stole from an unlocked aircraft. On the day he took off in a stolen single-engine plane from an airfield located on Washington state's Orcas Island, it was his first flight ever. He flew through harrowingly gusty winds over the Cascade mountain range before crash-landing in a field outside Yakima, Washington. Miraculously, he walked away. As if that wasn't gutsy enough, he would repeat this crazy feat four more times. To say that he was driven by aspiration seems an understatement.

When Colton Harris-Moore flew those planes, they were important instruments in bringing his possible self to life. Aspiration is a powerful force. While you may not be willing to risk your life in such a daring way to accomplish your own aspirational goals, you probably are prepared to take risks and invest in selected activities that give you a sense that you are making your aspirations more of a reality. Some of the brands we are most strongly attached to are the ones that we literally use as instruments in our activities to fulfill aspirational goals.

Russell W. Belk is a professor at the University of Utah who has spent most of his career studying and writing about the meaning behind consumer possessions. In a fascinating 1988 paper, "Possessions and the Extended Self," Belk argued that "we cannot hope to understand consumer behavior without first gaining some understanding of the meanings that consumers attach to possessions." He concluded, "We learn, define, and remind ourselves of who we are by our possessions."[10] To a large extent, much of the symbolic meaning behind our possessions is connected to the way we incorporate them into our self-concept. One of the ways that Belk suggested we make our possessions part of our extended self is through a strong desire. "It is no accident . . . that sexual relations have often been described as knowing or having another person, as it is our intimate knowledge of the other person that allows us to consider the person ours and a part of self." When brands become an extension of self, we incorporate them by coveting them. That strong desire makes us work for highly attached brands in ways we wouldn't for ordinary brands. We are often more invested in an attached brand precisely because we want it and it is hard to obtain. It's very gratifying when a brand makes us invest time, money, and energy to get into our life. In fact, after we acquire it, we're less likely to consider alternative brands. This finding works in reverse, too. As Park and colleagues found in their study on brand attachment, "The greater the attachment, the more difficult the behavior that consumer is willing to enact to maintain" his or her brand relationship.[11]

You don't need to read any of this research to see such phenomena at work. Sales of prestige branded cooking appliances such as Viking ranges and KitchenAid mixers have steadily risen in correlation with the growth of the Food Network. There are millions of aspiring chefs in homes all around the world who are willing to pay a premium for a Viking range because it authentically serves their aspirations to be great cooks. It doesn't matter that many of them never prepare anything more difficult than macaroni and cheese. Once they have this brand in their life, they don't want to be separated from it. Many owners of Viking ranges insist on taking them along when they buy a new home. The act of using this brand brings an aspiration to life because of its instrumental value.

SEPARATION ANXIETY AND DELIBERATE COMPROMISES

You can tell a lot about the degree to which consumers are attached to a brand by taking it away from them. Although we're willing to suffer a substitute for an ordinary brand on occasion if our preference is unavailable, when consumers are attached to a brand that is denied them, they can experience separation anxiety. Early in my career, I worked with an executive who drank Diet Coke all day long. She drank nothing else. When she was scheduled to travel to Paris for a meeting, she brought a six-pack of Diet Coke in her carry-on bag because she feared Air France wouldn't serve it. That's separation anxiety at work.

My team has measured separation anxiety in our client work by conducting deprivation studies. We recruit a few dozen respondents and we pay them to *not* use the brand for an extended period of time. During the deprivation period, we ask them to share their thoughts and feelings about life without the brand. In one study for an apparel brand, a respondent told us, "I don't feel like myself . . . it's weird because it's just some of my clothes . . . I know it sounds lame, but when I wear those clothes I'm me."

When we are truly attached to a brand, we're willing to make compromises in our other consumer behaviors in order to keep the attached brand in our life. I met a talented young photographer who had moved out of his parents' house for the first time to live on his own. He worked a lot of unrelated jobs to pay his rent. He ate ramen and spaghetti for just about every meal. Not surprisingly, he spent most of his money on his camera gear. He was a Nikon shooter, and he owned a professional camera body and a few expensive lenses. He told me he was willing to sacrifice food in order to have the best gear. This isn't surprising at all, but then I noticed his Beats by Dr. Dre studio headphones. I asked if they were a gift. He told me he had just bought them. In fact, they were his second pair. He forfeited funds he had been saving to upgrade part of his camera kit so that he could buy the new headphones. When I asked why he did this, he told me that music inspired his photography and he couldn't imagine listening to music on anything other than his "Beats." This compromise behavior is key to brand attachment. We'd rather go without something else—even something connected to our livelihood—than go without our access to the brand that's part of our extended self.

COMFORT FROM CLOSENESS

In the same way that you can measure brand attachment by how anxious a consumer becomes when the brand is taken away, we can measure how much comfort and satisfaction consumers report as a result of having the brand in their possession or in close proximity. The more consumers view the brand as an extension of their own identity, the more they want the brand nearby.

You might not have the budget to stock your wine shelf with Opus One, but if you can buy one bottle of it, everything else on the shelf is more satisfying to you. You might purposefully put off opening that bottle because it's worth more to you on your shelf than in your belly. Having Opus One in the collection with the other wines is enough to validate your aspiration that you are a wine connoisseur.

The recent reemergence of the Moleskine brand of high-end journals and day planners is another example. The brand goes to market as the notebook used by "Vincent van Gogh, Pablo Picasso, Ernest Hemingway, and Bruce Chatwin." It is a brand that had faded into obscurity until reimagined as more than a pad of paper. Today, it is used by many professionals who keep it close because it is one of many "indispensable creative tools that help define who we are, identifying us wherever we are in the world."[12]

Which brings me back to the Barefoot Bandit. It's awfully dangerous to play armchair psychologist and speculate on Colton Harris-Moore's motives. But I found the nature of many of his crimes striking. Most burglars break into a home, steal what they can sell, and leave as quickly as they can. Harris-Moore broke into homes and then made himself comfortable. He took showers, ate meals, and slept in the empty beds. While many of Harris-Moore's suspected crimes included theft of cash and illegal use of credit cards, he is also believed to have kept some of the items he stole. In the now famous self-portrait of him, he is wearing a Mercedes-Benz branded polo shirt. When he was captured in the Bahamas he was carrying a Walther PPK handgun in his backpack. It's not the greatest weapon for a fugitive, but it was the gun that was famously used by Agent 007 in the James Bond franchise. Living on the run, Harris-Moore couldn't take a lot with him, but the few things he did take seemed to have brand significance. Perhaps they provided a sense of comfort. Perhaps the mere possession of the brands made the risk taking worthwhile.

Regardless of Harris-Moore's deeds and motives, humans have a history of imbuing possessions with so much meaning that we want them close at all times. Whether it's the lucky rabbit's foot we must have in our pocket or the personal artifacts we find buried with the ancients, it's in our nature to view some of our possessions as essential parts of ourselves. What's changed is how we've transferred that meaning from an object to a brand. After working on various smartphone-branding projects, I've noticed a clear dividing line in early adopters. There is always a segment that must have the latest gadget, regardless of the brand affiliation. For them, the comfort comes from the newness of the device itself. In fact, these fickle early adopters are also known as "first droppers," because they are usually the first segment to move on to a new technology. But there's another, growing segment that wants the newest device from their preferred brand. This segment even defends and rationalizes poorly designed devices from their brand of choice. To them, it's the brand in their pocket, not the object itself.

PRIDE AND BRAND DISPLAY

There is perhaps no stronger sign of brand attachment than the willingness of consumers to show off a brand. When a brand connects strongly with our self-concept, we often want to use it as a way to signal who we are to the rest of the world. Historically, the degree to which we're willing to wear brands comes in waves. During the 1980s, brand display was critical to conspicuous consumption. People enjoyed draping themselves with brand identities, creating odd tapestries reminiscent of NASCAR uniforms. By the millennium, the distaste for wearing a brand became so intense that for a while we saw the rise of a backlash movement in which people rejected anything that was branded. But the wearable brand never went away completely. It simply became more discreet. Whether used to show others you have status and style—as you might when carrying a signature Louis Vuitton handbag—or to display your commitment to quality—as you might with a Montblanc pen—we're often attached to brands because they help us project our identity to the rest of the world. Sometimes this leads to problems for the brand's maker.

A colleague recently told me that fashion brand Bebe was considering whether to discontinue production of its logo line of T-shirts. These shirts, available online and in most stores for about $20 to $30, feature the word *Bebe* in the center of the chest. It was rumored that some of Bebe's management team were troubled to see housekeepers and nannies in local neighborhoods wearing Bebe T-shirts in the performance of their duties. They were worried that the brand would be perceived as less special because it was so accessible that you might find it on someone who was pushing a stroller or cleaning windows.

CEO Manny Mashouf had publicly stated that his goal was to position Bebe as a fashion icon worthy of premium pricing. In an investor conference call in 2010, he cited this goal as his rationale for partnering with public personalities like Kim Kardashian, who he believed provided the brand with celebrity cachet. Many of the women wearing the Bebe logo T-shirt might indeed identify with the brand's image, which projects woman in every advertisement as a desirable sex object. Unfortunately, while many of these women consider themselves stylish, sexy, and sophisticated, they probably can't afford many of the products in Bebe's line. The comfortably priced logo T-shirt allows them to possess the Bebe brand and present themselves to the world as part of its culture.

Whether or not the story is true, it raises interesting questions. How much should a brand manager limit access to a brand to preserve its cachet and image factor? And if limiting access could contribute to broader socioeconomic issues, how much should the manager weigh that factor into her decision? As I write this book, 53 percent of American girls are "unhappy with their bodies" at the age of 13. That number increases to 78 percent by the time they are 17.[13] The media and our fashion leaders have created an aspirational body image that only 5 percent of women can realistically obtain. Nevertheless, consumers are so conditioned to the aspiration that weight-loss products and programs have grown to become one of the most profitable segments of the economy. Many of the women buying the T-shirts won't ever have the body that Bebe celebrates in its branding and advertising. Yet those same consumers are attached in some way to the brand. The T-shirt is an accessible way to consider themselves part of the culture. If Bebe purposefully eliminated items that allowed these women access to the brand culture, would it be contributing to a societal issue? Should it care? How long can it sustain a brand that glorifies 5 percent of the population while hoping to profit from the other 95 percent?

These are questions few brands consider, but I believe they will have to address in the future. Pepsi faced significant criticism in 2011 when it introduced a "skinny" can for Diet Pepsi. In an introductory print advertisement that ran during Fashion Week in New York, a very thin model with very skinny arms is seen sipping the product from the narrowly thin new can. CMO Jill Beraud described it as "a perfect complement to today's most stylish looks." Interestingly, the new can contained the same amount of fluid and the same amount of calories as the traditional can. It didn't take long for consumers to voice their opinion on social media. One blogger said, "Now, even a soda can tells women that their butts will always be too big."[14]

I'm not trying to say that a brand must be democratic, nor am I arguing that a brand is obligated to be accessible to everyone. However, because of what we know about brand attachment, brands must consider the implications of their actions when they choose to limit consumer access or when they send a signal about access that contradicts the realities of brand attachment.

INDEPENDENT VS. INTERDEPENDENT

When consumers use brands to display their sense of self, they often make a statement about their relationship with the rest of the world. A brand can help consumers demonstrate how much they wish to fit in (as in the Bebe example) or it can help them signal how much they stand out. When your consumer audience celebrates interdependence—that we're all connected and that the more we work with others, the higher the benefit—your brand serves as a common bond.

However, some consumers attach themselves to a brand because they see it as symbol of disruption. They see it and themselves as iconoclasts who are out to destroy traditions and previously accepted ideas. The brand demonstrates how they don't follow anyone's rules; nor do they care if they are accepted into the mainstream. When Alexander McQueen's fashion lines first debuted, many in the fashion elite were shocked. McQueen built a name for himself by creating provocative styles like low-rise pants, dubbed "bumsters." He staged fashion shows with controversial names like "Highland Rape." The early followers of McQueen's fashion lines wanted to stand out. They took delight in his creative approaches to design, and they saw his brand as a form of rebellion—an opportunity to signal their autonomy and fierce independence.

Brands that successfully attach to independent-minded individuals have a way of evolving into symbols of interdependence. After all, when consumers see those cheeky, fashionable people bucking the trends and standing out with pride, they're often persuaded to follow the lead. Maintaining the "badge value" of the brand between these two mind-sets is tricky and requires a strong, dedicated commitment to realizing the brand promise. It also requires reason. Many brands use disruption to achieve their brand promise. It is hard to sustain attachment with a brand, however, when it appears that its promise is focused more on disruption than on the delivery of its real benefits. In fact, many brands have risked their valuable following because they took disruptive tactics to an extreme. People for the Ethical Treatment of Animals (PETA) is famous for disruptive "shock" advertising that calls attention to animal rights issues. But some of its most faithful supporters felt distanced from the organization when it began running advertisements featuring nude models holding crucifixes, and billboards that contained photographs from the Holocaust accompanied by the headline "To Animals, All People are Nazis." While these ads certainly attract public attention, many critics worried that they also alienated some of the most fervent animal rights supporters—people who believe in PETA's cause but don't want to be associated with the controversial approach.

Brand architecture is often the way a brand can continue to satisfy independents while broadening access for interdependents. Some brands solve this problem through brand architecture—by segmenting the brand into one tier that disrupts and innovates and another tier that makes those innovations mainstream. Martha Stewart developed a billion-dollar empire by developing tiers for her product lines that allowed her to cater to a high-end, quality-conscious audience on one end of the spectrum while serving a mass-market audience through relationships with retailers like Macy's and Kmart.

OPPOSED

When attachment to a brand is particularly strong, we often find consumers with strong *oppositional loyalty,* which is a tendency to develop an adversarial view toward rival brands. The bitterness hard-core Apple loyalists felt toward Microsoft led to the infamous Mac and PC campaigns, in which actor Justin Long personified Mac and author/comedian John Hodgman portrayed PC. The campaign was so successful that Microsoft eventually responded with a derivative campaign of its own: "I'm a PC." The kind of vitriol that surfaces in discussions between Apple and Microsoft loyalists is emblematic of strong brand attachment. The more consumers view the brand as part of their own identity, the more they're willing to defend it and attack anything that threatens it. Threats to the brand are like personal threats to the brand loyalist.

Strong oppositional loyalty can create a stronger brand community, where the most attached consumers feel compelled to bond with others who are as strongly attached. They use the opposition as a focal point for their relationships. Brands with strong oppositional loyalty enjoy a consumer base that is willing to work far more on the brand's behalf than it might for other brands. These consumers are more likely to promote the brand on their own in social media. They'll also go to great lengths to see that the brand succeeds, even if it means buying products and services from the brand that they don't need or wouldn't otherwise buy.

But there's a significant downside to oppositional loyalty that few marketers understand. When people are so invested in your brand that they are willing to attack your competition, they are much more likely to turn their attacks toward you if you let them down. In a 2011 study appearing in the *Journal of Consumer Research*, researchers found that the more consumers attached a brand to their self-concept, the more likely they were to engage in "antibrand behavior" when the relationship with the brand came to an end. In the same way that some people seek revenge after a bad romantic breakup, highly attached consumers are quite likely to attack and deride their former brand soul mates. They often say they feel betrayed by the brand, and they describe their feelings in exactly the same way they might talk about a damaged relationship with a lover.[15]

UNPOSSESSED BRANDS

It may not be so surprising that consumers buy and use brands to shape their self-concepts. But can a brand be part of a consumer's identity when the consumer doesn't even possess it? The answer, of course, is yes. It's common to find consumers who identify with brands they have never owned or used. Think of the number of car aficionados who identify with the Ferrari, Maserati, or Bentley brands. Most of them haven't even sat in one of those vehicles, let alone owned one. The same is true for fashionistas who identify with Chanel, Prada, and Giorgio Armani.

When brands that resonate with our identity are hard to possess, we compensate in other ways. In the real world it is often true that we are what we buy. Venture online and you quickly find that people seem to subscribe to the belief that we are what we post.

In a 2003 study, researchers Hope Jensen Schau and Mary C. Gilly researched the way people constructed online identities through the creation of personal websites, which required significant time and technical skill. Schau and Gilly concluded that "consumers add depth to their digital selves by using brands and logos as shorthand for more complex meanings." In case after case that they studied, they found instances of consumers who affiliated with specific brands even though there was significant evidence that the consumers neither owned nor used the brand in real life. Usage was irrelevant. The shorthand value of the brand and its cultural meaning provided a way for consumers to project parts of themselves to online audiences. What I found most striking about this study was the way in which people purposefully displayed brands to reveal who they'd like to be, even when it conflicted with who they actually were.[16]

Today, it requires far less time and skill to project an identity online. Social media sites like Facebook, Tumblr, YouTube, and Twitter have made it so easy that all you have to do is click the "Like" button or tell people you're following a brand. There's almost no risk. Every time you include a brand in your social stream, you're signaling to your world that this is what you stand for. Which brings me back again to the Barefoot Bandit. Why would thousands of people choose to identify with a notorious fugitive and an alleged criminal?

The easy answer to the question is that our culture has a history of glorifying outlaws. We've had naughty brands (Playboy), irreverent brands (Virgin), tricksters (AXE), and outright hostile characters (think of Apple's sometimes maddening, sometimes endearing "take it or leave it" approach to new product introduction). But dismissing Harris-Moore's Facebook fan base as nothing more than a widespread love of antiheroes misses the point.

Consumers who liked the Barefoot Bandit on Facebook were engaged in at least one identity-affirming activity. Some clicked the "Like" button because when they came across Harris-Moore's story, something inside them identified with the Barefoot Bandit. Perhaps they admired his flagrant challenge to law enforcement, or they saw him as the free spirit they'd like to be. For some reason, they said, "That's great. Fly on!"

The other possibility is that they liked his fan page because they wanted to signal to their circle of friends and acquaintances that their own personal brand is aligned with the brand of the Barefoot Bandit. As Schau and Gilly put it, these Facebook users activated "a type of cobranding, commingling brand logos, and creating relationships between brands." Aidin Stevens, an entrepreneur who profited from Harris-Moore's run from the law by selling T-shirts bearing his likeness, said he rooted for the Barefoot Bandit because "being good doesn't really get you very far. It's a kind of sucker's swindle . . . whether he's a mastermind or not, he was obviously never going to have the kind of opportunities that some people might have to have a Mercedes or to be a pilot."[17] Stevens proved his argument every time someone paid him $15 for a Barefoot Bandit T-shirt.

A couple of years ago, my family moved into a new home in Santa Monica. The move got us closer to all the things you might like to do in Southern California. We were closer to the beach, within walking distance of great restaurants and shops, and adjacent to the attractive westside scene. Everything was a bicycle ride away, which made the move particularly liberating for my teenage son.

We kept our bikes in a common garage that we shared with most of our neighbors. Shortly after we moved in, a thief broke in and stole our bikes. As an avid cyclist, I'd put quite a bit of money into my bike. It was a sizable financial loss, and I was angry. But I found it even more painful to see how it affected my son. He was deflated. It was as if someone had stolen his freedom.

The point of the story is that you shouldn't interpret any of my comparisons to Colton Harris-Moore as a glorification of a life of crime. As a victim of the kind of crime Harris-Moore pleaded guilty to committing, I understand why there are so many who have little sympathy for his story. Though I don't count myself among the thousands of his Facebook fans, a part of me identifies with his daring quest to seize some of his dreams. I grew up wanting to be a pilot, drawing pictures of planes just like he did. I enjoy flying on a plane to this very day, even though I work in a field where one can argue that I log far too many air miles. There's a part of me that enjoys the fantasy of taking the risk Harris-Moore took in order to make his dream real. But I wouldn't do what he did, and I suspect that 99.9 percent of his fan base wouldn't choose a life of crime, given the opportunity.

The story of the Barefoot Bandit is an allegory about the pervasiveness of brands in our lives. There was a time when we looked to other parts of the culture for meaning. Religion, for one, helped us align our identities with values and ideology. In the modern world, we have secularized many of the aspects of our lives that religion once governed, so much so that Pope Benedict XVI warned of the dangers of secularization in his inaugural address to the church. And where have we redirected our quest for meaning? Brands are surely one channel.

It is possible that Colton Harris-Moore attached so much meaning to brands that he elected to possess them the only way he knew how—to steal them. It seems likely that the meaning of some of those brands emboldened him to engage in extraordinarily risky behavior, literally putting his life on the line. Along the way, he defined a brand of his own, creating a brand mark and establishing an identity that influenced others. And in perhaps the most striking lesson, his brand became a link to people all over the world—people who aren't inclined to be criminals. Instead, they saw a part of themselves in his brand, and they used a very nonrisky channel (the online universe) to associate with his equity.

Brands are a part of the consumer narrative. To deny this is to turn a blind eye to the sometimes strange and often powerful way people attach themselves to brands. This context is a critical component of a brand strategy. You must understand more than your brand's functional value. You have to understand what it means thematically to the narrative your consumers are trying to activate. Sadly, for many of the great brands, this meaning was accidental at best. As we attach more and more meaning to our brands, it's worth your time to understand the compelling context your brand provides to the consumers who will make it their own.

When celebrities fall from grace, as they do from time to time, they will often say they never asked to be a role model. Whether it's a star, an athlete, or a politician, the public is rarely sympathetic to this argument. The fact of the matter is that once you enjoy the benefits of celebrity, you have an obligation to serve your fans if you want to sustain your relationship with them. Increasingly, those fans want you to be a role model. They want you to prove them right for aspiring to be like you and for attaching you to a part of themselves. Brands must live by the same obligation. It is simply insufficient to ignore this new social contract. If your brand enjoys high levels of attachment, you have an obligation to live up to what you promise. If not, you risk becoming irrelevant or—even worse—reviled and outcast.

....

CHAPTER SEVEN

EXPRESSING THE PROMISE

Brand Narrative, Brand Voice, and Communications Strategy

The parking lot of the Nokia Theatre in Los Angeles is not ordinarily a campsite. Yet on an unseasonably cold Monday night in June 2010, a crowd of people pitched tents and lounged on sleeping bags outside the downtown concert venue. More would congregate in the days ahead, each of them hoping for the same thing: to be one of nine thousand audience members to see the premiere of *Eclipse,* the third installment of the Twilight motion picture franchise.

In just five years after it first appeared on bookshelves, Twilight had become one of the most successful entertainment ventures of all time, selling more than one hundred million books, grossing more than $1 billion at the box office, and making pop stars out of a cast of actors who were virtually unknown before they flashed their fangs and pouty looks. In record time, Twilight became a massive brand.

The beauty of Twilight's success is that it is a recycled story. The vampire genre has existed for hundreds of years, resurfacing nearly every decade in a new novel, blockbuster film, or television incarnation. Before Bella and Edward enraptured audiences with their angst-ridden love story, millions of fans cheered on *Buffy the Vampire Slayer* and brooded darkly in an *Interview with the Vampire*. Despite the perpetual recurrence of the formula that drives vampire stories, audiences keep coming back for more. They love the *genre*. In fact, Twilight's success is an apt demonstration that stories are not powerful because they are original but because they play with our expectations. It is the way that a story line frames those expectations to surprise and delight audiences that creates box office magic.

In this chapter we'll explore the awesome power of storytelling and how it binds real brands to their audiences. We'll discover that just like a good genre film, a brand can rely on the expectations of a category to create its own unique narrative. We'll consider how a brand defines and presents its character through the auspices of a brand voice. Finally, we'll consider how the story is put to practical use through a communications platform that cuts through the clutter and persuades with simple, relevant messages.

BRAND NARRATIVE

In recent years, storytelling has received a lot of attention from the branding industry—and for good reason. Humans are narrative thinkers, the only species on the planet yet discovered that filters information and experiences through the lens of stories. Cognitive psychologist Steven Pinker reasons that "100,000 years of evolutionary reliance on story has built into the human genetic code instructions to wire the brain to think in story terms by birth."[1] When you think back on a past experience, such as a vacation or a job interview, you usually use narrative to organize the sequence of events, recall what happened, and describe it to someone else. We love stories because of their logic. They have a beginning, a middle, and an end, which magically satisfies our need to understand cause-and-effect relationships. That's why brands thrive when they wrap their promise in a story. They become more accessible, more easily understood, and far more familiar to us. In fact, neurological research has proven that stories actually affect our brains; stories cause our "mirror neurons" to fire, creating a stronger sense of a relationship with the storyteller.[2]

Narratives are so ingrained in our way of thinking that we are always on the search for them. We're primed to "uncover the story." Nassim Taleb revealed this phenomenon in his book *The Black Swan*. He showed that our propensity for a good narrative sometimes leads us to perceive relationships that don't exist at all. We crave a story so much that we will piece together unrelated information to rationalize what was actually random and unpredictable. It is precisely this instinct that allows brands to connect with a narrative, even when they don't spend a dime on advertising.

In Chapter 2, I argued that brands rely on cues to persuade our brains to recall information stored in our memory. The simplest cue can help us retrieve a vast number of ideas, attitudes, and emotions locked up in our heads. You might smell lavender and suddenly remember a touching conversation with a lost relative or your first kiss. Before the cue, those recollections were idling. After the cue, they fill your consciousness. This same cueing activates stories. That's why rumors exist. Most rumors begin life from the false interpretation of a cue. Once we're prompted by the cue, we piece the story together, filling the missing parts with juicy conclusions and probable suppositions. Trial lawyers convict and acquit defendants by convincing a jury of the story of the crime, despite gaps in the evidence. They rely on clues from the crime scene and witness testimony to validate the story they want the jury to believe. Most courts of law disallow evidence that relies on conjecture, but conjecture is so much a part of human thinking that judges can declare a mistrial if they believe the jury relied on it more than the evidence to render a verdict.

The conjecture that results from cues makes brand narrative possible. Consider the brand-related puzzle in Figure 7.1. You probably guessed the

FIGURE 7.1

slogan easily because you have been exposed to Nike's famous tagline long enough that guessing the missing letters (U, T, D, and T) required no effort. This "fill in the blank" tendency can be used in many creative ways. My personal favorite is "The Count Censored,"* a YouTube video that went viral because of a small, innocent alteration that editors made to a musical segment from *Sesame Street*. It shows the vampire-inspired character The Count singing a song about counting, but a clever editor has inserted a censoring bleep every time The Count says the word *count*. Here's an excerpt, with bleeps inserted:

> You know that I am called The Count
> Because I really love to (bleep)
> Sometimes I sit and (bleep) all day
> But, sometimes I get carried away.
> I (bleep) slowly, slowly getting faster
> Once I start (bleep)ing it's very hard to stop
> Faster, faster. It is so exciting.
> I could (bleep) forever and (bleep) until I drop.

If you laughed, shame on you! Yet you did what came naturally. You imagined what the missing word could be and created some mental tomfoolery. This is the functionality that makes brand narrative possible. It's also what brand managers tend to forget. Instead of engaging brand audiences by hinting at a story and letting their minds piece it together, many brand managers feel the need to spell everything out. They don't create narrative experiences. They lecture.

Brand narratives can take many forms, but they always contain three key parts: a genre, a narrator, and a message. Let's explore each of these.

---

*You can watch the video on YouTube at http://www.youtube.com/watch?v=b2h5yQgv58s.

THE ART OF THE GENRE

In much the same way that a movie about vampires can create an instant connection with audiences because of what they know about the genre, the story of the brand's category can cue a well-defined set of audience expectations. The brand can choose to conform to or play against those expectations, depending on its strategy.

When watching television, most of us recognize the category that's being advertised within seconds of the start of a thirty-second commercial. This is true even on occasions when we watch a commercial for the very first time. We know when we're about to see an automobile pitch. We anticipate the humor of a beer ad. We sense a feature demonstration when a gadget is being marketed.

Some of the most memorable advertisements succeed by playing with our expectations of their category genre. For example, in 2010 ad agency Draftfcb launched an amusing campaign for Miller Lite. The first few seconds of each spot in the "Dating" campaign played to the established genre of online dating services: couples describing the serendipity of how they met, juxtaposed with "slice of life" vignettes showing the same couple walking, dancing, and lounging through life. It isn't until halfway through the ad that it is revealed that the man has been talking about his passion for Miller Lite and not his significant other. Viewers who found the spot humorous reacted to the unexpected use of a genre they were conditioned to expect.

On the other hand, genre can be used to skip over the parts of the narrative the audience already understands about your category, so that you can focus your attention on one key point of differentiation. Think of it as framing an expectation by creating a variation on a song. We're all familiar with holiday songs, but many people pay money to hear a popular artist render a new version of "Jingle Bells" or "Silent Night." The relationship between genre and brand experience is much the same. When you purposefully build from genre, you possess the leverage to make it easier for consumers to understand what to expect from you and easier for you to create a distinctive experience.

Genre is most often expressed through verbal and visual cues. For example, Trader Joe's uses the unique genre of the trading post rather than the grocer. It has purposefully designed a system around the exotic visual language of tropical outposts and the casual communications style of an island host. The whimsy and playfulness lead to the narrative. Even though loyal customers do a lot of their weekly grocery shopping at their local Trader Joe's, they still describe the experience in the context of fun and discovery. Of course, the voice extends beyond the communications system. Frontline employees are hired based on how well they contribute to the genre experience. Customers rave about the friendly cashiers and baggers at their local Trader Joe's. The narrative works because the genre extends throughout the entire experience.

THE NARRATOR'S VOICE

A brand narrative expresses a point of view by telling the story with a distinctive voice. At the beginning of this chapter, I mentioned three different vampire stories: the Twilight series, *Buffy the Vampire Slayer,* and *Interview with the Vampire.* Each of these stories is different because of its narrator's voice. The Twilight stories are told from the perspective of a teenage girl in love with a vampire. *Buffy* is told from the perspective of a young woman who's destined to rid the world of all its bloodsuckers. And *Interview* is told from the perspective of a two-hundred-year-old vampire cursed with a conscience. Some say there are no original stories, only original storytellers. That's why it is critically important to define a compelling brand voice.

Alan Siegel, the chairman and founder of Siegel+Gale, introduced the concept of brand voice to the business community nearly three decades ago. Siegel noted that most companies littered the marketplace with "a cacophony of sound." A single company might communicate with the same consumer multiple times and sound entirely different in each communication. In one message the brand sounds like a friend, while in the next it sounds like a litigator. This cacophony causes dissonance. And Siegel believed that the dissonance created enormous distance between brands and their audiences. He became an outspoken champion for a clear and compelling voice for every brand, and he set about proving quantitatively how a distinctive brand voice leads to greater brand engagement and loyalty.

Brands communicate more today than they ever did when Alan Siegel began his crusade. In addition to all the traditional channels where we expect them to speak, they also engage in social media activities, broadcasting messages across an increasing number of devices, and imposing themselves on experiences that were once commercial-free. There's rarely a moment of brand silence, and, although many brands aim to strike a particular tone of voice, the real concept behind brand voice is getting lost. A voice defines the character of a brand—a character that narrates the brand's story.

We love to personify creatures and objects. I've always admired how Pixar first won the hearts of audiences by personifying a desk lamp. The innovative animation studio made us empathize with a utilitarian object. It made it a character in a story. The effect was so strong that Pixar chose the beloved desk lamp as its mascot. It's part of the corporate identity. It's human nature to project human personalities onto nonhuman entities. Whether it's the way we describe our dogs or name our cars, we create meaning in our stories by projecting human qualities onto the subject. This is equally true for our relationships with brands. A brand's voice connects it to humanity.

Time for another reality check: Brands usually aren't individual human beings. Unfortunately, overzealous managers, in their desire to create the illusion that a brand *is* a real person, have been known to cause consumer backlash. As I write this book, thousands of people have congregated in Zuccotti Park near Wall Street to protest corporate greed in a movement known as Occupy Wall Street. It has inspired similar protests around the world. Many of the protestors complain in interviews that brands are misleading people, hiding predatory motives behind projections of themselves as trust-worthy, relatable, human personalities. As we examined in Chapter 1, it is quite easy to manicure your appearance, say what people want to hear, and prey on the collective tendency to perceive human qualities in nonhuman entities. That strategy is not sustainable, and it isn't what we mean when we consider brand voice. A brand's voice helps us relate to the human values and the real benefits that make a brand worth our attention. When used ap-propriately, a brand voice helps us understand whom the brand is for, why it matters, and what distinguishes it from other options. It does this by guiding the brand's expression, not misguiding the audience's impression.

CONNECTING TO THE MESSAGING

Just like people, brands need to communicate to survive. In real life, people communicate with one another every day and transmit messages to influ-ence others' behavior and to sustain relationships. Brands are no different. A brand's communications strategy guides the way it persuades people and engages in ongoing relationships with its audiences. A messaging strategy serves as a kind of script for the brand's narrative. The challenge is to define a script that doesn't feel "scripted." The more the messaging strategy feels manufactured and mechanical, the less your audience will feel that it is sin-cere. On the other hand, without the script, you run the risk of delivering inconsistent messages that cast doubt on the brand's true intentions, charac-ter, and underlying promise. It's a delicate balancing act.

An understanding of the people who make up an audience and their needs, the capabilities of the messaging channel, and the motivation for the message should always govern a messaging strategy. Of these considerations, the audience need and the message motivation are perhaps most important. Let's address motivation first.

Brands send out messages for one of three reasons: They wish to at-tract attention to themselves, they wish to educate, or they wish to persuade.

Though it is possible for a single message to attempt all of these objectives, the best messages are focused on just one aspect. Attracting attention is the easiest of the three. Many of history's great advertising campaigns were the equivalent of drumbeating. Virgin Active was seeking attention when it ran this banner ad on websites: "Want to see what Madonna's favourite vibrator looks like?" The reveal featured a Power Plate vibrating exerciser, which you could find at any Virgin Active club (and, yes, Madonna reportedly did use the equipment because it was said to be twice as effective at burning tummy fat).

While the brand messages that provoke our attention may entertain us or compel us to take notice for a bit, they primarily serve to build or sustain awareness. These messages are to a brand narrative as a movie poster is to a movie. It hints at the story, but it isn't the story. The messages that build familiarity and preference are typically educational messages and persuasion messages.

An educational message is not the equivalent of a public service announcement. The best educational messages include a call to action, but they do so by helping the audience to develop a stronger sense of familiarity with the brand and why it matters. These messages work by revealing new information and dramatizing its relevance through situational context. For example, in 2007 my team at Siegel+Gale was asked by Microsoft to help it reposition the Windows brand. Windows was the most successful operating system brand of all time, installed on more than 90 percent of the world's computers. But over time, the Windows brand had lost its voice.

Microsoft had determined that the promise of the Windows brand was to be compatible with your whole life, and our messaging imperative was to educate people on how much Windows contributes to life's routine. We found a voice for the brand by focusing on real people and real stories. We borrowed this tactic from the great orators of politics and culture. When he was president, Bill Clinton often mesmerized national audiences during his State of the Union addresses by linking a real person in the United States to an issue he wished Congress to address. By referencing the plight of real people, Clinton educated a broad audience and increased our comprehension of the topic. This, we believed, was what Windows needed to do. We encouraged Microsoft to stop talking about endless features and start talking about how real people use those features to "make their whole life compatible."

We began playing with some examples to illustrate what we meant for the client team. Microsoft supplied us with the following copy it was already using to describe Windows Live, a cloud-based extension of the Windows operating system:

> Windows Live Spaces is a terrific tool for sharing your memories online. It is your virtual home on the internet for your family and friends to visit! Like any home, we should probably put up a few photos. Windows Live Photo Gallery gives you the power to share your photos directly to your Windows Live Space for friends and family to see from afar. Unlike many online photo websites; Windows Live Spaces even has the ability to directly download an entire photo album! It is easier than ever to share your photos!

Using our messaging strategy, here's how we reimagined the copy:

> For lots of little reasons, Beth Adams takes lots of little pictures. Lots and lots, actually. A gigabyte a day. Beth runs a daycare center, and a few years ago, she had a brainwave: snap photographs of the kids being cute and share them with the parents. Great idea. But just an idea, until she discovered she could reach out to almost any parent, anywhere, easily, with Windows Live Spaces. Now, Beth uploads images to her Windows Live Space and broadcasts them to parents in a single mouse click. She creates downloadable photo albums for each classroom. And since the world is compatible with Windows, she knows that the pictures—and the smiles— will come through for everyone.

The strategy and the illustrative copy samples we wrote were well received by the client. They served as a point of inspiration for the very popular "I'm a PC" campaign created by Crispin Porter + Bogusky. Microsoft found that people developed a much stronger understanding of what Windows could do as a result of the strategy. Shortly after the campaign launched, Windows enjoyed a large and measurable increase in intent-to-purchase scores.

Educational messages are not isolated to sales pitches and brand-building campaigns. The most important educational messages are linked to customer service. Every time you send a customer an invoice, you are delivering a message. If clients cannot make sense of your invoices or statements of account, you've failed at your attempt to help them comprehend. Very little attention is paid by most brands to the messages that relate to postsale activities. These include calls to customer service, instruction manuals, and interactions with the brand in social media.

The third type of message is the *persuasive* message. Persuasive messages adhere to the words of David Ogilvy: "If it doesn't sell, it isn't creative." Most of the messaging connected to advertising and promotion is designed to persuade people to behave in a specific way. You want them to try your brand, buy your brand, and use your brand. You also want them to recommend your brand to someone else. To do this, your messages should reiterate relevant benefits that are, at best, completely aligned with your promise or, at a minimum, not in conflict with it.

Anytime consumers evaluate a decision to do something you suggest, such as buy your product or service, they consider three buckets of knowledge: First, they consider how much they know about what they're buying. Second, they consider what they know about the brand selling them the product or service. Third, they consider what they know about the sales tactic. Let's face the facts: Our world is littered with sales messages; we live in the most media-saturated environment of all time.[3] We're quite aware that brands are trying to sell us things, and we're also quite aware that many brands do not have our best interests in mind when they make their pitch to us. As we weigh all the costs and benefits of a sales pitch, we increasingly ask ourselves the questions: What's the catch, and what's in it for the brand?

Consider some of the tactics to which we've become accustomed. You can get a discounted cell phone, but you'll be locked into a two-year contract with steep penalties for early termination. You can get a credit card with a 0 percent interest introductory rate, but the issuer can change the rate to 29 percent if you are a day late with your payment or you exceed your credit limit. You can buy a very cheap printer for your computer, but you'll pay quite a bit for ink cartridges that don't last very long.

It's not my intent to pick on any specific category or brand, but rather to draw your attention to tactics marketers use frequently to persuade consumers to buy—with the result of heavy regrets. Earlier, I mentioned Occupy Wall Street. That movement has been driven by extreme consumer frustration and a growing sense that brands are duplicitous. And persuasion knowledge is only going to get stronger in the years ahead. The next generation of adult consumers has grown up with the Internet, mobile phones, and social media. They are very sensitive to persuasion tactics, and they aren't shy about rebelling against them. In a 2011 global study of more than seven thousand young adults published by McCann Worldgroup, justice and authenticity were among the three most common values that transcended international borders and motivated brand loyalty.[4] The study found:

> From a young person's point of view, the worst thing a brand can do is make a promise it doesn't keep. Given their focus on truth and authenticity, youth want brands to adopt a form of justice that is a) credible and b) true to the brand. They want brands to do the right thing in a way that seems right for that brand. Anything that seems cynical or piecemeal will be quickly dismissed.

Additionally, 90 percent of the respondents in the study said that they would "make a point of telling their friends about unjust behavior from a brand."

This audience is highly skeptical, media savvy, and very vocal. They scrutinize a brand's every action. To succeed in messaging to this audience, not only must you deliver on your promise, you have to be cognizant of their persuasion knowledge. If your message doesn't address what they know about marketing tactics, it will be dismissed or misinterpreted.

THE POLITICALLY INCORRECT REALITIES OF VOICE

The goal of brand voice may be to guide expression, project whom a brand is for, and conjure a story that explains why it matters. But you'd have a hard time backing that up by looking at how some brands establish their voice guidelines. For example, here are four voice attributes defined by a professional services brand I came across: caring, compassionate, intelligent, and charismatic. While it's a little unfair to show these words out of the context of the rest of the brand platform, I offer them up to illustrate how most guidelines do little to help people articulate a voice that conveys a brand narrative. If I asked you to draw me a picture of someone who matches this description, what would you draw? What if I asked you to write a headline for a print advertisement? There's nothing wrong with the four words, and they very well may reflect the traits that people use to describe people inside your brand, but they leave a lot of ambiguity about how anyone should conceive of the brand's voice.

There are three dimensions of a voice that can help a lot. Unfortunately, they are controversial. Gender, age, and socioeconomic characteristics are among the most helpful cues people use to understand the voice of a brand. I think a lot of marketers and managers shy away from discussing these dimensions because they fear being politically incorrect. It's politically correct to be gender neutral, age agnostic, and made for the masses. But whether or not a marketer specifically intends to define a brand's gender, age, or social class, consumers assign them on their own. Harley-Davidson is perceived as masculine, while Acura is often described as feminine. Apple is thought of as young, while IBM is perceived to be "mature." Target is described as upper middle class, while Walmart is perceived to be blue collar. Although these characteristics may be used to describe the brand's voice, they don't describe whom the brand serves. There are an awful lot of blue-collar shoppers who prefer the Target brand, and I know quite a few people over the age of 50 who use Mac computers. A lot of women enjoy movies with men playing the heroes, and a lot of men enjoyed *Erin Brockovich*.

One final note on the gender dimension of a brand's voice: Research demonstrates that it can have a powerful effect on perceptions of category fitness, strength of brand attachment, and the success of brand extensions.[5]

One of the most useful ways to think about your brand's character is to compare it to a relevant narrative archetype. Every culture has its archetypes: the Nurturing Mother figure; the Commanding Father; the Innocent Youth; the Fool. Psychologists have used archetypes for years to model personalities and behavior. And, of course, archetypes are one of the great pillars of literary theory. As Margaret Mark and Carol S. Pearson chronicled in their book *The Hero and the Outlaw,* you can employ an archetype to shape your brand's voice using a character role model that will be familiar to every audience in any corner of the world.[6] The real beauty of using archetypes to articulate your voice is that they truly relate to behavior. When you connect an archetype to your brand promise, you have a better chance of delivering brand experiences that are "in voice" because it's easy to imagine how the archetype would behave in any given situation. Like genre, archetypes prime us to preload a set of expectations about behavior, attitude, and personality. These archetypical expectations help people on the inside of a brand understand what is required to bring the brand to life as much as they cue customers on what to expect in the brand experience.

FROM DESCRIPTIVE TRAITS
TO TRUE CHARACTER

After working on many brand strategies in my career, I find it amusing how often clients and strategists obsess over the words they choose to describe a brand's voice. I've sat in meetings where people argued for hours about five words. I've also led exercises to fine-tune those words, creating scales that attempt to guide people to the proper context for a voice attribute. For example, if we suggested that "irreverent" was one way to describe the brand, we might add that *irreverent* means the brand is "humorous, daring, and juvenile." Perhaps we'd offset that by saying that *irreverent* does *not* mean the brand is "disrespectful, destructive, or mean." These scales can certainly help people strike the right tone, but they're never quite as useful as we'd like them to be. The descriptive word charts always feel a little vague to me, and no matter how you clarify them, they're always open to some interpretation. You and I might have very different perceptions of the word *irreverent*. And even if we agree on what it means, it can't be the secret to your brand's voice.

The fact is, if a brand voice helps us connect with the brand's humanity, it's got to be deeper than a few descriptive words. You'd probably have a hard time using five words to describe your mother to me in a way that helps me understand her character. So why should we think that we could describe a brand's character so succinctly?

When I was a Cub Scout, one of my troop leaders advised us boys to focus on our character, not our personality. He said the boy who focuses on developing his personality might win a popularity contest, but the boy who focuses on building his character will triumph in life. That sounds like a cliché you might find on a Successories poster, but it stuck in my head when I was an impressionable youth hoping to make something of myself. It sticks in my head today when brand managers ask me how to create a more vibrant brand identity. The best brands develop a voice that reflects their character, not desirable personality traits. We can think of many ways to describe that character, but the truth is that it is always revealed through actions. Research demonstrates that most consumers perceive and understand a brand's personality through the character of its branded experiences.[7] You'll find your brand voice by imagining how the brand responds to the needs of those it serves, not by analyzing how people characterize it.

Most of the leading branding agencies begin their work with a client by immersing themselves in a comprehensive discovery process. One part of that process is usually a series of stakeholder interviews. We can spend months interviewing employees, customers, partners, investors, and other stakeholders who know the brand and help us understand its behavior. We go through this process whether we're branding a product, a service, or a company. We ask a lot of questions to gain a better understanding of how the brand behaves. What does it do? How does it do it? How do people interpret that behavior? How much does their interpretation differ from what's intended? We pay attention to what people say, but we also observe what they don't say, what they leave out or say without words. While the strategy team nearly always leads this discovery process, I often insist that designers and creative personnel participate, too. Because no matter how hard I try to describe what I've observed, it never compares to what the creative team experiences directly with their eyes and ears. When they observe the brand in action, they find it easier to develop a voice that truly reflects the character of the brand. They translate the character into names, logos, and a patchwork of creative expression that brings the real story of the brand to the surface.

It's usually very hard for clients to replicate this discovery process on their own. They're too close to the subject matter. Does that mean that brands must always hire an agency to find their voice? Absolutely not. Just like people, some organizations are more grounded than others, and the more grounded brands come by their voice naturally, without self-consciousness. They might not execute the voice perfectly in every way, but because it is such a natural part of their character it always feels authentic. In my experience, when there's a "natural brand," three factors are invariably at play:

* *Simplicity.* Nothing gets in between character and voice more than complexity. Every layer a brand adds—every minor exception it decides to address—leads it away from the essence of its true character. Brands that come by their voice naturally deliberately limit those layers and exceptions.
* *Consistency.* Natural brands have a fairly consistent culture—whether that's a corporate culture or just a product team. They're very particular about whom they hire and they're disciplined about whom they retain. By doing this, they come by their voice naturally because it reflects the authentic commonality of the culture behind the brand.
* *Emphasis on delivery.* Natural brands are obsessed with what goes into the delivery of their experience, often at the expense of marketing and communications. The best brands I've worked with and studied have not always been the strongest marketers, but, boy, do they sweat the details of whatever it is they're branding. They send out mystery shoppers to ensure that the service experience lives up to expectations. They reengineer their products at the eleventh hour because something "just isn't right."

The third aspect has always intrigued me most. These natural brands occasionally ignore consumer research because they believe in what they've done and they're certain the public will come around eventually. And they're usually right. If there were more brands like these, we wouldn't need many brand consultants to help brands find their voices. But these conditions are rare, so I remain gainfully employed.

Four Seasons Hotels is one of the best examples of a brand that comes by its voice naturally—a brand that has risen to the top through its actions and *not* by its marketing prowess. To be perfectly honest, Four Seasons isn't a great marketing organization. I know because I observed their practices with my own eyes when they *did* hire a branding consultant—my firm. But Four Seasons doesn't need to be that great at marketing because its brand is so true to its character that customers are more than happy to share stories about their experiences. Word of mouth and repeat business have built the Four Seasons into one of the great brands of our time. Everything at Four Seasons revolves around service. In fact, the brand governs its business operation by measuring against the promise of delivering guest experiences that are "beyond compare." This practice is embedded in the culture and promoted every day by CEO Isadore Sharp.

In his book, *Four Seasons: The Story of a Business Philosophy,* Sharp describes two pivotal decisions that created success for his brand. First, he made the strategic decision to focus on a specific corner of the hospitality market. "We will offer only midsize hotels of exceptional quality, hotels that wherever located will be recognized as the best."[8] He opted to keep the business model as simple as possible so that nothing got in the way of his vision, and the model has remained virtually unchanged to this day.

It was his second decision, however, that truly distinguished the brand. Sharp realized that he could not defend his brand on capital assets and image alone. Better-funded competitors could build bigger rooms with more opulent furnishings, and they could outspend him on advertising and promotion. So he decided that his brand had to deliver on service. "Service, I believed, was our win-or-lose arena." You won't find a service-oriented slogan scribbled on any Four Seasons marketing collateral. That's because exceptional service is more than just marketingspeak. It's a discipline practiced throughout the company. If you were to try to replicate the success of the Four Seasons brand only by studying its personality traits—its iconography, imagery, and the tonality of its marketing communications—you would fail. Like a Cub Scout developing his personality but not his character, your brand might win a popularity contest, but it won't triumph in the long run. Again, the best brands develop a voice that reflects their character, not just a bunch of desirable personality traits.

Sharp claims the brand is really about the Golden Rule. "We demonstrate our beliefs most meaningfully in the way we treat each other and by the example we set for one another. In all our interactions with our guests, customers, business associates, and colleagues, we seek to deal with others as we would have them deal with us."

The Big Five Personality Traits

If you're on a mission to create a more distinctive voice for your brand, don't spend time listing traits that will make it more popular. If you're thinking about launching a new brand, don't waste your time studying the types of personalities you'd like to emulate. Instead, look to your actions: What do you intend to do? Why does it matter? How will you deliver against your promise in real-world situations where a customer or someone on the outside interacts with your brand? That's where the voice will emerge. The more you focus on the point of interaction, the more authentic and engaging the voice will be.

For more than one hundred years, psychologists have attempted to deconstruct human personalities. They've been on a hunt to identify universal traits—traits that are stable over time and distinctive enough to account for all the variations between us. In 1989, researchers Robert McCrae and Paul T. Costa, Jr., published a framework in the *Journal of Personality and Social Psychology* that became the benchmark for all personality research that has followed.[9] McCrae and Costa found that every human personality could be reduced to five traits:

- Neuroticism
- Extroversion
- Openness
- Agreeableness
- Conscientiousness

Each of these traits is actually a scale in its own right. For example, some people score very low on neuroticism, being described as calm, relaxed, or unemotional, while others score very high, being described as nervous, emotional, and anxious. By measuring the strength of each of the five attributes for an individual, you can scientifically describe that person's personality. The social sciences community refers to this helpful scale as "The Big Five Model."

It didn't take long for marketing researchers to ask the question: Can you develop a similar scale for brand personalities? In 1997, social psychologist and marketer Jennifer L. Aaker delivered a comprehensive quantitative study that answered yes. Aaker wanted to "develop a framework of brand personality dimensions and a reliable, valid, and generalizable scale to measure the dimensions." A total of 631 subjects rated 37 brands on 114 different personality traits.[10] After conducting rigorous statistical analysis, Aaker found that consumers perceive five distinct personality dimensions in brands:

- Sincerity
- Excitement
- Competence
- Sophistication
- Ruggedness

Three of Aaker's factors correlated strongly with human personality traits. Sincerity in brands bore a strong resemblance to agreeableness in people. There were similar correlations between exciting brands and extroverted individuals, and competent brands and conscientious people. Recent research has explored whether or not brands are favored more by people with analogous personality traits. The results aren't clear. In my opinion, brands appeal to a wide variety of consumers regardless of their personality alignment for precisely the reason many friendships consist of two personalities that are polar opposites.

The brand personality scale is a good place to start for measuring and perhaps defining the traits of your brand's character. It's validated by ample research and shown to be true across cultural boundaries and product categories. However, it's worth noting how dominant the sincerity trait is in Aaker's research. Sincerity explained more than 26 percent of the variance in the brands that she studied. It was connected to descriptors such as "honest, genuine, down-to-earth, wholesome, and real." While her study did not specifically link these descriptions to brand preference, the fact that consumers often used sincerity as a way to describe a brand is relevant in its own right, and it reinforces the point I made earlier in this chapter. Your brand voice is a reflection of your character, and your character is revealed through your actions. When you consistently demonstrate that character in brand experiences, your personality will probably be evaluated as being more sincere than that of other brands.

CONSTRUCTING THE MESSAGING STRATEGY

It's time for a new approach to branded communications. Most messaging strategies are horribly mechanical. They include matrices that segment messages by audience and provide boilerplate descriptions of a company or product in various word lengths (e.g., a one-hundred-word description of the company versus a twenty-five-word description of the company). You might very well need a matrix to keep track of your messages and most companies need a consistent way to sign off on a press release, but these tools aren't the way to bring a brand narrative to life. They won't help people reveal the character of the brand through the messages it transmits. Worse, these relics of branding's past don't address how a brand should behave in a two-way conversation. You can't use these tools to guide a frontline employee who must respond to a brand issue on Twitter or Facebook. I can assure you, if that employee writes a stock line from a messaging matrix, she will not be well received.

We have to stop thinking of a communications strategy as something you write once. It has to be addressed every day. You can create guidelines and foundational principles, but the message from the brand has to relate to the audience and to the context of the situation, and that requires ongoing work.

Start by profiling your audience. Do this by creating "personas"— descriptive declarations about the most typical needs, attitudes, and behaviors of key audience segments. A good persona helps people inside the brand understand audience sensitivities, their prototypical self-concept, and common aspirations. I've come across a lot of attempts at personas that are nothing more than demographic profiles, detailing the statistical average for age, race, gender, and household income. Frankly, these statistics have limited value. Personas, on the other hand, help you understand your audience's worldview. What are their beliefs? How does the brand fit in? What do they expect from the brand? What do they know about your brand's tactics? What have they come to expect from the category? Have they been burned in the past? Where are their pain points? When your team members have a good understanding of this perspective, they'll be better prepared to listen and engage in a way that engenders confidence.

Once you have profiled your audience, don't stop. Increasingly, social media are excellent tools for understanding the sentiments of a brand audience. A lot of brands have used social media to determine whether people are making positive, negative, or neutral comments about them. That's fine, but you can also participate in social media conversations that help you gain a greater sense of context. And there are more powerful analytical tools emerging that can help you understand more about the audience. If you make this a continuous process, your personas will evolve and your team will have a better sense of who their audience is. They'll develop a stronger relationship with the audience, and they'll be more likely to behave in an authentic way.

Finally, your communications strategy needs to clarify your motivations. It's one thing to create a stock set of brand messages. It's quite another to take a step back and determine your purpose for messaging in the first place. Depending upon whether or not you choose to attract attention, deepen understanding, or persuade audiences to take action, your message will change. Nothing about this process is easy. However, the fluidity of brand messaging allows for occasional missteps. If anything, your branded communications will become stronger when you learn from mistakes and continue to evolve your approach. As Einstein said, the definition of insanity is doing the same thing over and over hoping for a different result. It's time for brand communications strategies to be flexible and connected to an authentic narrative that reveals the true character of the brand. Only then will consumers be willing to trust.

CHAPTER EIGHT

NAMING AND IDENTITY DEVELOPMENT

At the start of this book, I described the difference between brand behavior and brand identity. With each new chapter, I have attempted to persuade you that a brand's behavior should always be guided by a credible promise that results in a consistently strong experience. Brand identity allows brands to get credit for such an experience by giving them a signature. In the same way that you look to the bottom of a painting to identify the artist, a brand identity helps us connect an experience to a brand.

Identity is not only the sexiest part of branding, it's also the most accessible aspect of the discipline. You might have a hard time getting people to debate the finer points of a brand's promise, but ask them what they think of the name and logo and they've always got an opinion. Because names and logos are so easy for a layperson to evaluate, they may lead to absurd discussions and management decisions. In Chapter 1, I provided two examples—Congress hoping a flawed policy would get better if it had a new name and Gap's crowdsourcing of its graphic identity. Let me illustrate in a different way.

Imagine going in for a job interview and being flatly rejected because your potential employer doesn't like your name. You introduce yourself as Joe, and the interviewer launches into a discussion about how the name Joe is so commonplace, uninspired, and completely undifferentiated. As you take stock of what's just been said, your interviewer then asks if your given name is Joe or Joseph. When you say the latter, you're berated for cheapening your brand by shortening your name. Your interviewer fires up his laptop and begins lambasting you on social media because you have disgraced your heritage by introducing yourself as Joe when your parents intended for you to be known to the world as Joseph.

Let's imagine another scenario. This time, you're at the bank signing the loan documents for your first house. You sit across from the banker and review a lengthy mortgage agreement. Once you're satisfied that all is in order, you sign your name, whereupon the banker begins laughing at your signature. She criticizes your handwriting and then begins offering you suggestions on how you could improve your signature. Maybe she takes the pen right out of your hand and draws you a few examples.

If either of these situations occurred for real in our personal lives, we'd be mortified, incensed, and possibly litigious. But these situations happen all the time in the world of brand identity. People feel they are entitled to critique and participate in a brand's identity. In many of these cases, brands have no one to blame but themselves. Starbucks made a habit of saying that its brand belonged to its customers. It should have shocked no one that there was a considerable outcry when Starbucks decided to change its logo in early 2011. Observing the frenzy in social media, *The Economist* noted, "much of the rage in the blogosphere is driven by a sense that "they" (the corporate stiffs) have changed something without consulting "us" (the people who really matter)."[1]

Yet a brand's identity fulfills the same function as a person's. You should be no more inclined to change your brand name and logo because people criticize it than you would be to change your own name and signature. Your brand identity reflects your brand's true character because of who you are and what you do, not because of its design. You should change your identity only if you determine that it somehow creates the wrong cues or because you believe that it no longer represents what the brand stands for. Period.

In this chapter, we're going to study the two dominant parts of brand identity: names and logos. We'll explore how a name can be loaded with meaning from the start or how it creates meaning by its application. We'll also discuss the changing role of the logo and the realities of how a logo inter-acts with the system that supports it. Throughout, we'll continually return to our central theme: A brand identity is a signature for a brand experience.

NAMING

Naming is a part of branding that people relate to because it seems so easy. Anyone can come up with a name. If anyone can name a child, why can't anyone name a business, a product, or an ingredient technology? Well, the truth is, anyone can. Jerry Yang and David Filo were doctoral candidates in electrical engineering at Stanford when they came up with the Yahoo! brand name for their Web guide. It was an acronym for "Yet Another Hierarchi-cal Officious Oracle," but the two Internet pioneers liked the name because of what the word stood for: a person who is "rude, unsophisticated, and uncouth." They didn't hire a naming consultant, and they created one of the most valuable brands in media.

However, Yahoo! was once a power brand because of what it did and what it stood for. Yes, the name was distinctive, and, yes, it had hid-den meaning. But the reason Yahoo! rose from obscurity to fame was the value it delivered—helping people navigate the Internet. Until 2004, most Internet users started their Web journeys with Yahoo! But that year Google (which was also named by its engineers) went public and changed history. The search capability Google offered, coupled with tools and technologies that competed head-to-head with Yahoo!, altered Yahoo!'s fate rapidly. Yahoo! has struggled to demonstrate its value ever since, and its stock price has steadily declined. The company's board recently signaled that it would be open to a sale. If the Yahoo! brand name was responsible for Yahoo!'s suc-cess, is it also to blame for its fall from grace? Of course not.

I once got into a heated discussion with a Silicon Valley venture capitalist about this very topic. After our team had worked with one of the companies his firm was backing, we delivered a report that detailed all of the challenges in the brand's value proposition. We'd been hired to develop a brand platform and a name. Before we could start the naming process, we needed to secure the VC's approval on a brand promise. He told us we were wasting his time and money. He just wanted a great name, not our opinion of the value proposition. We parted ways soon after, and the members of his team created a name on their own. They did a fine job, but about six months after they launched, the business failed. The market didn't understand what the service did or why it mattered. A nice name couldn't save it.

Overthinking a Name

On the other end of the spectrum: managers who go a little crazy analyzing their naming decisions. Years ago, when I was working with Kodak, I witnessed this irrational preoccupation with names in high gear. In the days before digital imaging, Kodak discovered a gold mine when it introduced disposable cameras. For the first time, consumers didn't need to make an investment in an expensive camera to capture important occasions on film. Instead, they could walk into their local drugstore, purchase a disposable camera, shoot twenty-four to thirty-six pictures, and hand the camera off to the photo lab for processing. It was an innovation that created substantial profit for Kodak. The only challenge was figuring out what to call it.

Everyone referred to the product as a "disposable camera," but a debate began about the word *disposable*. Well-intentioned marketing executives asked, "Do we want people to think that our brand is disposable?" One manager told me, "The last thing we want is for people to think you can throw Kodak in the trash." Instead, the team agreed to call the product a "single-use camera," which sounded more prestigious and had the added advantage of describing the camera's functionality. The problem with this name was its acronym: SUC. By the time the management team finished its exploration, it settled on the somewhat awkward name of "one-time use camera." It worked, and the product was a hit, but whenever I did research with Kodak consumers to ask them about the products they used, they nearly always said they bought "disposable" cameras.

A brand is not a name. A name is certainly part of a brand's identity, but the name rarely determines a brand's fate on its own unless it is so charged with cultural meaning it can't overcome the negative association. Even then, many brands have reframed what we think about names that otherwise seem like bad ideas. When Apple launched the iPad, it was ridiculed by some of the leading experts on branding because they thought it sounded like the name of a feminine hygiene product. Public relations expert Peter Shankman remarked in the *New York Times,* "I'm waiting for the second version that comes with wings." The term iTampon spiked on Twitter, along with mocking tweets like "Heavy flow? There's an app for that!" Worse, many predicted that women would reject the product for its lack of cultural sensitivity.[2] Nearly two years later, the iPad is a must-have gadget, and few people make a connection to feminine hygiene.

There's something to be said for conviction. Leadership expert Warren Bennis famously said that "leaders are made rather than born." The same could be said for brand names. Many of the brand names we admire most earned their way into our hearts. My friend Nikolas Contis is one of the best namers in the industry. Working with him on projects while I was leading strategy teams at Siegel+Gale was one of the great pleasures of my career. Nik can easily spin out hundreds of name candidates for a client in a couple of hours, but his real gift is his uncanny ability to see the potential in the names under consideration. He looks beyond people's knee-jerk reactions, often insisting that his clients wait a few days to give him feedback after he shares name candidates with them. He tells them he wants them to "sit with the names for a while." The first time he did this with one of our clients, I had an anxiety attack. It isn't the way our industry works. We expect instant feedback from clients, and clients too often oblige us by dismissing great naming ideas because of a bad first impression. Working with Nik, I discovered that clients often saw the same potential we saw in a name when they lived with it for a bit. It's even more striking when you consider that we didn't tell clients which name candidate we preferred. They nearly always asked. We always told them they'd have to wait. It was shocking how often we agreed.

Here's the quickest way to kill a good naming opportunity: Submit it for testing. Design an online survey, recruit a random sample that is a statistically significant representation of your market, rotate the order of the names so that respondents aren't biased by the first name they see, ask them to tell you how much they "like" or "dislike" each name, have them force-rank the options, and then tabulate the results. You'll receive completely irrelevant findings that are as likely to lead you to the worst candidate as they are to the best. This method of name "validation" ignores the fact that some of the greatest names make no logical sense. A study like that would probably reveal that Amazon is a horrible name for an online retailer and Apple is a poor choice for a technology company.

My colleague Alan Brew wrote a wonderful blog piece about people's growing obsession with children's names. In his article, he noted the opinion of Bruce Lansky, an expert who has written eight books on baby names. According to Lansky, "People who understand branding know that when you pick the right name, you're giving your child a head start." But Alan quite pointedly and eloquently rejected this notion:

Before our daughter was born in 1998 we had hopes and dreams and guesses at what she might be like, and in the end we called our bundle of abstractions Nicole. Why? It was the one name on which my wife and I could agree wholeheartedly. Now, at the age of thirteen, Nicole has given her name a rich, complex and beautiful meaning simply by wearing it.

And that's the truth of the matter with all names. Regardless of any inherent meaning in a name, the Theory of Reverse Association will always apply: the bearer of the name will determine its ultimate meaning. Just like Elvis, Adolf, Enron, Google, Barack . . . and Nicole.[3]

Finding a Good Name by Playing with Sound

Finding a name for a brand is getting harder and harder to do because branding has proliferated. In most categories, the obvious, descriptive, straightforward, and easy-to-understand names have been taken. This explains the explosion in nonsensical names such as Hulu, Bing, and Altoids—names that mean nothing at all, but can easily be owned. Inventing words is one way around the trademark challenge, but it isn't an easy approach and it usually requires you to trust your instinct. Allow me to illustrate.

Sometime during the hot, humid summer of 1960, Reuben Mattus chose to branch out from his family business to start a venture of his own. It was a life-changing decision, but entrepreneurship came naturally to Reuben. He'd helped his mother build a business in the Bronx selling ices from a horse-drawn carriage when he was 10. Reuben had a knack for good ideas, and he genuinely enjoyed experimenting with ingredients and tinkering with his recipes to create flavor combinations that led to modest profits. But Reuben wasn't one to rest on his laurels, and at age 44 he embarked on a new business venture: He wanted to launch a new brand of ice cream.

Reuben had been experimenting with butterfat. While many grocery store brands were using cheap ingredients, artificial flavorings, and mass production processes to generate profit margins, Reuben focused on high-quality ingredients—real cream, egg yolks, imported Belgian chocolate, and whole vanilla beans. He was convinced that he could sell more ice cream if he made it taste richer and creamier, and he was satisfied with the first three flavors he planned to introduce. But he didn't have a name. So he and his wife, Rose, a savvy marketer in her own right, found themselves brainstorming names on their living room couch.

Reuben thought the name should sound European because he believed it would lend the product credibility. He was right. By the late 1950s, American consumers were beginning to buy "vichyssoise" brands, a designation the *New York Times* coined to explain the way Americans paid more for products that sounded as if they originated across the Atlantic.*

Reuben and Rose played with many combinations of syllables and sounds. Legend has it that Reuben, while staring at a box of Duncan Hines cake mix, began rearranging the first letters of each word to form a new name—Huncan Dines—and that this was the origin of the funny-sounding name he chose for the product that would rocket his ice cream to the upper echelon of food brands. But in her autobiography, Rose set the record straight. Reuben invented the brand name by narrowing the linguistic playing field. He picked a European country, played with its language, and created a new, totally fabricated word for his ice cream. He chose Denmark because it was "the only country which saved the Jews during World War II." That's how Reuben named Häagen-Dazs.

Reuben didn't speak Danish, which you'll soon discover if you try to use a Danish dictionary to translate the meaning of Häagen-Dazs. The Danish language doesn't even use umlauts, though the name features one on the first "a" in the first word. While Reuben's nonsense name probably eased the trademark process, it really shines because of what it says without even trying. The sounds and syllables of the Häagen-Dazs name are cues that prime most people to expect a thicker, richer, creamier ice cream, even if they've never tasted the product. Reuben's name takes full advantage of a useful phenomenon known as *sound symbolism.*

Sound symbolism is a linguistic process that every member of the human species apparently shares. It works because, for reasons we don't entirely understand, certain sounds are connected to common human perceptions and emotional meanings. Don't confuse sound symbolism with onomatopoeia—words that sound like what they name, such as *croak, clap,* or *bark.* Sound symbolism is a subconscious process that connects individual

---

*Interestingly, the word *vichyssoise* is an American construction, invented by the management of the Ritz hotels to lend credibility to a cold soup they introduced on their upscale menus in 1917.

parts of words to ingrained meaning. Most people aren't even aware that they're linking sound with meaning, but a number of studies make a strong case that the phenomenon exists. On the surface level, it explains why we find so many similarities in the world's diverse set of languages. Researcher John Ohala noted that many languages use words with a disproportionate number of high-frequency acoustic sounds to convey "smallness": The words *teeny* (English), *chico* (Spanish), *petit* (French), *mikros* (Greek), and *shiisai* (Japanese) all roughly translate to "very small." Conversely, Ohala found that words with low acoustic frequency were used in the same languages to convey largeness: *humongous* (English), *gordo* (Spanish), *grand* (French), *makros* (Greek), and *ookii* (Japanese).[4]

Those who subscribe to sound symbolism will tell you it is more than coincidence that all those words share similar sounds. Linguistic researchers have been studying the phenomenon by examining the physiological process of sounding a word to its perceived meaning. They map the movements of our tongues, our lips, our teeth, and our vocal chords and look for patterns between those movements and the resulting word meanings. The research is fascinating because of the near-universal way certain sounds stimulate our emotions and conjure mental associations. One study noted the negative connotations most languages attach to the *sl* letter pair. That sound in English, made largely by the tongue touching the upper part of the mouth, is connected to words like *slut, slovenly, slime, sleaze, slick, slow,* and *slouch.*[5]

Reuben Mattus instinctively chose two words that were prepacked with subconscious meaning. Both words, *Häagen* and *Dazs,* rely on very low frequency sounds. The double *a* (particularly when accented with an umlaut) creates what researchers refer to as a "back vowel"—a sound that is created when the highest point of the tongue is in the back part of the mouth. The *ä* in Reuben's "Häagen" is, in fact, one of the deepest back vowels we can voice. That's significant because research has found that we associate that sound with perceptions of heaviness, thickness, richness, and slow movement.

In a 2004 study, two sets of respondents were shown two nearly identical names for a fictitious ice cream brand that was reported to be very smooth, thick, and creamy. For one set of respondents, the name discussed was Frosh. For the other set, it was Frish (which uses the far front vowel *i*, associated with perceptions of small, light, and lively). The respondents shown the name Frosh were more likely to match the name to the product than those shown the name Frish.[6]

Though he probably didn't know it scientifically, and he certainly couldn't prove it at the time, Reuben Mattus chose vowel sounds that did more than conjure imagery of European craftsmanship. His manufactured "Danish" name cued sensors in the brain to anticipate an ice cream that was deliciously creamy, thick, and rich. Of course, Häagen-Dazs became a success because Mattus created a product that was so delicious it set a standard for all premium ice cream brands that followed.

Coining Words and Extending Meaning

As far as naming goes, sound symbolism is not the only useful approach. We can also borrow from the lexicon of root words that sit idly in our minds, waiting to be joined to prefixes that play with their meaning and context. During the past fifty years, linguists have unearthed a wealth of information about how our brains process and serve the words that drive our language.

Modern linguistics theory suggests that we use language through two linked processes. One process stores morphemes—the smallest roots of a word that still contain meaning—in a dictionary-like stack called the *lexicon*. The morphemes stored in our lexicon are sounds such as *pre, post, un, mal,* and *for*—all of which can be combined with other morphemes to create words. The second mental process our brain needs for language is the ability to adhere to rules that form our grammar. When our brains combine the morphemes stored in our lexicon with the grammatical rules that govern our language, we can transfer ideas from one mind to another with meanings largely intact. This mental machinery allows us to construct words that are nonsense in one situation but have meaning in another. Many companies have used this approach to name themselves and their products. For example, when European pharmaceutical companies Sandoz and Ciba-Geigy merged in 1996, they used Latin root words to name their new company Novartis. Though it is a coined word that previously didn't exist, we sense that it contains meaning. It translates as "new skills."

Any headline writer can tell you that selecting the right word makes all the difference. A single word can have great power. Sadly, the business world is littered with lazy word constructions such as *productize, upping,* and *value-added.* It's unfortunate because coining a new word to express an idea can be one of the simplest ways to capture its essence in an instant. Consider that Shakespeare is said to have invented about 1,700 of the words that appear in his poems and plays. He is credited with coining words that were either new to his audiences or used in novel ways. Many of these words we now take for granted such as *dwindle, ensnare, frugal, howl, hurry, leapfrog, monumental, obscene,* and *submerge.*

Text is usually a noun referring to a manuscript, but in the age of wireless communications we now use *text* as a verb, meaning to send text messages on our mobile phones ("text me with your location"). Digital security providers merged *malicious* and *software* to coin the term *malware.* Malware is infectious software that interferes with a computer's performance. Millions of Americans are now all too painfully familiar with one of the banking trade's concoctions. *Subprime* mortgages are high-interest loans designed to service the needs of customers with imperfect credit and the term now carries the additional meaning of "disastrous." Public speakers now address audiences through Web-enabled seminars, or *webinars,* and so on. In each case, an idea is simplified through clever wordplay. Sometimes this repurposing of words can lead to a great brand name. *Droid,* the smartphone from Motorola that is based on Google's Android operating system, changed the context of a word in so many ways it is arguably one of the most inventive brand names in recent memory. The word has an obvious connection to Google's brand, but it is also derived from the realm of science fiction to describe robots that closely resemble humans. George Lucas is credited as being the first to shorten the word, in the Star Wars franchise. Motorola has attempted to extend its usage with a popular (and sometimes intimidating) campaign that proclaims "Droid does," projecting the power of superior artificial intelligence.

People "tweet" when they post messages on Twitter, the microblogging service. Twitter's creators prescribed the term. Individual Twitterers have *followers*. Conversations can be indexed with *hashtags*. The company concocted all of these designations. But the ultimate signal that the lexicon has caught on is the number of derivatives the brand culture has produced. If someone posts someone else's tweet, they are said to *re-tweet*. A community of Twitterers is a *Twitterverse*. If you meet someone you converse with on Twitter, you're attending a *Tweetup*. And if your behavior is erratic and prone to short outbursts, you might be described as *Twitterish*.

Stepping outside of the digital realm, you have to admire Swiffer, a platform of household cleaning products from Procter & Gamble. The word means nothing on its own, but when you hear it and see the product you instantly know what it does. Though the language of Droid, Twitter, and Swiffer is hardly the same as the poetic stage speech of Shakespeare, in each case singular words are used to connote meaning that is derived from clever use of context.

LOGOS

While it's harder for a layperson to design a logo than it is to coin a name, there are plenty of armchair designers who have been liberated by software that allows them to play with type, mix colors, and alter shapes. Technology has unleashed the creativity in people that previously seemed inaccessible. Many of the candidates submitted to 99designs.com are from inexperienced or part-time visual artists, and on the whole everyone benefits. I believe the more people learn to express themselves visually, the more they unlock great ideas. But the burst in our collective creative expression has also changed the context for the design of logos and visual identity.

Fifty years ago, logo design required uncommon skill. Logos were hand-drawn, refined for mechanical reproduction, and challenged by the limitations of print and media. Many of yesterday's innovative logos wouldn't cut it today—not because they were poorly designed but because they were designed for the constraints of their media. As technology improved our ability to create and display visual identities, the entire branding environment expanded. Some of the most mediocre identities today can do more with color, texture, and depth of field than the truly great logos of the past. The result is a jumbled landscape where it's hard to differentiate among the ever-increasing number of logos. Our new design capabilities have lifted the tide for all boats, but they've also generated a creative global warming crisis.

I am not a designer, nor do I profess to understand the nuances of "great." But as a strategist who has collaborated with phenomenal design minds over the years, I can tell you that, while logos and visual identity have evolved a great deal, the principle behind them remains the same. Like a good name, a logo is *not* the brand. It is a signature for the brand that can develop symbolic meaning over time through consistently linked experiences.

Arguing for marketers to pay more attention to the experiences that accompany logos over time, researchers Linda Scott and Patrick Vargas noted that "a view of logos as ideographs standing for a complex statement of qualities, voice, and events would be more consistent to our understanding about the way advertising writes these meanings onto the brand image."[7] In their view, you might think of a logo as a ball of string. Every message or experience such as an advertisement or a purchase occasion, adds context to the core of the logo, making its symbolism and meaning bigger and bigger as time goes on. Like a name, a logo's symbolism is usually made over time, not born. That explains how some of the simplest and most commonplace geometric shapes have become meaningful signatures for a brand.

The logo for Bass ale has the distinction of being the first registered trademark under the United Kingdom's Trade Mark Registration Act of 1875. It is officially trademark number 1. It's not a fancy logo. It's a red triangle. It stands out because it stands for something: one of the best pale ales in the world.

In the United States, one of the earliest brands was very literally a brand. The King Ranch in Texas developed an international reputation for raising some of the world's finest cattle. Buyers paid a premium price for the Texas longhorns branded with the famous "running W" of the King Ranch. The crude squiggly line of that branding iron remains the hallmark of the ranch to this very day, even though it is now better known for its real estate investments. Buyers parted with cash because they had been conditioned to link the symbol to meaningful value: superior breeding and delicious beef.

Clients often express a desire for a logo that is loaded with symbolism. They want it to act like an advertisement in its own right, to change the way people think about the brand because the mark taps deep, symbolic roots. Some of branding's design giants such as Saul Bass, Paul Rand, and Walter Landor crafted the world's most powerfully evocative logos, imbued with rich, symbolic imagery. However, there's very little evidence to suggest that a symbolically infused logo negates the need for advertising and promotion. In fact, there's quite a bit of evidence to suggest that a symbolic logo becomes relevant to the brand only through repeated and consistent association with brand experiences. The great work of Bass, Rand, and Landor endures because their logos were so often commissioned by organizations that consistently applied the logo and brand mark to great brand experiences.

Leveraging the Symbols of Visual Identity

Eighty miles north of Las Vegas, Nevada, lies a serpentine ridge of sand and rock known as Yucca Mountain. Undulating like a cross-stitched scar in the desert, it is hardly noteworthy but for its unique geology. Yucca Mountain is formed of layers of a volcanic by-product known as *tuff*, which many experts say is the best type of material in which to entomb radioactive waste. The unassuming hunk of petrified ash and pumice in Nevada became the subject of a prolonged, contentious political debate until 2009, when the Obama administration officially abandoned it. During the twenty-two-year clamor to prove or disprove Yucca's eligibility, activists on each side commissioned a vast body of research. One study in particular asked a question that few had considered before: How do you mark such a dangerous site to ensure that future earthly inhabitants know it is hazardous and should not be disturbed?

On the surface, it sounds like an absurdly simple question to answer. Carve the universal radioactive symbol into the tuff and be done with it! However, consider the fact that most of the radioactive waste to be stored in a place like Yucca Mountain has a half-life of more than one hundred thousand years. To put that number in perspective, anthropologists estimate that modern humans began migrating out of Africa about seventy thousand years ago. That's a full sixty-four thousand years before recorded history began. If you buried radioactive waste in the year that humans first migrated to other corners of the world, it would still be dangerous to dig up today. In that span of time entire languages were born and died. The symbols of many civilizations rose and fell. Will the offspring of our offspring's offspring interpret three interconnected triangles connected by a circle as a sign of imminent danger?

Perhaps the answer is a symbol that's more primal, like death. The skull and crossbones always means danger, doesn't it? Not necessarily. Death symbols such as the skull and crossbones can be powerful harbingers. Back in the colonial era, the flag of the sea captain Edward Teach, better known as Blackbeard, struck fear in the hearts of men sailing the Caribbean. It was said that the sight of Blackbeard's flag caused ships to surrender without a shot being fired. The symbols of Blackbeard's flag were packed with meaning. It contained a skeleton holding an hourglass in one hand while piercing a heart with a spear in the other. Its message was clear to anyone of the era: mercy to those who surrender, violent death to those who do not. But were you to encounter Blackbeard's iconography posted on a mountain today, you might mistake it for buried treasure—and dig yourself to death!

Symbols can be infused with great meaning, but they usually require a layer of cultural context to do their job. In Blackbeard's time, the skull and crossbones on a vessel on the high seas was contextually linked to danger. Three hundred years later, following a romantic legacy of storytelling from Robert Louis Stevenson to Walt Disney, the symbol on a mound of dirt is contextually linked to fortune. Today, skull symbols are used to brand a variety of different products, from Skullcandy headphones to Yale's secretive Skull and Bones membership society. There are plenty of logos that triumph because of the symbolic cues they incorporate—the Nike swoosh, the Starbucks mermaid, and the Olympic rings are but a few. However, symbolic logos work only when they can adapt to the context of their business. As a signature, a logo has to evolve with the brand. Starbucks has actually changed its logo four times in its four-decade history. The symbol has remained mostly the same, but subtle changes have been made to reflect the brand's changing context. In the most recent refresh, the maiden was emphasized, the overall design simplified, and the word *Starbucks* dropped from the graphic identity completely.

More important for a brand than logo design and symbolism is consistency. A brand's graphic signature should appear only when a great brand experience is unfolding. That experience can be an emotionally exciting advertisement, or it can be a visit to a local showroom. To build meaning into a logo, you link it to the delivery of experiences promised by the brand. Unfortunately, many brands fall so in love with their logos that they stamp them everywhere, even in places where there is no brand experience or, worse, places where the brand is challenged. My good friend and former colleague Matthias Mencke illustrated the result of this haphazard approach. Matthias created an illustration for a client project that dramatically demonstrated the jarring disconnect audiences experience when brands aren't smart about using their signature. He took three symbols that everyone understands and juxtaposed them with words that represented the opposite meaning (Figure 8.1).

Matthias's point was that, as a brand's logo begins to stand for something, it's critically important that it be linked to environments, messages, and experiences that support that meaning. His illustration also reminds us that it's hard to change the meaning associated with a symbol we've been

FIGURE 8.1

conditioned to understand. Sometimes it is easier to change the associated brand experience as a means to shifting what we perceive about a brand.

Moving from Symbol to System

In much the same way that many human cultures evolved away from pictographs to phonetic alphabets, brands rely less today on all-encompassing symbolic logos than on a proprietary visual language. Branding is becoming more about the creative "kit of parts" that, taken together, expresses the brand's identity and visual signature. To illustrate how this works, let me give you an exercise.

Fully extend your arm in front of one eye and extend a finger. Do you see it? That's a trick question. You have a blind spot in each eye where the optic nerve literally passes through your retina. There are no photoreceptor cells on this part of your eye, but you don't see a dark spot in your world because your other eye provides information that allows your brain to complete the picture. Even if you had only one eye, you would still see a complete picture because our eyes are constantly scanning our visual field. The brain pieces it all together for us.

The same wiring in your head that allows you to discern your finger from patterns of light allows your brain to discern the presence of a brand with only hints of branded imagery. The impressionist painters of the nineteenth century understood how this worked. They offered priority to color and shape over line, a break from centuries of fine art tradition. They applied colors side by side rather than mixing, letting the mind blend the colors and interpret the subject. They focused on capturing the subject with short, imprecise brushstrokes rather than laboring over perfect lines and attempts at realism. The great art of Renoir, Monet, Pissarro, and Cézanne was purposefully imperfect, as are the intentional flaws to be found in Zen art. In fact, it is the imperfection that makes these works of art so valuable, often commanding significant premiums over comparable paintings by realists. These works of art employed the theater of our mind to fill in the gaps, the broken pieces of line, the unblended color, the hastily sketched form. To me, the striking part was how easily patrons could discern the artist by the way he chose to provide the impression. These patrons didn't need to look at the signature at the bottom of the canvas. They could tell a Renoir from a Cézanne because of the artist's stylistic choices and visual language.

One of the earliest brands to truly embrace this approach was MTV. Though the cable channel had a distinctive logo that became iconic in our culture, it also relied on a visual system that changed constantly. If you removed the MTV logo from an MTV-branded experience, the brand's signature was still evident.

Another example: Today, Burberry, the London-based fashion apparel maker, has created a simple visual language that makes it stand out. Its signature plaid pattern is instantly recognizable and reminds us of the brand's presence. The pattern is not a logo. It's a motif, and it actually changes quite a bit. We have been conditioned by Burberry to look for plaid to know that its brand is the author of the experience.

OWN YOUR IDENTITY

I've spent a lot of time in this chapter beating a drum about the role of brand identity. Looking back over these pages, it dawned on me that you could get the wrong impression. You might mistakenly think that I believe a brand's name or visual signature is inconsequential. Wouldn't that just be typical from a strategist! I can assure you that nothing is further from the truth. I am constantly inspired by great names and beautiful logos. Some of the visual identity work I have been lucky enough to experience in my career is art in its own right. The teams that create it are smart, passionate designers who have dedicated their lives to making a brand's identity stand out and mean something to the audiences they serve.

Our world is becoming more and more designed. Entire industries are transforming because design is changing the way we experience a brand. Design matters. I would never try to persuade you that the design of a visual identity doesn't matter, nor would I argue that the arrangement of letters in your name is inconsequential. However, I urge you to understand the role of brand identity. Whether represented by a name or a logo, your brand identity serves as a signature. It represents the experience your brand promises to deliver, and it should be present when the brand is performing at its best. It should also surface whenever your brand communicates with your audience and restates its promise. Your identity gains meaning only through consistent application, not through birth. Resist the temptation to change your identity simply because you received feedback from your audience that it doesn't quite suit their taste. Your identity must never be subjected to a beauty pageant mentality. If your signature inspires your organization, then your signature stands for your organization. Own it.

....

CHAPTER NINE

THE TOUCHING
EXPERIENCE

How to Deliver on a Promise at Meaningful Touch Points

t was a White House first. On April 28, 2009, 293 photos were uploaded to a newly created "official" photostream on Flickr.[1] These behind-the-scenes images captured by White House photographer Pete Souza delighted photo enthusiasts and social media evangelists alike, but the event may be more significant because it was the peak of validation for the Flickr brand—a brand that didn't exist when the previous administration entered the White House.

Flickr began life as a feature for another product. It was designed to allow users of a massive multiplayer online game to share photos during their game play. According to cofounder Caterina Fake, "Had we sat down and said, 'Let's start a photo application,' we would have failed."[2] Instead, the team members focused their energy on building a simple way to share photos and have fun. Before long, they realized that they'd stumbled onto a unique business opportunity. They scrapped the game concept and launched Flickr in February 2004. It grew so fast that Yahoo! bought the company a year later for a reported $35 million price tag.

When our team at Siegel+Gale created the brand platform for Flickr, we were drawn to the service's overall experience. Though it lacked some of the features found in established photo-sharing services offered by Kodak and Shutterfly, Flickr's simplified approach and elegant user interface did something else: It inspired people to share photos and engage in conversations. Commented one loyal user: "To say that I'm addicted is an understatement. Flickr makes it easy to indulge this bit of voyeurism while making it easy to engage in a little bit of exhibitionism myself . . . which is why I have my camera with me virtually everywhere I go now."

When you dug under the surface, Flickr promised users new perspectives about the world as seen through the lens of shared photographic experiences. Functionally, it delivered on its promise by making it easy for people to upload, store, and organize their photos. But emotionally the brand won a legion of fans because it created an exceptional experience that was rooted in fun, self-validation, and social interaction. It was Flickr's experience that drew users back for more.

Flickr followed the central tenet of great brand experiences: It surpassed the expectations of its audience. It did more than meet the bare minimum to deliver on its promise. It delighted its users. Its experience conjured their emotions, engaged their minds, and created a sense of community they couldn't find on any other photo-sharing site. While other services were busy adding features for photo editing and distribution, Flickr religiously developed a truly immersive and incomparable experience.

In this chapter, we'll explore what makes a brand experience compelling and how winning brands align their experience with their promise to engage and inspire audiences. We'll also deconstruct the critical building blocks of experience so that you can better understand how to construct and refine one of your own.

WHAT IS BRAND EXPERIENCE?

It's pretty easy to define brand experience by pointing to brands that deliver it—Apple, Four Seasons, Lexus, Starbucks, JetBlue, Target, Williams-Sonoma. But it's a lot harder to describe what it is about these branded experiences that makes the brands great. The whole concept of what a brand experience is has remained somewhat elusive, even to researchers and industry practitioners. Brands have been delivering great experiences for a long time, but until recently they haven't had much data or practical advice to help them improve how they do it.

Brand experience lives entirely in the mind of your audience. That's why it's so hard to define and discuss. A brand experience is not a package, it is not a retail environment, and it is not an advertisement. All of those elements contribute to brand experience, but none of them *are* the brand experience. A brand experience isn't tangible. It's the by-product of our thoughts, our feelings, and our behavior. It's also highly personal. There's no way for me to know whether or not your experience with a given brand matches my experience. We can talk about it and provide each other with descriptions of what we experienced, but it's nearly impossible for me to transfer the precise emotions, streams of thought, and sensory memories that come to my mind when I recall my favorite brand experiences.

Throughout this book I have reminded you how brands create equity. To generate brand equity you deliver an experience that meets or exceeds the expectations set by your brand promise. What I haven't told you is what makes a great brand experience. A great brand experience surpasses your audience's expectations when you deliver on your promise, and it lingers in your audience's memory well after that moment of interaction. In other words, the best brand experiences surprise or delight us when we encounter them, and they leave a strong impression afterward. In fact, brand experience is the primary means by which we actually process a brand's true character and personality.

Fortunately, because we know brand experience contributes so much to a brand's equity, researchers have begun to give it more attention. In a 2009 study that appeared in the *Journal of Marketing,* the branding community received a useful framework for measuring the strength of a brand's experience. Using quantitative methods, this study divided brand experience into four components:

- **Sensory:** when a brand makes a strong impression by appealing to our five senses
- **Affective:** when the brand conjures strong feelings or sentiments
- **Intellectual:** when the brand makes us think more, or induces us to think in a specific way
- **Behavioral:** when the brand stimulates us to do things or change our behavior as a result of the experience[3]

Each of these four factors could be independently traced to what differentiates one brand experience from another. They are also reliable predictors of brand attachment and brand preference. For simplicity's sake, you need to remember only three: A brand experience influences what we think, feel, and do as a result of interaction with the brand. *Think, feel, do.* You might not realize how much brands influence what you think, how you feel, and why you do what you do as a result of their presence. American Express makes a lot of its members think more about their financial well-being and the way they transact than other payment brands. Hallmark and Disney can make us emotional just by mentioning their names. And Starbucks has forever changed the way we order a coffee.

To truly surpass the expectations of your audience at the point of delivery, these three dimensions of experience differentiate the okay brand experiences from the really great brand experiences. Let's consider each in turn.

When Experience Makes Us Think

When loyal Flickr users talk about their experience with the Flickr brand, they very often describe how the service expands what they know about photography. In fact, learning and sharing were two of the primary factors that led to Flickr's success. The brand encourages people to share their work and engage in conversations that broaden their knowledge of the subject. Not surprisingly, many of those conversations revolve around how to improve photographic techniques. Flickr also stimulates users' thinking about the subjects that are photographed. Many of the most popular groups on Flickr are collections of photographs about subjects, such as food, aviation, human rights, and nature.

Consumers of Patagonia sportswear are drawn to the brand's conservationist nature. Its website, direct-mail communications, and in-store environments call attention to specific environmental issues such as water conservation and sustainable materials use. Though the brand's promise undoubtedly relates to the delivery of premium-quality activewear and gear for outdoor sports enthusiasts, it's steeped with intellectual experiences. When you engage with the Patagonia brand, its hard not to consider its unique state of mind. A few years ago it dressed its store environments with posters that demonstrated the difference between farm-raised and wild salmon. As you browsed for a fleece sweater, photographs of raw fish surrounded you. Patagonia experiences make you think about natural resources and the human behaviors that affect them.

In a very different way, REI encourages its customers to "get out and play." It creates a brand experience that induces people to think about their freedom to roam. Every REI retail location is a makeshift adventure camp, complete with a rock wall that customers can climb to put gear to the test. The sheer size and orientation of an REI store might actually stimulate customers to engage in a thought process that is broad and connected to freedom. Architects have known for some time that people who occupy environments with high ceilings report greater happiness and feelings of positivity than people who occupy places with low ceilings. That's why so many office environments ditched drop ceilings in favor of exposed ventilation ducts. Though the ceiling may look a little less finished, the added height makes workers feel more content. In fact, a 2007 study in the *Journal of Consumer Research* found that ceiling height adds to the intellectual side of brand experience: High-ceiling environments were more effective at stimulating people to consider themselves in situations where they might do something they hadn't done before.[4] Looking at the REI experience through this lens, you can argue that the very nature of its retail environment creates an intellectual experience that makes people think about how they might go out and play. It may make them more likely to connect the promise of the brand to activities they had never considered before.

Perhaps the most stunning piece of research pertaining to the way brand experience makes us think arrived in 2008, and it's not surprising that Apple was the focus of its attention (given that Apple is currently cited as one of the strongest brand experiences overall). A lot of people imagine themselves being creative. Creativity is one of the most frequently cited behavioral aspirations, so much so that people spend millions of dollars every year to buy products and services that they believe will help them realize their creative potential. In this landmark study that appeared in the *Journal of Consumer Research,* participants who were exposed to the Apple brand experience actually behaved more creatively in a structured activity than participants who were exposed to another brand.[5] Because of the study's rigor, it quickly circulated among the world's news organizations and provided statistical proof for a notion many people had speculated about for years. Apple enthusiasts claimed that creatives worked better on a Mac, and here was conclusive proof that it was true. Apple, it seems, really does make us "Think Different."

Stimulating Senses and Emotions Through Experiences

It's a common turn of speech to say a picture is worth a thousand words. The Flickr brand won legions of fans in part because its experience made it easy for users to access and share a library that contained millions of photos—photos that allowed people to communicate in ways words never could. Users fondly described their photo-sharing and exploring experiences as "addictive" and "fun." Where the experiences of other photo services were seen as utilitarian and functional, Flickr led users on an emotional adventure, and that's why its experience was so beloved.

Great brand experiences are usually linked to emotional benefits. Years ago, when I was a manager at Disney, I witnessed the way people reacted to the brand experience of another photographic pioneer: I was assigned the task of managing all of Disney's brand activities in its relationship with Kodak, one of its most important strategic partners. During my first trip to Walt Disney World to review Kodak-branded experiences, I observed guests at a Kodak-sponsored attraction at Epcot called Honey, I Shrunk the Audience, a 3D movie experience. As guests waited in line just outside the attraction, Kodak presented a five-minute slide show set to "True Colors," the popular Cyndi Lauper ballad. The slide show featured powerful images of people in various life moments, captured by Kodak photographers on vibrant Kodak media. As I watched the film, I felt myself welling up with tears. To my surprise, as I looked around the room, other people were actually crying. I asked my Kodak colleagues how much of that experience people attributed to Kodak and how much was attributed to Disney. They shared survey research with me that showed how guests described the True Colors preshow as one of the most memorable parts of the attraction experience. When asked why they liked it, many guests cited the positive emotions and sentiments the show made them feel and how much it made them want to take pictures. And the best part was that guests linked the experience to Kodak, which they described as a brand they could trust with their memories. Though not every brand can afford a Disney-blessed slide show in front of a captive audience, there are many brands that leverage such experiences today in stores, on the Web, and, of course, through advertising.

The feeling we get from a good brand experience is very important because we tend to remember things that are the most emotionally charged.

In the business world, emotional experience is often dismissed and devalued. We're too prone to believe that people make choices using only their rational minds. Yet neuroscience is proving just how wrong this assumption really is, even in business-to-business settings. António Damásio is one of the most respected neuroscientists in the field today. He has written several best-selling books that detail how our emotions and rationality rely upon one another. Damásio countered conventional logic when he said, "We are not thinking machines; we are feeling machines that think."[6]

Researchers have known for years that consumers are more open to brand engagement when they're in a positive mood. That's why so many advertisements rely on humor. When we're feeling good, laughing, amused, or even pleasantly surprised, our minds are more likely to remember the experience and connect it with a brand. Brand experiences can also win our favor by raising our pulse with excitement, waxing in nostalgia, and making us feel sexy.

The "feeling" dimension of brand experience is not limited to the state of our emotions. It also governs our sensory experiences. There's a great bit of Apple folklore that has to do with the debut of the first iPod. According to legend, not long before the product was publicly unveiled, when Steve Jobs plugged his headphones into the production model he didn't like the fact that the headphone jack didn't "click" into the outlet. He is said to have ordered the team to reengineer that part of the device so that there was a noticeable "click" whenever you plugged in your earbuds. Jobs believed it was an important sensory element of the product experience.

Our sensory perceptions of a brand experience matter more than we know. Auto manufacturers learned long ago to engineer heavier car doors so that they make solid thuds when shut. People want to hear a specific sound when they close their car door, and they want it to feel solid.

We have five senses—sight, sound, taste, smell, and touch—yet most brand experiences focus mostly on what we see. Although our visual sense is strong, some of the other senses have been found to make a more lasting impression in memory.

Maybe it's because of our ancient ancestors, but scent is a particularly powerful sensory memory. In fact, it's thought to be the strongest. One of the world's most popular smells is the smell of a new car. New car owners constantly cite it as an important emotional experience. Some owners describe how anxious they feel when they imagine the smell of their new car fading. Scent is not only an evocative part of experience; it also has the power to conjure strong memories. Ask anyone who's had a bad experience with tequila to tell you how the smell of the beverage affects them years after the fact.

Only a few brands seem to take advantage of the distinctive role that scents can play in their brand experience. Shoppers can find their way to an Abercrombie & Fitch store with their nostrils. Abercrombie engineered a proprietary scent that sales associates spritz liberally every hour while the store is open. The same is true for the W Hotels chain. You can't buy the scent of a W hotel in a home furnishings store. It is purposely guarded so that you associate it only with the hotel chain's destinations. A few years ago, my family and I went on vacation and stayed at a W hotel. At the time, my daughter Jordan had just finished several weeks of chemotherapy, and her stomach was prone to being upset. One night during our stay she got sick and didn't make it to the bathroom on time. We called for housekeeping. They came immediately and helped us return the room to normal. When they sprayed the signature scent, I was impressed by how quickly it changed the atmosphere in the room. I asked the housekeeper if I could hold on to the bottle in case Jordan was sick again. She was very polite, but she explained that she was not allowed to leave it with guests. I was intrigued by this, so the next day I asked the hotel manager why I couldn't hold on to the bottle. He explained that hotel personnel were required to sign out the bottles every day. They were expected to account for the bottles of W scent the same way bartenders must account for the spirits in their charge. W understands the value of the sensory experience.

Next to smell, sound also holds tremendous experiential power. I recently heard a story on NPR that traced people's experiences with certain songs and types of music to influential life memories. Again and again, people talked about the way that certain songs trigger a chain of memories. Many of them discussed how vividly they could recall minute details about their experience when they heard a specific song: where they were, what they were doing, how they felt. One respondent linked a song to his first sexual experience. Another described the day her mother passed away.

The music and sounds that accompany a brand experience can transport us and make a powerful statement that lasts in our memory. But we're not always deliberate in choosing those sounds. De Beers created a proprietary link to romance when it commissioned an orchestral arrangement that accompanied its popular "Shadows and Diamonds" advertising campaign. Southwest Airlines has become synonymous with its legendary "Ding!"

Taste is harder to integrate into a brand experience unless you're a food and beverage brand. Yet some brands have found ways to link their experience to food. The DoubleTree hotel chain distinguished itself for serving customers warm chocolate chip cookies upon arrival.

While touch is an incredibly important part of the sensory experience for many product brands, it isn't used as often as it could be for services. Starbucks gets it. Every Starbucks coffeehouse is filled with textures. The way a Starbucks retail location interacts with your body is just as important to the experience as the way its coffee tastes. Although Ben & Jerry's ice cream gained attention from its cause-related promise and unconventional marketing, one of the biggest differentiators was its product experience. Because founder Ben Cohen suffered from anosmia—a condition that causes a nearly complete lack of smell or taste—he added more and more textures to the ice cream recipes: cookie dough, brownies, bits of cherries. That textural element of the product is one of the key reasons it became such a powerful brand.

Perhaps no one understands how the five senses combine to create the best brand experience more than Virgin America. When it launched in the U.S. aviation market, things could not have been worse for the airline industry. On the heels of the September 11 terrorist attacks, most airlines suffered considerably and cut back the amount they spent to deliver experiences. Most airlines became flying buses. Onto this landscape, Virgin introduced a U.S. version of its legendary service platform.

When travelers check in for a Virgin America flight they are greeted at a stylishly designed check-in area complete with disco-driven house music. You begin your Virgin experience with the richness of sound. When you receive your boarding card, you literally touch something distinctive and proprietary. Virgin designed its own version of a boarding card. It's a different shape, it's smaller than other carriers' cards, and it's printed on a heavier stock. It's also bright red.

I previously described the Virgin America boarding experience. You enter a darkened plane with mood lighting and house music. Flight attendants wearing sleek black uniforms guide you to your seat. You sit on a light-colored leather seat, and you slip your belongings into acrylic pockets.

If you order food on a Virgin flight, you do so through a digital menu. I can't say I've ever noticed a Virgin America scent, but it wouldn't surprise me if it was introduced in due time. Virgin is an excellent example of a brand purposefully using all of the senses to accent the experience. And in so doing, they stir passengers' emotions. Many passengers say a Virgin America flight makes them feel more relaxed. Some say it gets them aroused. Most describe the experience as cool. They're all great ways to describe a brand that promises to infuse what it does with a rock 'n' roll spirit.

When Our Behavior Is Part of the Experience

Brand experiences are often the most memorable because the audience is engaged. Many of the greatest brand experiences either change the behavior of the audience or compel the audience to behave in a specific way. This was certainly true for Flickr. It allowed users to *do* certain things they couldn't have done as easily before. For example, the service made it easier for users to exhibit their work to a broad audience of people with similar interests. Photographers started using Flickr to distribute their work to people they knew, but soon enough they were encouraged to post their photos to groups of people they *didn't* know. The service made it easy to follow interesting photographers and keep a collection of "favorite" photos. And the service encouraged users to participate in the community with its popular "interestingness" feed. Every day, based on a carefully guarded algorithm, several dozen photographs were selected because they were interesting to the Flickr population. If you were passive, you could simply click through the interesting photos that appeared each day. If you were looking for a few clicks of fame, you worked hard to have your photo selected.

Though it is often the butt of many jokes, the fact that people have to assemble IKEA furniture is an important part of the brand experience. We may curse the crazy names, the limited instructions, and the funky maneuvers we have to master with an Allen wrench, but the experience also makes us more invested in the inexpensive furniture we assemble. The furniture and the experience have meaning because of the behavior the brand induces.

Go into a Starbucks and order your favorite coffee. You'll use a specific vocabulary. Starbucks engineered its own language, and we willingly put it to use. That's part of what makes the Starbucks brand experience memorable. In fact, Starbucks influences a lot of our behavior at its retail locations. We stand in line. We sit in overstuffed chairs. We tip our barista. All of that activity influences our perception of the brand.

While the Flickr brand experience increased the variety of our behavior, many brands create memorable experiences by constraining what we can do. You can't buy a meal on Southwest Airlines. You also can't reserve a specific seat location. Southwest doesn't fly to all the major airports, nor does it allow you to fly first class. And an awful lot of people positively *love* the Southwest brand experience. The fact of the matter is that we often perceive greater value in the experiences that constrain our options. Sometimes we feel less overwhelmed because we didn't have to sort through many choices—the brand lessens our sense of responsibility. Sometimes we feel a greater sense of accomplishment because the experience focused our attention. In either case, the brand experience makes us more aware of our behavior, and that behavior differentiates the brand at the point of delivery and in our recollections.

THE RIGHT WAY TO PLAN BRAND EXPERIENCE

It's one thing to describe the components of brand experience. It's quite another to consider how to orchestrate a great one in real life. Conventionally, a lot of brands think of experience linearly, whereby the experience unfolds moment to moment and every moment counts. A good analogy for this model of brand experience is a movie. It has a beginning, a middle, and an end, and everything contained within the movie matters. The problem with this view of brands is that it can be overwhelming. I used to tell my clients they had to make sure the brand delivered on its promise at every touch point throughout an experience, but that's a ridiculously daunting, and probably inefficient, task. Here's why.

Right now, as you read each new word of this book, your brain is engaged and digesting the words I share with you. However, unless I call your attention to a specific word or phrase, you probably aren't paying too much attention to it. You scan the text, and your brain absorbs information as quickly as it can, as long as I don't say something that confuses you or draw attention to something that snaps your brain out of scan mode and into analysis mode.

Although I'd like to imagine that every sentence I load into this book is packed with thought-provoking, memorable material, I know that certain parts of what I share are going to interest you more than other parts. Not only that, but your attention will waver from time to time, until an exception comes along that snaps your conscious mind back into the present. In the meantime, your mind may wander here and there. Maybe you're hungry, and you start thinking about what to have for lunch. You keep reading while your mind ponders food, but you're not as engaged.

That's the reality that the moment-to-moment view of experience doesn't really address very well. It's the kind of thinking that leads many marketers to overbrand—saturating their experiences with logos and brand messages because every moment counts.

The only argument in favor of the moment-to-moment view of experience comes from a body of research that suggests we perceive a lot about brands even when we're not paying attention to them.[7] I can share a series of logos with you—some you have seen before and some you have not. Imagine I let you look at this page of logos for only ten seconds and then ask you to write down all the brands you saw. You would probably list only the ones with which you were familiar, leading us to think you didn't see the new logos. However, the next time you see the logos you didn't know, they'll feel familiar to you. If I asked you to recall the brands you saw that day, you might not remember seeing ones that were new to you. But when you see one of them again, something about it will feel familiar. That's part of the strange way your mind works: You process more information in an experience than you realize. This phenomenon lies at the heart of the controversy behind subliminal marketing. People rightfully feel violated when they suspect that a marketer has manipulated their perceptions. But in this instance, the logo wasn't hidden at all. It was right there in front of you; it just wasn't relevant to your experience, and you weren't engaged enough to remember it consciously even though it did stick somewhere in your memory.

The movie model of moment-to-moment experience design is where most managers go, but the most effective method of experience design focuses attention on *recalled* experience. The best way to understand this context is to think back to a time when you shared a personal experience with someone else. Did you walk the person through every mundane part of the experience? *I got up and put on my slippers. Then I walked twelve steps to the sink and brushed my teeth, first on the top bridge of my mouth, and then on the bottom bridge. . . .* Your audience would be snoring by this point in the story. Instead, when you describe an experience, you focus on specific moments in time.

After you finish this book, you won't remember everything I've shared with you. You'll remember only certain parts. It's possible that you really like some of those parts. It's also possible that you took issue with other parts. Regardless, the places where you liked something or were dissatisfied with something are the parts of the experience you will *recall,* not the rest of the material. Imagine we are keeping a running graph of your interest—maybe a long piece of paper tape that spits out of your head with little marks like an EKG that a doctor takes to track your heart rate. When something piques your attention during an experience (good or bad), the line on the running tape spikes. Otherwise, it flatlines. Those peaks are all that you'll remember from your experience with my brand.

Here's the really interesting part: Whenever the line peaks on that tape, your brain takes a snapshot of the key drivers of experience. It is in this moment that you imprint a memory of your feelings, your thoughts, and perhaps even your specific behavior. It's as if your brain decides that it needs to remember your experiential vital signs because your attention is focused at this moment in time. Researchers Barbara Fredrickson and Daniel Kahneman developed an apt analogy for this conceptualization of our experience. They suggested that our recalled experience is more like a photo album than it is a movie. In the movie metaphor, memory provides comprehensive coverage of experience. But most of us don't recall our experience comprehensively. We recall key moments as though they were captured like photographs tacked to a wall in our brain. Whether good or bad, the strongest emotional attachment we have to a brand can be measured by the peaks.[8]

This structure is the most useful way to design and manage your brand experience. Diagnostically, you want to identify the moments people remember most frequently. If you're launching a new brand, you make assumptions and refine your model as you go. This is why prototypes and tests can help you work out the kinks before you formally launch your brand experience.

What do the mental photographs have in common? By studying the commonality of your audience's mental photo albums, you can focus your attention on the parts of the experience that need the most improvement as well as the parts of the experience that must be preserved or enhanced. Strategically, you can decide which parts of the experience are most closely related to your brand promise. And you can focus your investment on branding those aspects so that they become more memorable and proprietary. In essence, you can decide which photographs you want consumers to paste into their mental albums.

Avoiding Interruptions

What impedes a brand's ability to deliver a great experience? Let's return to the two mental models I just gave you. Imagine a brand experience as an EKG line that spikes when something catches our attention, good or bad. Every time there's a significant peak, our brain captures a snapshot that allows us to picture and remember the essence of the moment. If we went back over our tape and looked at the peaks that were associated with the negative parts of our experience, the most common culprits would be interruptions.

Interruptions are the parts of a brand experience that draw our attention to anything that is irrelevant or in conflict with the brand promise. The interruptions not only distract us from the desired thought, emotion, or behavior we're trying to induce, but they get imprinted in our memory as well. The sad part is that a great experience, filled with many exciting and positive peaks on our EKG tape, can be thwarted by a single interruption. I often use an analogy from the theater to illustrate why. The fourth wall is an imaginary wall between the stage and the audience that acts as a dividing line between the play and reality. In most plays, especially those that attempt to portray reality, the fourth wall is essential for the audience to suspend its disbelief. If an actor who suddenly looks out at the audience breaks it, we're reminded that we're sitting in a darkened room watching a bunch of actors pretending to be someone else. No matter how strong the rest of the performance, we just got a dose of reality—and we'll probably say something about it when we have coffee later. An interruption is anything that breaks the fourth wall of a brand experience—anything that might draw the audience's attention away from the experience you promise.

Too many brands ignore this vital facet of brand experience. They spend millions of dollars crafting a great strategy and designing a vibrant brand identity system, only to have the entire investment wasted because at critical moments in the experience the audience is jarred away from what really matters. You don't have to look very hard to find these interruptions. Spend some time with wireless service carriers. All of the major service brands spend heftily on their brand design and identity. They mount impressive advertising campaigns and invest in their image on several fronts. Yet, in most cases, a visit to one of their stores, a call to the phone center, or time spent on the website aggravates the most patient brand loyalist. Although some are better than others, the category is challenged by consistently poor brand experiences—and interrupters are the prevailing cause of dissatisfaction.

Each year, my colleagues at Siegel+Gale publish their Global Brand Simplicity Index. In the 2010 edition of the study, respondents overwhelmingly stated that simplicity allows for greater peace of mind and less stress. The best brand experiences make it effortless for a consumer to connect with the brand's promise. That's why your first step in any brand experience effort should be to find ways to reduce information and interactions that create anxiety. It's often easy to find them. Secret shopper initiatives are very effective approaches that allow you to uncover problematic touch points in an experience. These might include store visits, calls to customer service centers, and inquiries through e-mail and digital touch points. Sometimes, you can identify the problem spots by taking time to read the material associated with your brand, which may include product instructions, marketing collateral, and perhaps the biggest smoking gun of them all, the monthly statement. The simplification step should come before you attempt any other part of experience improvement.

Determining a Hierarchy of Touch Points

We manage brand experiences by manipulating touch points. At any moment in time, something in a particular experience has the potential to stimulate what we think, feel, and do. Our role as managers is to determine the touch points that contribute most to a great brand experience and then determine the most appropriate way for the brand to get credit for that *brand touch*. Every time you are exposed to a brand during an experience, you've been touched by the brand. If you are sitting at home and you see a television advertisement for the brand, that's a brand touch. If you make a call to a customer service number and the agent answers on behalf of the brand, that's a brand touch. If you go to the store and see the brand's package on a store shelf, that's a brand touch. The same is true for visiting a branded store or a sponsored event.

A branded touch point is anything you might interact with during the experience that features some recognizable part of the brand's identity (logos, names, distinctive shapes, colors, typography, etc.). As managers, touch points are the places where we can deliberately change the experience. Some touch points overlap and contain one another. For example, if you play with an iPad in an Apple Store, both are touch points. It just so happens that the Apple Store is a touch point that contains several other brand touch points. This type of overlap is important when you are diagnosing or planning brand experience. It's not important how much they overlap. It's important which ones register. We tend to remember the touch points that are either at the peak or at the end of our experience.

Perhaps the most challenging aspect of developing a brand experience strategy is to decide which touch points matter most. In your prioritization efforts, you should rely on the hierarchy shown in Figure 9.1. Foundational touch points are mission critical. They are the touch points where the brand truly delivers on its promise. If you are managing a bicycle brand, every product model in your line is a functional touch point. If the product doesn't perform as expected, no amount of advertising or brand snazziness will

FIGURE 9.1

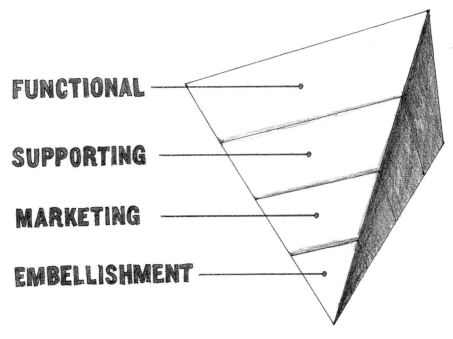

FUNCTIONAL

SUPPORTING

MARKETING

EMBELLISHMENT

compensate for its failure. Your audience experience comes to life every time someone sits on one of your bikes and takes it for a spin. In service industries, the functional touch points are often linked to people. For example, a waiter in a restaurant is an important, functional brand touch point. If I have a bad experience with a waiter at your restaurant, it has the potential to seriously interfere with my total assessment of your brand experience (of course, the food is an important functional touch point, too).

Invest plenty of time in fine-tuning your functional touch points. Trace the steps of your audience to determine where they get their money's worth and where your research demonstrates that your audience expects the promise to be delivered, and never stop fine-tuning these elements of your experience. The functional touch points are where the proverbial rubber meets the road. Many brands ignore this. They'll focus on communications or design touches that are largely irrelevant to the delivery of value. To succeed, you need to sweat the details on the most functional elements of your brand experience.

One level down on our hierarchy are the supporting touch points. They do exactly what you'd think they do: They provide support to the core function of the experience. Supporting touch points are necessary, highly influential, often overlooked, and surprisingly unbranded. When you offer a product or service, it's inevitable that someone will have an inquiry, a problem, or a need that isn't central to the value proposition. But if it isn't addressed, it can make a brand experience awful. Software companies discovered this fact shortly after the PC boom in the 1980s. They rushed to put new versions of software on the market but didn't work as hard to create intuitive documentation or field a large enough customer support staff. They soon realized that these two touch points were critical to customer satisfaction and great experience, but they were also expensive. For years, most of us used bad software and expressed our frustration at the poor service and support function. This colored our experience with brands like Microsoft and Intuit.

The winning brands carry the brand experience forward to their supporting touch points. They consider how the brand behaves when there are exceptions in the experience. When you pick up the phone and call a customer service representative, what do you remember thinking? When you receive a bill, what draws your attention? When you have to figure out how to assemble that prefabricated piece of furniture, how does it feel when you thumb through the instructions? You don't have to overbrand supporting touch points, but you do have to consider how they impact the total brand experience. You do want to find ways to lessen the painful parts and create a little pop when the audience least expects it. If you ask Lexus customers about their favorite part of the Lexus experience, they'll tell you it's having their car serviced. Lexus has transformed the way the entire industry thinks about the part of owning a car most of us hate—the trip back to the dealership for a repair or a routine maintenance check.

Another level down on the hierarchy are marketing touch points. Look, brands have to promote themselves. Every brand, in some way, shape, or fashion, has to generate communications that try to persuade the audience to engage with it. These touch points certainly make an impression on the brand. They can prime us with strong feelings, thoughts, and behavioral cues. But remember that marketing touch points are not central to the delivery of value, nor do they usually provide us with necessary support. More often than not, they are soliciting new opportunities to engage with customers and sell incremental products and services. Going back to our bicycle brand analogy, if your bicycles are shoddy, no amount of Madison Avenue spin will improve your brand experience. If an award-winning advertising campaign creates a strong brand narrative, it's going to fall apart when your bike does. Marketing touch points are important to the total brand experience because they set expectations and project a brand's story. But they will not make a poor experience better.

Finally, a branded embellishment is a special class of touch point on the hierarchy that provides value through accents. It offers form and not necessarily function. It is the experiential touch point that piques our interest because it is just plain beautiful or because it adds something to the experience that makes it more emotionally compelling to us. Embellishments like the unique scent of a W hotel room or the analog clock on the dashboard of a Lexus are not core to the brand's functional value, and they aren't a mode of communication. Yet they are often the memorable parts of our brand experience that add quite a bit of proprietary value. The key to contemplating experiential touch points is to remember that simplicity wins. If you begin adding experiential elements that needlessly complicate the experience, you risk being unmemorable or confusing your audience.

THE INCREASING ROLE OF GETTING SOCIAL

Although researchers are conflicted about whether social experience is separate from the other dimensions of brand experience, there is no question that consumers are told how important social connectivity is in the age of digital media. If Facebook succeeds at becoming the world's first trillion-dollar business, the social aspect of experience will certainly be hard to contest.

When most pundits talk about brand experience, they describe it in isolation. That is, they talk about one consumer interacting with one brand in a fairly pristine brand environment. Of course, this is rarely the case. We are social animals. We shop together, consume together, and talk about our shopping and consumption experiences after the fact. This tendency is the force that's transforming the design of digital applications. You would be hard-pressed to introduce a new piece of software today that does not include some kind of social functionality.

As it pertains to brand experience, social interaction can actually transform our perception. Recent research suggests that the photos you would tack on your mental wall when experiencing the brand alone might be quite different from those you would post when experiencing the brand with others.[9] Go back to our movie analogy. Let's imagine that you're watching a romantic comedy alone in your pajamas on the sofa of your living room. When the movie is over, you'll remember certain scenes that made you laugh, cry, or grimace, depending on the quality of the film. However, if I put you in a crowded cinema with an enthusiastic crowd, you might have different memories of the film. Laughter is contagious. Perhaps something struck you funny in the crowded theater that would not have if you were sitting at home alone. And because we tend to remember things that make us laugh more than, say, things that bore us, the social experience would have created different brand experience peaks for you. You might also evaluate the whole brand experience more favorably because of the social aspect than you would have in isolation. This is the power of social interaction in a brand experience.

PUTTING THE PIECES TOGETHER

Left on their own, all of these facets of brand experience are nothing more than parlor tricks. In fact, if you're not careful, you can harness all of these insights to create the type of phony, positioning-derived brand I've decried throughout most of this book. But I hope you'll consider the equation that lies at the heart of our time here together: *that great brands succeed by creating experiences that meet or exceed the expectations set by a brand's promise.* Those experiences are not flat, one-dimensional constructs. A brand experience is realized through multiple touch points and extends into the three dimensions—how people think, what they do, and how they feel. It's not enough to say that you are going to deliver a great widget that will enable people to be more creative. You have to create an experience that makes this true. A good part of that obligation rests in the utilitarian functionality of your product or service. But there's an equally important part of it that lives in the mind of your audience. As you design, make, and support your product or service, you must consider how people will think, feel, and act in the mental snapshots that coincide with the peaks of their experience.

....

CHAPTER TEN

BRAND INSIDE

Why People Are the Key to Your Brand Strategy

The examples are numerous. Some have become cliché. We've heard of the Nordstrom salesperson who accepted a tire as a return from a customer, even though Nordstrom does not sell tires. Or the Southwest pilot who sacrificed an on-time departure to hold the plane at the gate so that one of his passengers could catch the only available flight to take him to his father's funeral. These customer service gems highlight many coaching anecdotes and training seminars on service excellence. They have developed a life of their own because they inspire us and remind us to follow that age-old axiom: The customer is always right.

Most managers have been told that great customer service leads to better business performance. Conventional wisdom prescribes that you should focus your attention on the people who directly interact with customers, as they are where the brand truly comes to life. That's certainly true. But everyone inside a brand matters. When brands fail, the culprit is always human error. From the executive suite to the front lines to the investment base, the best way to sustain a real brand is to align the people behind it with the brand promise.

GOLEM BRANDS

Without the engagement of the entire brand culture, brands can behave like the golems of Jewish folklore. They look and behave like humans, endowed with magical personalities and wondrous talents, but they fail to live up to human expectations because they lack a soul. When you hold the golem brands to account, you find yourself sifting through phone trees, decoding complex statements, and getting lost in cluttered websites. The golems of the brand universe troll around in social media, drawing attention to themselves with catchy promotional offers and popping up in the press for making themselves wealthier. It's enough to make you hate all brands. Sadly, this dim view is shared by millions of consumers. In December 2010, Harris Interactive polled more than two thousand Americans with a simple question: "Which industries are generally honest and trustworthy?" To the seventeen industries listed, which included banks, hospitals, supermarkets, airlines, and computer companies, nearly half of those polled responded, "none of the above."[1]

Our tolerance for lip service has completely eroded, and it isn't purely a factor of poor customer service. It's driven largely by a failure to align people inside with the promise of the brand. British Petroleum won our hearts and minds with a refreshing rebranding campaign that promised to go "beyond petroleum" and improve the quality of our lives by investing in sustainable energy solutions. A leaky pipe in Alaska first made us question BP's intent. Then, a preventable catastrophe in the Gulf of Mexico summarily ended our willingness to believe anyone at BP. If BP were truly aligned with their promise, neither incident would have occurred. Employees across the company should have had an incentive to deliver on the promise of the brand.

Legions of Toyota owners received the proverbial punch to the gut when they learned that the substance of the Toyota promise—exceptional safety and quality—was in question as a result of a widespread safety recall the company initially contested and then downplayed. It was not until CEO Akio Toyoda apologized on Capitol Hill that the company appeared to be willing to live up to its promise and lay blame where it belonged. "We pursued growth over the speed at which we were able to develop our people and our organization, and we should sincerely be mindful of that," Toyoda said.[2]

Growth. Investors demand it, and business managers are trained to pursue it aggressively—sometimes at the expense of any other objective. Growth is necessary for most businesses, but it should be balanced with the delivery of customer value. The value customers receive should serve as the business's engine for growth. Growth and brand alignment should not be mutually exclusive concepts, nor should they be in conflict with each other. They should be joined at the hip. In fact, history is full of brands that grew as a result of their unrelenting commitment to exceed the expectations of their stakeholders—which include investors as much as customers—at every touch point. Why can't more brands achieve the same results?

Lessons gleaned from the field of corporate finance shed light on how growth becomes a branding challenge. The modern corporation relies on three critical stakeholders: owners, managers, and customers. Owners provide capital for managers to run businesses that deliver benefits to customers. It's simple until you consider the scale and structure of large companies.

Publicly traded corporations are owned by millions of shareholders. They could not function if every investor had a say. Instead, they elect a board of directors to look after their collective interests. The board's job is to ensure that investors achieve a return on their investment. It does this by hiring a management team to run the venture's day-to-day operation. Here's where the trouble starts. The CEO and his or her team are essentially agents for the owners. In theory, everything a manager does should serve owner interest. But we know this is often not the case. When a manager's actions are not aligned with investors' interests, we call the result an *agency cost*. For example, imagine that I am the founder of a regional chain of gourmet ice cream parlors. I built my business from one small creamery to ten stores because of great attention to detail and a commitment to quality. There's an archive of news stories documenting great feats I accomplished to inspire my customers. I know a good many of them by name. But, after twenty years in the creamery business, I want to try something new. So I retire as CEO and hire you to manage my growing franchise. For argument's sake, let's say that my business generates $10 million a year in profit, and it's growing at a rate of 5 percent per year. When I hire you, I agree to pay you $500,000 a year to grow the company.

Now, I'm sure you're a hard worker and have great intentions. But like most people, your top priority is keeping your job. Your chief goal is to deliver $10.5 million in profit by the end of the year. If you do that, you know I'll be happy because I'm accustomed to about 5 percent growth. So, that's what you do. It turns out, however, that you missed a couple of opportunities. For instance, my biggest rival went bankrupt, and we could have acquired his chain of seven stores for pennies. But you didn't take that step because you weren't sure it would generate enough growth to satisfy my expectation for this year's earnings. It might have got in the way of your profit target for the year, so you elected to focus on discounts and aggressive sales promotions. You hit your number, but you missed an opportunity that might have been in my long-term best interest. That's an agency cost. Here's another example: Imagine that you *do* go after the acquisition opportunity and shortly after you complete the deal you knock the roof off your sales targets with an innovative marketing tactic. You double sales! You also buy yourself a plush, top-of-the-line Bentley using company funds to shuttle between the many locations of the growing ice cream empire. You justify the expense as necessary so that you can manage effectively. Maybe a Prius would have done the job just as well. The extra money you spent on that car could have gone into my pocket. That's an agency cost. It signals that our interests are not aligned.

Many companies try to mitigate agency costs by creating financial incentives for senior executives. By awarding stock options, restricted stock, and lucrative performance bonuses, investors hope their management teams will make decisions that match their investment interests. And the abiding investor interest is nearly always growth. The leaders of most of the world's big brands are motivated to grow, grow, and grow some more. The incentive compensation models work, but they create noteworthy challenges. Enron, WorldCom, and Washington Mutual all relied on incentives to stimulate unprecedented financial growth and reduce agency costs—with devastating results. As we know, none of these brands exist today.

The trouble with all of the growth-oriented models is that it's just a given that everybody's behavior aligns with other stakeholder interests— stakeholders such as customers, nonmanagement employees, partners, and government. While many companies invest heartily to get everyone who's on the inside to think about growth and shareholder returns, they spend less time linking that growth to the promise of the brand. One BP oil spill or one massive Toyota safety recall can permanently break the covenant between you and your stakeholders. If you keep your promise to investors at the expense of the experience you deliver to customers, employees, and suppliers, growth will surely evaporate.

The alarming fact is that BP and Toyota might be among the lucky brands. Their sudden catastrophes couldn't be ignored. Their investors and management teams were forced to address situations that exposed how poorly the brand experience was aligned with its promise. BP has now tied its employee bonus programs to safety records, and Toyota has launched a massive overhaul of its manufacturing processes. BP and Toyota are under intense public scrutiny, and the odds are that they will repair their brands in time. But many brands break promises every day in the pursuit of a growth mandate. They lose a customer here, dissatisfy one there, all while making quick, cosmetic fixes so that they can grow enough to generate returns that satisfy investors. They push on with bad behavior while their brands slowly become less valuable, until one day someone asks, "Why are we now number two in our category?" or "How did a key competitor leap past us?" or "Why do customers seem so apathetic about what we do?" Without a catastrophe to focus everyone's attention on how the brand isn't living up to its promise, the brand slowly devolves into a golem.

It doesn't have to be this way. And people are the solution. Every brand has an obligation to align its promise with the behavior of all of the people inside.

THE TROUBLE WITH BRAND ALIGNMENT

Brand alignment is not a new discipline. It usually follows a rebranding initiative. Employees have to be trained to understand what the new brand means and exposed to how it should look and feel. While there are multiple variations on the theme, the basic premise remains the same: Brand alignment prepares internal stakeholders to behave in a branded way. Unfortunately, most brand alignment programs fail for one or more of the following eight predictable reasons.

1. The branding team. Brand strategies die when the branding or marketing team has sole responsibility for the brand. I can spot this flaw in a client organization quickly. We sit down to kick off the project, and the only people in the room with us are people with the word *brand* on their business cards. When it is time for us to do interviews with internal stakeholders, we're only provided access to marketing personnel. When we ask to meet with senior decision makers, we're told they don't have time. That's usually when I get up on my soapbox and try to convince the clients that the project is destined for failure—that they'd be better off paying me to take a vacation, because the investment will generate about the same results.

At the beginning of this book, I shared the case of Washington Federal. When we kicked off that project, CEO Roy Whitehead was in the room with us. So were his direct reports—all of them, including the heads of every business unit. At each milestone in the rebranding process, Roy and his team took time out of their busy schedules to review and discuss the strategy. When it was time to implement the strategy, Roy personally introduced it to the rest of the organization.

2. A waterfall design. A typical brand alignment approach uses a water-fall design that assigns time periods for training and implementation needs after a rebrand. Inevitably, these plans focus on a big launch followed by a sustained period of workshops, communications, and hands-on events designed to inspire employees and instill the brand promise. It's called a water-fall design because each new phase trickles down from the previous phase. It's linear, mechanical, and focused on dependencies. While a waterfall design may be a useful conceptual model for thinking about a linear process for aligning an organization, it has two very limiting vulnerabilities.

First, a waterfall design is event-driven. It's anchored to a series of one-time changes. You launch, and then you train, and then (we hope) you measure. Anytime you roll out a change in your brand strategy, you will certainly have these one-time events. But brand alignment is not always a sequential series of educational and inspirational mile markers. It's no wonder so many well-intentioned brand strategies gather dust on office cubicle walls. Six months after the new material is introduced and the waterfall chart is complete, people are back to focusing on growth targets. As logical and orderly as a waterfall approach may seem, at some point it bottoms out and you'll lose the momentum and effectiveness you want to achieve.

The second vulnerability of the waterfall approach is that it considers only what it takes to introduce the brand to the organization, not the way people behave. It doesn't consider what it takes to motivate people or to persuade them to change their behavior. It just lists a series of required steps and the order of rollout. It lives by the assumption that "if we train them, they'll behave differently." Maybe. But maybe not. It depends on what you're training and how it's presented. Perhaps the people you want to train have insights that can build on the strategy and evolve it into something new that strengthens the organization's ability to exceed stakeholder expectations (and, again, when I say "stakeholder" I mean *all* stakeholders, including investors). The waterfall design rarely accounts for the decidedly nonlinear feedback loop. Strategy is not static. It changes by necessity. The approach to implement the strategy must be fluid.

3. Compulsion. My job is hardest when I know a company has already completed one or more rebranding efforts. Why? Because people groan when they are told to attend a meeting with "the brand consultant." More often than not, they end up hearing an outsider tell them what they've been doing wrong—an outsider who has only a faint idea of what they do every day, and who won't pay the price if the strategy fails.

Most brand alignment initiatives are about as inviting and engaging as sexual harassment training. They are positioned as a mandatory effort and delivered as a dry and one-sided lecture. Brand alignment should be an engaging experience that connects the people on the inside with the promise of the brand. A good alignment initiative should get people thinking and doing. It should create useful opportunities to enlist employees and other stakeholders as advocates. If it feels like a chore or a sermon, people will be less inclined to pay attention and make it part of their daily job.

4. Form over value. A typical brand alignment initiative places a great deal of emphasis on aesthetics. People are trained on how to use the logo correctly. They're taught how to go about naming. They may even take classes to learn how to write in the brand's voice. These are all necessary and useful exercises, but they tend to overemphasize the form of a brand rather than its value. Alignment initiatives of this sort condition people to think of the brand as a marketing asset. While it certainly is, brands become real when they deliver on a promise. The symbols, names, and other forms of brand expression are reminders that link the value to marketing assets. The best brand alignment initiatives provide people with resources and inspiration to change *the way* they deliver value.

5. Narcissistic navel-gazing. Brand alignment initiatives are perhaps at their worst when they become the corporate equivalent of self-psychology. Too much time is spent looking backward at history and brand evolution. Too much attention is paid to internal reflection and rationalizing why things are the way they are. Don't get me wrong. History can be a powerful motivator. Brands such as Coca-Cola, Disney, and General Electric have remarkable heritages that are essential parts of the brand promise. But I've also seen many brand alignment initiatives that devolve into propaganda that glorifies the past without helping stakeholders understand what they must do today and tomorrow to deliver on the promise. I've seen just as many initiatives fail because the team couldn't break with the past to make new progress. I'm generally a congenial guy, but a few of my clients have seen another side of me—the side that has little patience when a client resists a good idea because ancient history in their organization has proven it can't be done.

6. Training wheels. Because so many brand alignment initiatives are viewed as one-time events that are connected to the launch of a new identity system, they are commonly implemented through a series of workshops and training programs. The workshops and training can be valuable, but, as you might assume, many of them are focused on the tactical implementation of the identity system. Participants are taught how much clear space to use around the logo. They learn how to rewrite copy so that it adopts the brand's tone of voice. They study different ways to stage the logo and implement elements of the visual identity system, such as the typography, color palette, unique shapes, and imagery.

All of this hands-on activity with the brand's identity serves a role and adds value. But it doesn't do much to change the way people think or behave. Training and workshops can be an effective way to jump-start a broader process of behavioral change, but rarely do they make much change on their own. Even the best brand alignment workshops that focus on brand values, the brand's value delivery system, or the retooling of brand experiences often have finite shelf lives that expire before the work is done. Alignment requires constant follow-up to achieve required changes. The leading cause for failure in a brand alignment initiative is too much emphasis on the initial training front with no support after the fact.

7. Conflicting agendas. Some time ago, I led a corporate rebranding initiative for a large professional services firm. The company operated as a partnership, and within our first few interviews with partners it became evident to us that the client's management team was not aligned around a single vision for the company. Some of the partners candidly derided the branding initiative. We had been hired by one of the most influential of those partners, and many of his colleagues suspected that the branding project was a power play.

Our team worked diligently to find common ground. We defined the client's brand according to the values and promise that we believed were evident. In fact, when we revealed our findings and shared our suggested platform with the partners, we received strong support and nearly unanimous agreement. I made a point of reconnecting with those partners who had cast doubts early on. Each of them told me they liked the work and planned to support the program. It was great, until the time to implement the brand strategy. Within weeks, the rollout was being sabotaged. Some of those influential partners who'd said they would support the brand quietly planted poison pills whenever they could. The reason: They didn't want to support the brand because doing so would empower the partner who hired us. Even though these partners would tell you they wanted a stronger brand for their company, they didn't want it badly enough to retire petty political issues. This was an extreme occurrence of a common situation: when execution of a brand strategy fails, not because the strategy is flawed but because managers have ulterior motives. This is every bit as true for product branding strategies as it is for corporate branding strategies. I witnessed a terrific brand strategy and identity for an online social media service hit the waste bin because a powerful manager did not want to give anything to a colleague she competed with. She kept raising minor, irrelevant objections to the work, and she cited arbitrary precedents to cast doubt on its merit. In the end, the leaders above her rejected the brand strategy because they wanted to make a compromise that silenced a star executive. You have to be sensitive and realistic about these scenarios. A big launch event and a series of work-shops won't make them go away.

8. The pursuit of perfection. Finally, a lot of brand strategies fail be-cause managers focus so much on making minor details 100 percent perfect. Perfection can be the enemy of great. A few years ago, one of my teams wrestled with a client who was too much of a perfectionist. She was known for carrying a clipboard with a giant checklist. The team referred to her as Clipboard Karen (though Karen is not her real name). We had an exten-sive list of activities to complete for this brand implementation effort. To succeed, we had to prioritize and focus on making some of those activities flawless, while allowing others to be "good enough." We nearly didn't make it because Clipboard Karen wouldn't allow the team to move on to a new task until she believed the current task was perfect. She continually delayed the schedule and created unnecessary discussions, to the point that even her senior managers questioned her judgment. There's beauty in the pursuit of perfection, except when it gets in the way. Your brand can die because you are too rigid and too much of a perfectionist. Increasingly, the best branding efforts thrive imperfectly.

When brand alignment was first adopted in business practice, its pri-mary function was based on command-and-control principles. A brand was thought of primarily as an asset that needed to be protected in order to pre-serve its value. The conventional method of value preservation was to create a control structure that dictated how to use the brand. Alignment initiatives codified rules and control systems to ensure that the brand was not misused. It worked at the time, but it is a less effective approach today.

A good brand alignment initiative should focus on core principles and behavioral guidelines, not rules and controls. As a result of an alignment process, people should feel more empowered to use brand assets and more comfortable applying brand principles in their daily behavior. Nothing kills perceived ownership of a brand faster than a lecture on what not to do.

On a separate note, many brand alignment initiatives falter because they are designed to vest control of the brand into a centralized group—usually a brand management team. While I like brand management teams (after all, they are often my clients), the best are those who hope that their job will one day be redundant. In a perfect company, the brand is so well understood that the idea of having a team dedicated to managing it seems superfluous. I realize that's a lofty goal, but I've been fortunate to work with brand managers who share this point of view.

Many brand management teams use alignment initiatives to preserve their function. I once had a client tell me he was worried that if we empowered other divisions to own the brand, he'd be out of a job. He meant well, but that's exactly the kind of thinking that makes many alignment initiatives terrible. They are self-serving to the brand management function.

IT'S THE PEOPLE, STUPID

In 1991, political strategist James Carville provided candidate Bill Clinton with a famous piece of advice: "It's the economy, stupid." In the case of a branding program, no surprise, it's the *people*. To make a brand strategy work, the people behind the brand have to behave in a branded way. It doesn't matter if the brand we're discussing is a product brand, an ingredient brand, a service brand, or a corporate brand. If the brand strategy doesn't influence the behavior required to deliver the brand experience, then the brand promise is at risk. If a high-tech manufacturer's engineers don't understand the value their brand promises, they will find it harder to develop relevant technologies and innovations, or to prioritize which technologies get integrated into the product. If service personnel at a hotel don't embrace the value proposition that's central to their brand promise, they will be less likely to contribute to a rich and powerful guest experience. Alignment is essential if you wish to engage the people who ensure that your brand meets or exceeds audience expectations. Don't forget that your brand has to meet and exceed the expectations of your internal audience as much as it surprises and delights audiences on the outside. Strong brands find it easier to attract good people. They enjoy lower rates of turnover. And they boast higher levels of employee satisfaction. Satisfied employees sustain strong brands.

I just outlined eight common scenarios in which brand strategies fail in execution. Let me put a finer point on the root causes so that you know where to focus your attention. When a brand fails, you can trace the cause to one or more of the following five factors:

- **Ignorance:** The people inside simply don't know what the brand stands for, why it matters, or how to deliver on its promise.
- **Doubt:** Internal audiences aren't convinced that the brand is what it claims to be, or they don't believe the organization can deliver on the promise it claims to make.
- **Incompetence:** The people who have to deliver the brand experience don't have the necessary skills to fulfill the brand's promise.
- **Poverty:** The organization doesn't provide the resources necessary for teams to create great brand experiences. For the record, the resources that are needed aren't always financial. Many a good brand strategy died because people didn't have enough *time* to bring the strategy to life, or enough *information* to monitor their progress, or enough *support* from within the organization.
- **Lack of incentive:** Either people aren't motivated to deliver the value promised by the brand or they may actually have an incentive to behave in ways that conflict with the brand promise.

When you implement a brand strategy, shift focus from marketing and creative development to human resources and organizational development. The creative evolution of the brand certainly continues. But to do it well, you need to inform and inspire the people who breathe life into it every day. To do that, you have to make sure that people know the brand promise, that they believe in it (better: that they are inspired by it), that they are trained and developed to deliver on it, that they have ample resources to get it right, and that they are motivated by a sustainable system that actually *rewards* branded behavior. When an organization is truly aligned with its brand promise, people on the inside are motivated to go beyond the behavior that is prescribed. They take initiative, and they provide frequent feedback that allows the brand to consistently excel.

The audience you need to influence is broader than you think. To succeed, you have to engage frontline employees—the people who are closest to the customer and the brand experience—and influence the senior and mid-level managers who will lead by example. A good brand alignment program is truly balanced throughout the organization and considers three pivotal inside audiences:

- **Employees:** This includes executive leadership as much as or more than the front line. The best brand alignment strategies go beyond organizational hierarchy. They target thought and opinion leaders throughout the organization. Quite often the most important participants in brand execution are a mix of people from different management levels. Although their paychecks and leadership responsibilities might not look the same, they have uncommon influence over the behavior of people within the organization.
- **Partners:** I've always found it a bit odd that critical suppliers and marketing partners are often the last to know about a brand's new strategy. Most businesses today rely on a delicate ecosystem of related buyers and sellers to deliver on their promise. When you deliver your brand experience, you will increasingly rely on people who live on the perimeter of your organization. They aren't technically inside the brand, but they participate in fulfilling the brand promise. They are so integral to the brand's ability to deliver a great experience that it's critical for you to consider them and include them in the brand alignment process.
- **Investors:** Imagine that you agree to let me drive your car. While I've got it, I repaint it bright red and trick it out with racing accessories—all without asking your permission. When I return the car to you, it doesn't

look anything like it did before. You probably would not lend me your car again. It's ludicrous to think that we might alter something that doesn't belong to us without at least consulting with the rightful owner. But that's exactly what a lot of organizations do when they implement a brand strategy. No one bothers to share the work with investors—the true owners of the brand. There are many good reasons why the information doesn't flow. In a publicly traded company, there are often concerns about publicly disclosing strategies that could benefit competitors. However, you don't have to share your brand strategy at a big public investor event. Sometimes a private meeting with a few members of your board is enough to engage their thinking and get their support. You can also tailor the message of your strategy so that critical investors understand how you plan to deliver compelling experiences. It is better to engage investors than ignore them. Some of the best ideas I've heard for strengthening a brand originated from an owner. After all, owners arguably have the most invested in the brand's success.

CREATING LEVERAGE

Where to Focus Your Efforts

I began this chapter by describing a number of reasons that brand alignment initiatives fail. The short version of the story is that a lot of them don't spend enough time thinking about engagement and implementation. Brand alignment is most often an afterthought. If more managers invested as much time and energy implementing brand strategies as they do designing them, more brands would consistently deliver on their promises. As a rule of thumb, spend twice as much time and money on implementation as you do on development, regardless of your size and structure. If you're a small business and you spend six weeks and $10,000 creating your brand strategy and designing a brand identity, plan to spend at least another twelve weeks and $20,000 training your employees and putting the strategy into place. My larger clients are often speechless when I make this recommendation, but they shouldn't be. Think of what's required to put a brand strategy into action.

Here's the most important reality check to consider when thinking about brand alignment: It needs to be a transformational process, rather than a transactional process. One of the most interesting and comprehensive studies to quantify this fact was published in 2009 in the *Journal of Marketing*. Based on a thorough review of the data, the study team concluded:

> Managers would do much better by opening their minds to a Transformational Leadership approach, which would entail behaviors such as articulating a unifying brand vision, acting as an appropriate role model by living the brand values, giving followers freedom to individually interpret their roles as brand representatives, and providing individualized support by acting as a coach and mentor. This would allow followers to experience the feelings of relatedness, autonomy, and competence in their roles as brand representatives, which would ultimately spill over into the commitment, authenticity, and proactivity that characterize a real brand champion.

The study differentiated this model of transformational leadership from a transactional leadership model that focuses primarily on contingent rewards (clarifying expectations and offering rewards when expectations are met) and management-by-exception (monitoring and reprimanding deviances from prescribed performance standards). The study didn't dismiss the value of transactional leadership. In fact, the data suggested that successful transformational brand alignment initiatives incorporate some layer of transactional elements. But the data stunningly demonstrated that organizational behavior changed with greater significance when a transformational leadership approach was emphasized.[3]

How exactly does an organization adopt a transformational leadership approach? In my experience, there are six key areas you might address in your implementation plans to achieve the goal.

1. Build organizational understanding. Unless you're a business of one, your brand strategy will only be as strong as your organization's weakest link. It takes only one employee to break the brand's promise and create a reputation problem. Successful implementation programs include everyone, take no assumption for granted, and repeat the message again and again until it is second nature—especially for the teams that control critical touch points. Great programs build understanding by keeping the message simple and by being explicit about what the brand promises—and equally explicit about how that promise is delivered in experiences. Most important, the best implementation programs work hard to keep the branding effort relevant: They tie delivery of the brand promise to meaningful rewards for promise keepers.

A little while ago I had the great opportunity to tour the operations environments of several Southwest Airlines stations. Operations are critical to Southwest's promise. Customers are only so forgiving when flights are delayed or the overall experience is irregular. All Southwest employees understand how their individual roles connect to the brand experience, and they hold themselves accountable individually and as a team. Every year, Southwest contributes a set percentage of the airline's profit to an employee bonus pool. That's significant when you consider that no other U.S. airline has been as consistently profitable as Southwest. The profit pool is allocated democratically, based on the performance of individual teams. When I toured Southwest stations I was struck by how well individual teams connected their performance to the brand experience—and how they connected that relationship to their potential for reward at year-end. Southwest employees understand that a great brand experience leads to a healthier business, which leads to better rewards for everyone.

2. Recruit well. The best brand implementation strategies make human resources a high priority, beginning with recruitment. My clients often won-

der why recruitment would be a higher priority than efforts to retrain existing personnel. The answer is that it can take a long time to change existing
behavior, but you can cast for the desired behavior now. You can end a po-
tentially vicious cycle by hiring people who are best suited to deliver the
brand promise. Set the standard on the recruitment front, even if you don't
have many open positions. The process of defining the ideal employee profile alone will improve your efforts to change the behavior of existing personnel. That's not to say you should ignore your existing personnel. Instead,
it's a recommendation to follow the lead of great brands that cast well.

Frances X. Frei is a professor in the Technology and Operations
Management Unit at Harvard Business School and the chair of the MBA
Required Curriculum. She has dedicated her career to the study of great
service brands. In her many writings and lectures, she often describes a
common denominator: Great service brands tend to hire for attitude and
train for skill. In working with brands that deliver exceptional brand experiences, I have observed a strong corollary: The brands that consistently
deliver on their promise are meticulous about their recruitment efforts. It's
not uncommon for employees at these organizations to go through several
rounds of interviews before making the cut. In many cases, positions go
unfilled for some time because the managers of these brands would rather
wait until they find the right cultural fit than hire someone who might
jeopardize the brand experience. This is as true for the managers of large,
corporate brands as it is for the managers of small product brand teams.
These leaders, and their crews, understand the same principle that theater
directors have known for centuries: Ninety-nine percent of directing is
casting well.

It may seem senseless to invest time in your recruiting process when
your company is small and not growing quickly. However, if you're investing in your brand, this is one step you cannot afford to overlook. Even if you
won't make another hire for more than a year, invest some time in defining
what it takes to land a job working for your brand. Set the right internal
expectation by how you change your casting.

3. Lead from the front. As general of the Third Army in World War II, George S. Patton issued a written directive to all of his direct reports advising them to "always lead from the front." Patton rejected the notion that commanders lead battles from a headquarters tent, far removed from the hazards of the enemy line. He ordered every commanding officer to be seen taking the same risks as the men who followed them. Brand leaders would do well to heed Patton's advice. If you want to change the behavior required to improve a brand experience, immerse yourself in the experience itself.

When I was an executive at Disney, I had the unique opportunity to participate in an experience known as The Disney Way. I traveled to the parks and spent time doing the work of frontline cast members. I worked in a food and beverage location during a peak traffic period. I worked with a maintenance crew. And I suited up in costume to sign autographs as one of Disney's animated characters. The experience was intended to help me better understand what it's like to create great Disney brand experiences. It was as much of a reality check for me as it was an inspiration. From that point on, when I dealt with teams in all the various places where Disney operated, I had a better understanding and respect for what it took to deliver the "magic." It was a rite of passage that also helped me gain the respect of colleagues who would have to act on my direction.

Especially in large corporations, most branding initiatives are pushed from the top down. "Corporate" personnel dictate brand rules for "staff" to execute. Too often, the rules are irrelevant to the business operation, making the brand rollout a farce. The best brand implementation programs are completely integrated between the executive suite and the front line. Frontline employees are enlisted from the start, and senior leaders invest the time and effort to observe the strategy in action from the front.

4. Coach the brand. The best brand alignment efforts create brand coaches, not brand cops. The brand cop mentality is a sad vestige of another era. There was a time when corporate America vested a brand management group with the power to change or kill marketing and product development efforts that were deemed a danger to the brand. I watched many of these brand cops in action. They always started with good intentions. They always committed to being a resource instead of a barrier. Inevitably, however, they'd evolve into the ivory tower that perpetually said no. Big, expensive advertising campaigns would get held up because a few members of the branding team weren't satisfied with the way the brand message was incorporated. It didn't matter that the campaign wasn't intended to be a brand spot. If it didn't fit within the rules of the brand strategy, it was up for debate. I encourage everyone in an organization to raise their hands when they think something is "off brand," but it's quite another matter when the branding function becomes so troublesome that people would gladly prefer a way around it. Your brand should not be a tax on the groups that create value. As you can imagine, this kind of effort to protect a brand created nothing but contempt from business managers, who had very real growth targets. This, in part, is why chief marketing officers have historically had the shortest tenures in business. Many have disproportionate influence relative to their actual accountability.

Brands that consistently deliver on their promise do not isolate the role of branding to the marketing office. While there may be in-house branding specialists who help to coordinate efforts, measure results, and manage the brand strategy's ongoing development, implementation is the shared responsibility of many leaders within the company. Instead of policing the organization to ensure that the brand strategy is enforced, these multidisciplinary teams serve as coaching resources. They make it their job to proactively identify areas where the brand could be strengthened. They don't issue orders. They collaborate with the true owners of critical touch points to find solutions. There is no singular approach to doing this well. I've witnessed a lot of variation in the way these teams coach, but there's no doubt they're coaching. They're helping people on the inside get better at their game instead of penalizing them for breaking the rules. And they embrace every opportunity to transform anyone inside into a brand advocate.

5. Recognize the best brand experiences. Here's a common scenario: A company invests a significant amount of time and money to design
its brand strategy and brand identity. Everyone applauds how well the promise is defined, and they gush over the beautiful new visual identity. Maybe a
massive event is staged to introduce the brand to everyone inside, and a series
of workshops and training activities follows. Here's the best part: The effort
is working! Unfortunately, nobody knows it because little has been done to
measure progress and even less is done to celebrate success. Many companies
launch a new brand at a meaningful event such as a shareholder's meeting.
The new brand dominates the agenda of that event, and everyone attending
is told how and why the brand is important. One year later, at the next shareholder's meeting, no one talks about brand. This common event is painful to
me, especially because there is often great news to share in follow-up!

When you don't take the time to recognize the accomplishments of
your brand implementation, people imagine the worst. So assume that all
ambiguous information is interpreted negatively. The larger the investment
you make in your brand, the more you should feel obligated to find and celebrate great brand experiences. Virgin CEO Richard Branson does a great
job of reminding his team where Virgin is winning. Southwest Airlines
CEO Gary Kelly does the same. I'm not suggesting that you need to paint
a picture that's rosy when there's more work to be done. However, you'll
make significant progress if you find the time to focus people's attention on
where the brand is working.

Legendary theater director William Ball often told a story about his
experience watching Academy Award–winning director Francis Ford Coppola in action. He said Coppola had a great tendency to isolate the moments
when an actor was doing something really, really well—even when the overall performance was poor. Ball noted that Coppola minimized the amount
of criticism he provided and overemphasized what was working. Coppola
could be salty. It wasn't as if he was sugarcoating a bad performance. Instead,
he recognized improvement and encouraged the parts of a performance that
were absolutely *right*. When you're leading a brand transformation, you owe

it to yourself and your organization to recognize when delivery of the brand experience is fulfilling the brand promise.

6. Develop a social network for the brand. Your brand is a currency. It grows in value the more it is exchanged. If you want it to really permeate every part of your organization, make it accessible. Make it something everyone can touch, feel, and share. I mentioned at the very start of this book that branding has become part of our vernacular. Brands are as interesting to the people inside your organization as they are to the people on the outside. Make that fact part of your advantage. Encourage people to speak up and share ideas for improving the brand's ability to deliver on its promise. Reward those who suggest good ideas. And reward those who uncover issues that affect the brand experience. You will succeed when a majority of the people in your organization feel they individually own the brand.

In recent years, a lot of brand managers have lost sleep worrying about the rise of social media. They've fretted over how their brand should participate on Twitter, Facebook, and YouTube. But they've become even more anxious about how their employees behave on social networks. It's getting harder and harder to draw the line between the individual who works for a brand and the brand itself. A couple of years ago, Cisco faced this challenge when a new hire made a social media gaffe. After receiving an offer from a Cisco hiring manager, she posted the following message on Twitter:

> Cisco just offered me a job! Now I have to weigh the utility of a fatty paycheck against the daily commute to San Jose and hating the work.

Within hours she had incurred the wrath of many new colleagues. They ridiculed her, threatened to have her fired, and dubbed her the "Cisco Fatty." Suddenly, the Cisco brand was in jeopardy because the actions of Cisco employees painted a less than favorable picture of its culture. In response, the company issued a social networking philosophy that provided guidelines to employees on how to protect Cisco's reputation and when to comment on matters that relate to the brand versus their personal lives. At the time, it was considered one of the most forward-thinking guidelines for a corporate brand. Instead of cracking down on employees, Cisco went one step further. It created social@Cisco, a site that aggregates brand-related social media posts from hundreds of Cisco employees. By encouraging smart conversations about the brand, Cisco made employees more engaged in the brand's reputation and success.

FROM A CODE OF CONDUCT TO A CAMPAIGN FOR THE BRAND

It's time for a new mode of thinking in brand alignment. When we introduce a new brand to customers, we launch a splashy campaign. But when we introduce that same brand to employees, we delegate brand cops who will crack down, compel, and control. I tell my clients they need to think of an internal brand launch as though it were a political campaign. Political campaigns change how people think and create a groundswell of public interest. An internal brand campaign should do the same. There's much that political science can teach us about transforming a branded organization, including how to frame the mandate and the narrative.

Every four years, when American voters cast their ballots for the highest office in the country, pundits wonder about mandates and they frame the narrative of the candidates' campaigns. *Framing* and *mandating* the narrative are critical buzzwords for an internal brand campaign. Your mandate is a better brand experience—framed by the narrative of your strategy, which is tailored to key audience segments. We have already discussed the importance of a brand narrative, but in this instance we're focusing it on the people inside. You begin your campaign by articulating why change is necessary. What benefit will be created? What promise must be kept? How will it be delivered? You can't effect change unless you can clearly answer these questions for your employees, partners, and investors. As you develop your strategy, you must consider how you frame these questions for two groups within your organization: *supporters* and *the unconvinced*. We can further divide these two macro groups into four subparts, as follows.

Supporters

- **Evangelists:** These are the people who do more than believe in the mandate. They're willing to get out there and convince others of its necessity. Your job is to provide them with the narrative that will help them grow the base. You should identify your potential evangelists early in the process. You'll often find them while you're developing the brand strategy. You'll know who they are by their ability to persuade you of the brand's opportunities and merits. You'll also know them by the influence they have in the organization. While you'll certainly find brand evangelists living in the C-suite, you're likely to find even more working close to the action. Don't mistake official status with evangelistic potential. Some of the best brand evangelists line up with the majority of the organization. That's why they wield power.

- **Followers:** These are people who believe in the mandate and are mostly willing to do what it takes to see it through. They need a narrative that articulates what they can do to make a difference. In the age-old will/skill analysis, these internal audiences have the will, but they usually need skills and resources to be effective.

The Unconvinced

While it's not the most appealing segmentation name, the "unconvinced" comprises anyone in your organization who's not yet on board with the strategy. The campaign to the unconvinced is the battleground for a winning brand implementation effort. It addresses two subsegments.

- **Detractors:** Though this is generally a very small segment in most organizations, an influential detractor can greatly impede brand implementation. Most detractors, for whatever reason, don't believe the strategy reflects the true promise of the brand. Maybe they have a conflicting agenda or maybe they're misguided, but they are strongly opposed to the change you wish to make. If not addressed, they will create a counternarrative that can derail or diffuse your effort to act on the mandate.

- **The undecided:** This is often the largest audience to address, particularly in big organizations. Most of the undecided aren't opposed to the change you wish to make; they just don't understand the mandate. In my experience, most people in an organization who have no opinion about the state of the brand are that way because no one has taken the time to help them understand why the brand matters. No one has linked a promise to the brand's experience. No one has illustrated how the delivery of that experience creates value that is relevant to the undecided employee. This is where you focus your narrative.

Creating the Campaign Headquarters

Political campaigns create hubs of activity. To launch an effective internal brand campaign, you must do the same. It doesn't have to be a physical place, although many are. You can create central hubs online or through well-defined social circles. Many organizations create brand steering committees or task forces. When they work well, they become hubs for others in the organization to connect with the brand campaign. When they don't work, they're just task-oriented bureaucracies. Your campaign headquarters should be focused on the way to address the four audiences. Every time this task force meets at or through the headquarters hub, it focuses on key audiences, the message those audiences need to receive, and the tactics required to overcome obstacles. Task force members always have a concrete task in front of them—perhaps it's fixing a branded touch point or introducing a new subbrand—but they consider how to attack that task by developing a strategy to win the biggest number of hearts and minds within the organization. This last point is essential. It's what makes the campaign approach different from the command-and-control approach. The team is focused on how to change the way people think.

Polling

Many of my clients don't blink an eye about ordering research before they introduce their brands to the external market. But they invest very little in understanding how people on the inside view the brand's situation. In a political campaign, polling is essential. It's how decision makers determine where to focus their energy. It can be a valuable tool in your internal campaign for the brand. Quite honestly, it doesn't have to cost a lot. You don't need perfect statistics. You need barometers of readiness. You need to understand how ready people are internally to make the changes you want to make.

There are many forms of research that you can and should use in an internal campaign. What is the overall opinion of the brand? How convinced are people that the brand needs to change? Who opposes changes in the brand? Why? How well do people understand what the brand stands for? Do they believe it?

You poll to focus your efforts, and you poll to measure results. If you don't take a pulse from time to time during your brand campaign, you won't have any idea what's working and what's not. That doesn't mean that all your research has to be quantitative and rigorous. Some of the most effective polling techniques include small focus groups, quick online polls, social media barometers, and informal interviews. The point is to be on a constant search for data.

Seeding

It takes resources to win elections. The race for the campaign war chest precedes the ballot box in a presidential election. The same is mostly true for an internal brand campaign. You need to secure plenty of resources to support your drive to achieve the mandate and influence how people think. Resources can be broader than money alone, however. Time is critical. Your leaders should be willing to invest their time and commit others' time to see the brand campaign through to completion. They also need to provide access to facilities and technology that enable you to persuade effectively. Finally, if you really want to win an internal brand campaign, you have to motivate people to behave in a branded way and offer very public rewards for exemplary delivery of the brand promise. This comes back to my earlier missive on recognizing achievement. A brand campaign should celebrate success publicly. The best brand campaigns celebrate when people take initiative on their own to deliver a brand experience that goes beyond what is promised.

Messaging

Most internal messaging tactics are anemic. Remember: Ambiguous information is interpreted negatively. That's why you have to overcommunicate. At the beginning of your messaging campaign, focus on building comprehension about the mandate and generating familiarity with the brand promise. But as you go along, your messaging efforts need to reflect what you learn from polling. Here are some of the common requirements of an internal messaging campaign:

- **Recognize achievements:** A little good news is better than no news. Political strategists are known for making mountains out of molehills. This might not be your best strategy, but you need to keep the conversation going by sharing what's been accomplished.
- **Provide insights:** Your campaign must frequently share what you've learned and shed light on what the learning means. If you gather new research that relates to your brand experience, find a way to share that with your internal team and suggest its implications. Most people like to be led; they're motivated when they believe their leaders are thinking

about how to win. When you share insights, you do both. Truly transformational leadership rallies around ideas.

- **Repeat the objectives:** From time to time you have to repeat the mandate because it's easy to lose sight of it. Make a point of reminding people that the brand is a priority, and provide people with updated, relevant examples that illustrate why.

- **Demonstrate commitment:** Whenever you can, connect the brand to the way your organization delivers on its promise. Too many internal brand campaigns overemphasize the brand's marketing activities alone. That leads people to think that the brand lives only in advertising and promotion. But when you can show the brand in action—in a nonmarketing context—you change the discussion.

Galvanizing

Last, you need to make the brand accessible to the organization. You have to let people own it. A good campaign makes it easy for people to get involved. You do this in three key ways:

- **Enlist human resources:** If your organization has a human resources department, make it a reliable partner. Connect the brand to recruitment, training, and retention efforts. Human resources can serve as brand ambassadors, even when the branding focus is a product or service team within a larger organization. I've met many HR managers who champion small teams that are making a big impact. Since these people often are the first interface with potential employees, they can do a lot for your cause.

- **Lobby influential stakeholders:** Remember those detractors? Sometimes your best strategy is to keep them close. I watched as one of my clients carefully managed a very public detractor in his organization. He reached out early and put resources on the table that made it more attractive for the detractor to play along than to wage a war. Such behavior may feel inappropriate, but if you believe in your cause, these compromises are part of the game. In my experience, many detractors change their tune when the brand campaign begins to demonstrate results.

- **Stage symbolic events:** Don't underestimate the value of theatricality. If you really want to galvanize your base, stage events that make the brand's presence palpable. Although many people groan when they think of a corporate retreat, those same individuals return to their jobs with enthusiasm the week after. These symbolic events can be used in a smart way to emphasize the brand campaign and unite people around a common cause.

MEANS WITHOUT AN END

When we think of brand alignment, brand engagement, brand implementation—whatever words we use to describe the process of putting a brand into action—we are tempted to think of it as having an endpoint. Resist this temptation. Brand alignment doesn't have an ending. It's an effort that continues for as long as your brand exists.

After we launch a new brand for a client, I often ask the client to start thinking about version 2.0. Most look at me like I'm crazy because they've heard me preach the folly of constant rebranding. But Brand 2.0 isn't another rebrand. It's about how the brand needs to adapt and evolve. Within days of a brand launch we can already sense where the brand may need additional fine-tuning. As people inside the organization embrace the brand promise and think about how to translate it into brand experience, their shared perspective advances the brand in ways we didn't see when we were working tirelessly to get the brand to this point.

Throughout my career, the best brands I've observed share a common commitment to continuous improvement. The brand can always be a little better, a little more relevant, a little more inspiring. One of many terms I have borrowed from computer programming is *agile development.* In an agile approach to software design, you create an inventory of changes and developments that you want to make in the next software release. Then you set the team to work on implementing every item on the inventory. As team members progress, they come across other features or changes they want to make. The agile manager adds those feature suggestions and changes to a backlog that will be addressed when the inventory is completed. I encourage my clients to do the same to encourage ongoing brand development. Create a backlog as you go. Make it the point of conversation with brand leaders. Then focus on the next inventory that must be accomplished. The more you do this, the more the brand becomes relevant to people who don't spend their day thinking about brand equity for a living. It becomes a conversation about what you do, why it matters, and why anyone should care.

Real brands make people better because of what they stand for. Great brands get better because people stand up for them every day. Make branding a meaningful and continuous cause, and your brand will enjoy a long and productive life.

NOTES

CHAPTER ONE: REALITY CHECK

1. Sam Dillon, "Democrats Make Bush School Act an Election Issue," *New York Times,* December 23, 2007.
2. Sam Dillon, "Rename Law? No Wisecrack Left Behind," *New York Times,* February 22, 2009.
3. Andrew Rotherham, "A Contest! Name That Law!," *Eduwonk.com,* February 12, 2009, http://www.eduwonk.com/2009/02/a-contest-name -that-law.html.
4. Frank Newport, "Americans Doubt Effectiveness of 'No Child Left Behind,'" *Gallup,* August 19, 2009, http://www.gallup.com/poll/122375/ americans-doubt-effectiveness-no-child-left-behind.aspx.
5. "Front Row: 4 Questions for Marian Wright Edelman," *Ebony,* January 2004, 20.
6. Lindsay Goldwert, "No logo: The Gap's logo change and crowdsourcing tactics draw consumer and online ire," *New York Daily News,* October 7, 2010.
7. John D. Sutter, "The internet kills Gap's new logo," October 12, 2010, http://articles.cnn.com/2010-10-12/tech/gap.logo.social.media_1_new -logo-twitter-accounts-facebook-post?_s=PM:TECH (accessed January 30, 2011).
8. Juli Weiner, "New Gap Logo, Despised Symbol of Corporate Banality, Dead at One Week," *Vanity Fair,* October 12, 2010.

9. Mike Isaac, "New Gap Logo Hated by Many, Company Turns to Crowdsourcing Tactics," *Forbes,* October 7, 2010.

10. "Design a Better GAP Logo (Community Project)," October 25, 2010, http://99designs.com/logo-design/contests/design-better-gap-logo-community-project-54693.

11. Mike Monteiro, "Off the Hoof: Dear Gap, I Have Your New Logo," October 7, 2010, http://weblog.muledesign.com/2010/10/dear_gap_i_have_your_new_logo.php.

12. Trefis, "Holiday Sales Data Could Bring Cheer for Gap's Stock," January 8, 2011, http://community.nasdaq.com/News/2011-01/holiday-sales-data-could-bring-cheer-for-gaps.

13. Tülin Erdem and Joffre Swait, "Brand Credibility, Brand Consideration, and Choice," *Journal of Consumer Research,* June 2004.

14. Peter S. Goodman and Gretchen Morgenson, "Saying Yes, WaMu Built Empire on Shaky Loans," *New York Times,* December 27, 2008, A1.

CHAPTER TWO: WINNING THE MEMORY GAME

1. Jochim Hansen and Michaela Wänke, "Truth from Language and Truth from Fit: The Impact of Linguistic Concreteness and Level of Construal on Subjective Truth," *Personality and Social Psychology Bulletin,* October 14, 2010.

2. Starbucks website, http://www.starbucks.com/about-us/our-heritage, October 2011.

3. McCann Worldgroup, *The Truth About Youth,* May 2011.

4. Simon Dumenico, "Why Facebook Is Becoming the Media World's Black Hole," *AdAge,* October 3, 2011.

5. Jenna Wortham and David Streitfeld, "Amazon's Tablet Leads to Its Store," *New York Times,* September 28, 2011.

CHAPTER THREE: THE BENEFIT OF YOUR BRAND

1. Torsten Bornemann and Christian Homburg, "Psychological Distance and the Dual Role of Price," *Journal of Consumer Research,* October 2011.
2. E. Tory Higgins, James Shah, and Ronald Friedman, "Emotional Responses to Goal Attainment: Strength of Regulatory Focus as Moderator," *Journal of Personality and Social Psychology,* 1997.
3. John Deighton, *Dove: Evolution of a Brand,* Harvard Business School Case Study, March 25, 2008.
4. Dylan Byers, "Huffington to Talk 'Cause Marketing,' " *AdWeek,* October 3, 2011.

CHAPTER FOUR: LEVERAGING PORTFOLIO VALUE

1. Arul Mishra, "Influence of Contagious versus Noncontagious Product Groupings on Consumer Preferences," *Journal of Consumer Research,* June 2009.
2. David M. Boush and Barbara Loken, "A Process-Tracing Study of Brand Extension Evaluation," *Journal of Marketing Research,* February 1991.
3. Tom Meyvis and Chris Janiszewski, "When Are Broader Brands Stronger Brands? An Accessibility Perspective on the Success of Brand Extensions," *Journal of Consumer Research,* September 2004.
4. Alokparna Basu Monga and Deborah Roedder John, "What Makes Brands Elastic? The Influence of Brand Concept and Styles of Thinking on Brand Extension Evaluation," *Journal of Marketing,* May 2010.
5. Boush and Loken, "A Process-Tracing Study."
6. Huifang Mao and H. Shanker Krishnan, "Effects of Prototype and Exemplar Fit on Brand Extension Evaluations: A Two-Process Contingency Model," *Journal of Consumer Research,* June 2006.

7. Catherine W.M. Yeung and Robert S. Wyer, Jr., "Does Loving a Brand Mean Loving Its Products? The Role of Brand-Elicited Affect in Brand Extension Evaluations," *Journal of Marketing Research,* November 2005.

CHAPTER FIVE: POSITIONING BRANDS FOR CONTEXT

1. Dennis W. Rook and Sidney J. Levy, "Defending the Dowager: Communication Strategies for Declining Main Brands," in *Brands, Consumers, Symbols, and Research: Sidney J. Levy on Marketing* (Thousand Oaks, CA: Sage Publications, 1999).
2. Martha Lagace, "Gerstner: Changing Culture at IBM—Lou Gerstner Discusses Changing the Culture at IBM," *HBS Working Knowledge,* December 9, 2002.
3. Elizabeth Holmes, "Abercrombie and Fitch Offers to Pay 'The Situation' to Stop Wearing Its Clothes," *Wall Street Journal,* August 16, 2011.

CHAPTER SIX: BRAND ATTACHMENT

1. Mark Ebner, "Wanted: Colton Harris-Moore, An American Outlaw," *Maxim,* March 18, 2010.
2. C. Whan Park, Deborah J. MacInnis, Joseph Priester, Andreas B. Eisingerich, and Dawn Iacobucci, "Brand Attachment and Brand Attitude Strength: Conceptual and Empirical Differentiation of Two Critical Brand Equity Drivers," *Journal of Marketing,* November 2010.
3. Russell W. Belk, Melanie Wallendorf, and John F. Sherry, Jr., "The Sacred and the Profane in Consumer Behavior: Theodicy on the Odyssey," *Journal of Consumer Research,* June 1989.
4. Ibid.
5. Kathryn A. Braun-LaTour, Michael S. LaTour, and George M.

Zinkhan, "Using Childhood Memories to Gain Insight into Brand Meaning," *Journal of Marketing,* April 2007.

6. Michelle Krebs, "Chrysler, VW Win Big for Super Bowl Ads," *Edmunds AutoObserver,* February 7, 2011.

7. Hazel Markus and Paula Nurius, "Possible Selves," *American Psychologist,* September 1986.

8. Stephanie Clifford and Andrew Martin, "In Time of Scrimping, Fun Stuff Is Still Selling," *New York Times,* September 23, 2011.

9. "Chasing the Barefoot Bandit," *48 Hours/Mystery,* CBS, November 13, 2010.

10. Russell W. Belk, "Possessions and the Extended Self," *Journal of Consumer Research,* September 1988.

11. Park, et al., "Brand Attachment."

12. Moleskine website, http://www.moleskineus.com/moleskine-about .html, November 2011.

13. National Institute on Media and Family, 2009.

14. Natalie Zmuda, "Skinny Pepsi Can Launch Is Heavy with Controversy," *Advertising Age,* February 21, 2011.

15. Allison R. Johnson, Maggie Matear, and Matthew Thomson, "A Coal in the Heart: Self-Relevance as a Post-Exit Predictor of Consumer Anti-Brand Actions," *Journal of Consumer Research,* June 2011.

16. Hope Jensen Schau and Mary C. Gilly, "We Are What We Post? Self-Presentation in Personal Web Space," *Journal of Consumer Research,* December 2003.

17. Vanessa Romo, "At Large: Teen Bandit. Even Larger: His Legend," NPR, January 16, 2010.

CHAPTER SEVEN: EXPRESSING THE PROMISE

1. Luca Penati, "The Contribution of Neuroscience to the Art of Story-telling: 5 Lessons to Become Better Communicators," *Tech PR Nibbles,* http://www.techprnibbles.com, June 3, 2011.

2. Kaihan Krippendorff, "Barack Obama Is Tapping Into Your Brain," *Fast Company,* August 27, 2009.

3. Margaret C. Campbell and Amna Kirmani, "Consumers' Use of Persuasion Knowledge: The Effects of Accessibility and Cognitive Capacity on Perceptions of an Influence Agent," *Journal of Consumer Research,* June 2000.

4. "The Truth About Youth," study by McCann Worldgroup, 2011.

5. Bianca Grohmann, "Gender Dimensions of Brand Personality," *Journal of Marketing Research,* February 2009.

6. Margaret Mark and Carol S. Pearson, *The Hero and the Outlaw: Building Extraordinary Brands Through the Power of Archetypes* (New York: McGraw-Hill, 2001).

7. J. Josko Brakus, Bernd H. Schmitt, and Lia Zarantonello, "Brand Experience: What Is It? How Is It Measured? Does It Affect Loyalty?," *Journal of Marketing,* May 2009.

8. Isadore Sharp, *Four Seasons: The Story of a Business Philosophy* (New York: Penguin Books, 2009).

9. Robert R. McCrae and Paul T. Costa, Jr., "The Structure of Interpersonal Traits: Wiggins's Circumplex and Five-Factor Model," *Journal of Personality and Social Psychology,* 1989.

10. Jennifer L. Aaker, "Dimensions of Brand Personality," *Journal of Marketing Research,* August 1997.

CHAPTER EIGHT: NAMING AND IDENTITY DEVELOPMENT

1. Schumpeter, "Logoland: Why Consumers Balk at Companies' Efforts to Rebrand Themselves, *The Economist,* January 13, 2011.

2. Claire Cain Miller, "The iPad's Name Makes Some Women Cringe," *New York Times,* January 27, 2010.

3. Alan Brew, "Naming Nicole," on Name Droppings, www.name dropping.wordpress.com, September 25, 2011.

4. John Ohala, "An Ethological Perspective on Common Cross-Language Utilization of FO of Voice," *Phonetica,* Volume 41, Issue 1, 1984.

5. L.J. Shrum and Tina M. Lowrey, "Sounds Convey Meaning: The Implications of Phonetic Symbolism for Brand Name Construction," *Psycholinguistic Phenomena in Marketing Communications,* Psychology Press, 2007.

6. Eric Yorkston and Geeta Menon, "A Sound Idea: Phonetic Effects of Brand Names on Consumer Judgments," *Journal of Consumer Research,* June 2004.

7. Linda Scott and Patrick Vargas, "Writing with Pictures: Toward a Unifying Theory of Consumer Response to Images," *Journal of Consumer Research,* October 2007.

CHAPTER NINE: THE TOUCHING EXPERIENCE

1. Keith Axline, "Presidential First: White House Floods Flickr," *Wired,* April 29, 2009, http://www.wired.com/rawfile/2009/04/presidential -first-white-house-floods-flickr/.

2. Jefferson Graham, "Flickr of an idea on a gaming project led to photo website," *USA Today,* February 27, 2006.

3. J. Josko Brakus, Bernd H. Schmitt, and Lia Zarantonello, "Brand Experience: What is it? How is it measured? Does it affect loyalty?," *Journal of Marketing,* May 2009.

4. Joan Meyers-Levy and Rui (Juliet) Zhu, "The Influence of Ceiling Height: The Effect of Priming on the Type of Processing That People Use," *Journal of Consumer Research,* August 2007.

5. Gráinne M. Fitzsimons, Tanya L. Chartrand, and Gavan J. Fitzsimons, "Automatic Effects of Brand Exposure on Motivated Behavior: How Apple Makes You 'Think Different,' " *Journal of Consumer Research,* June 2008.

6. "The Adult Brain: To Think by Feeling," *The Secret Life of the Brain,* Episode 4, PBS, 2002.

7. Chris Janiszewski, "Preattentive Mere Exposure Effects," *Journal of Consumer Research,* December 1992.

8. Barbara L. Fredrickson and Daniel Kahneman, "Duration Neglect in Retrospective Evaluations of Affective Episodes," *Journal of Personality and Social Psychology,* December 1993.

9. Suresh Ramanathan and Ann L. McGill, "Consuming with Others: Social Influences on Moment-to-Moment and Retrospective Evaluations of an Experience," *Journal of Consumer Research,* December 2007.

CHAPTER TEN: BRAND INSIDE

1. Harris Interactive, "Oil, Pharmaceutical, Health Insurance, and Tobacco Top the List of Industries That People Think Should Be More Regulated," December 2, 2010, http://www.harrisinteractive.com/NewsRoom/HarrisPolls/tabid/447/mid/1508/articleId/648/ctl/ReadCustom%20Default/Default.aspx (accessed March 26, 2011).

2. Reuters, full text of Toyota President Akio Toyoda's testimony, February 24, 2010, http://uk.reuters.com/article/2010/02/24/toyota-testimony-idUKTOE61N04I20100224 (accessed March 26, 2011).

3. Felicitas M. Morhart, Walter Herzog, and Torgen Tomczak, "Brand-Specific Leadership: Turning Employees into Brand Champions," *Journal of Marketing,* September 2009.

INDEX

ABOUT THE AUTHOR

LAURENCE VINCENT (www.laurencevincent.com) has developed strategies for some of the world's most beloved brands, including Coca-Cola, Four Seasons Hotels, MasterCard, Microsoft, the National Football League, Sony PlayStation, Southwest Airlines, The Home Depot, and vitaminwater. He is the head of The Brand Studio at United Talent Agency, where he advises celebrity clients and corporations on brand strategy and implementation.

Prior to joining UTA, Laurence headed up strategy teams at several leading brand and marketing agencies, including Siegel+Gale, Octagon Worldwide, and Cabana Group. He began his career at The Walt Disney Company, where he led corporate strategy projects that leveraged Disney's brand equity to create innovative brand partnerships with companies such as AT&T, American Express, Coca-Cola, and Kodak.

His first book, *Legendary Brands,* was published in 2001 and established him as an expert in the field of brand narrative. He has been an outspoken champion for brand storytelling, and he has spoken and written frequently about the need for marketers to understand how their brand story affects the narrative of the consumer.

He holds an MBA from the Marshall School of Business at the University of Southern California. He also received his bachelor's degree from USC, where he attended the School of Cinema-Television.